For Doris Laslo

Carl Zigrosser

January 1943

SIX CENTURIES OF FINE PRINTS

Also by Carl Zigrosser: FINE PRINTS OLD AND NEW

SIX CENTURIES
OF FINE PRINTS

by Carl Zigrosser

New York · COVICI·FRIEDE · *Publishers*

COPYRIGHT, 1937, BY CARL ZIGROSSER

*All rights reserved. No part of this book may be
reproduced in any form without permission in
writing from the publisher, except by a reviewer
who may quote brief passages in a review to be
printed in a magazine or newspaper.*

PRINTED IN THE UNITED STATES OF AMERICA
BY J. J. LITTLE AND IVES COMPANY, NEW YORK

HALFTONE ENGRAVING BY POWERS REPRODUCTION CORPORATION

HALFTONE ILLUSTRATIONS PRINTED
BY S. A. JACOBS, THE GOLDEN EAGLE PRESS

TYPOGRAPHY BY ROBERT JOSEPHY

Contents

A BRIEF NOTE OF ACKNOWLEDGMENT: The following illustrations have been reproduced by courtesy of the Knoedler Gallery, New York: 18, 120, 128, 129, 131, 148, 151, 152, 154, 158, 160, 163, 164, 181, 187, 188, 189, 192, 193, 201, 203, 205, 207, 236, 238, 260, 264, 265, 294, 295, 296, 306, 307, 340, 341, 342, 349, 353, 359, 382, 388, 390, 406, 410, and 411. From the Metropolitan Museum of Art in New York: 57, 65, 73, 74, 75, 76, 126, 132, 133, 149, 150, 156, 161, 162, 166, 167, 173, 182, 183, 184, 185, 186, 215, 219, 224, 229, 230, 251, 275, 280, 284, 286, 288, 292, 299, 302, 314, 323, 330, 331, 337, 344, 345, 352, 356, 358, 368, 370, 372, 378, 381, 391, 450, 457, 458, 460, 461, 463, 464, 465, 466, 467, 470, 471, 473, 475, 476, 477, 478, 479, 481, 482, 484, 486. By courtesy of the Weyhe Gallery: 180, 216, 223, 258, 259, 266, 277, 278, 279, 287, 301, 308, 309, 311, 312, 313, 332, 333, 334, 335, 336, 351, 360, 373, 377, 380, 427, 428, 435, 438, 447, 448, 451. Illustrations 396, 420, 421, 422, 449 are by courtesy of the American Artists Group; 47 and 59 by courtesy of the Morgan Library; 123 and 472 of the Fogg Museum, 119 by courtesy of Prof. Paul J. Sachs; 404 of the City Art Museum of St. Louis; 134, of the Rosenwald Collection; 418, of the Guy Mayer Gallery; 423, of Mrs. Charles Whitmore of the Print Corner; 413, of Kennedy and Company; 310, of R. Fridenberg; 385, of Bernice Abbott; 384 and 386, by courtesy of Alfred Stieglitz and Camera Work; and numerous others by courtesy of the artists, of various publications and private collectors. And I wish to thank Mr. Fitz Roy Carrington and the firm of Knoedler and Company, Mr. William M. Ivins, Jr., and the entire staff of the Print Room of the Metropolitan Museum of Art, Prof. Paul J. Sachs and Harry Sternberg for many kindnesses accorded me in the preparation of this book. As far as the text is concerned I wish to record my indebtedness, both acknowledged and unacknowledged, for many ideas and opinions contained therein. In the words of Montaigne:

"I name not my borrowings, but I weigh them."

SIX CENTURIES OF FINE PRINTS

1. Introduction

THIS is the story of certain scraps of paper—scraps of paper, some old, some new, with curious marks of ink on them, but rare and precious in men's eyes, scraps of paper treasured in museums and cherished by collectors in many lands. These prints, for such they are, must indeed have something provocative and mysterious about them despite their ubiquity and matter-of-fact presence: they seem to be woven into the very fabric of our culture and civilization. What is this mysterious something that enhances so greatly the value of prints? It is not the intrinsic value of the paper and ink, for that is negligible. It is their power to move the beholder, not only to amuse or instruct him but also to stir the wellsprings of his being, to speak to him poignantly of his inmost thoughts and feelings, of religion, of sex, of war, of pride and pomp and power, of freedom and justice, of order and beauty. Prints share this power of evocation and inspiration with other great forms of visual art, but with the added virtue that, the print being a democratic form, its examples can be owned and enjoyed by many instead of a few.

Prints have had many apologists and defenders, but none more charming than the anonymous author of *Sculptura-Historico-Technica*, or *The History and Art of Ingraving*, of 1747:

When I reflect on the Usefulness of this Art, I am surprized to find so few Gentlemen professed Admirers of it. It requires a large Fortune to make a fine Collection of Paintings, and great Judgment to avoid Imposition, and understand their Beauties; but Prints are adapted to all Ages, all Ranks of Men, and all Fortunes; they cost much less than Paintings, the Knowledge of them is more easily attained; and they comprehend all Sorts of Subjects, they are equally as useful as entertaining. . . .

Prints divert Youth, and instruct them at the same Time, by the lively

9

Impression they make on their Minds; and this Instruction is not only more readily received but is more durable than that conveyed by Words. If you have a Child learn any Passage in Sacred or Profane History, by amusing him with a Representation of it, and explaining the Subject, he will rarely forget the Impression the different Characters that compose it will make on him. . . .

Prints are also as useful as entertaining; they represent absent things to us, as if they were present; they convey us instantly, without Hazard or Expence, into the most distant Countries, and make us as well acquainted with them as with our own; they communicate to us the Knowledge of many beautiful Objects in those Countries, which we must have been ignorant of, without their Assistance; and make us Contemporaries (in a manner) with the greatest Men of past Ages by giving us their lively Resemblance. . . .

Nothing is more proper to form a Taste than Prints: they give us a Tincture of the fine Arts; they assist us to arrive at the Knowledge of Paintings; for if we examine them attentively, they make us easily discover the different Manner affected by each School and Master. . . .

Lastly, there is hardly any Subject, with Regard to which we cannot either acquire some Knowledge, or enlarge that we already have, by the Help of this noble Art.

When our old author mentioned that prints can be both useful and entertaining, he hit upon a characteristic which distinguishes prints from most of the other forms of the visual arts—their potential duality. Prints, like literature and the printed word, can serve both science and beauty, in Coleridge's famous distinction between science and poetry, as the communication of truth and the communication of immediate pleasure (in its widest sense as emotive power); or, as Erasmus put it in praising the prints of Dürer, the natural aspect of a thing and the perfect symmetry and harmony. I am far from asserting that all the visual arts have a literary or didactic or scientific purpose—they have conventions peculiarly their own—but the graphic arts * are on the border line between science and art, and function in both. Fine prints as a class can serve beauty in a timeless way. They have an intrinsic appeal entirely

* The term, graphic art, is used strictly in this book to mean art forms produced by printing methods.

apart from the question as to whether they were made in the fifteenth or the twentieth century. They possess uniqueness, magic, a spiritual impress, the stamp of vivid personality, a singing quality of line or mass, some telling economy of expression that satisfies in a flash of immediate comprehension. But just as a work of art can splendidly evoke almost the whole gamut of the emotions, so it can also diagram or illustrate an idea. It can organize a group of facts into a telling picture. It can add to our knowledge in a graphic way. It can document contemporary life. Indeed, much of our knowledge of the past, its life, customs, manners, fashions, comes from the prints and illustrations of the time. In this respect photography has made an enormous contribution since its perfection less than a hundred years ago. In the past, prints were the only medium for illustrating flowers, birds, and other forms of natural history, maps and city views, pattern designs for lace, furniture, costumes, goldsmith's work, and all kinds of ornament in applied art and architecture. Graphic art is also the accepted vehicle for satire, caricature, humor, propaganda—all the various forms of comment and persuasion in pictures.

But what are prints anyway? The word, "prints," like charity, covers a multitude of sins. To some people prints mean mechanical reproductions in color, used for decoration, which one can buy, neatly framed, in drug or department stores. To others prints are the innocuous etchings that are given again and again as wedding presents. To still others they are the photographs that are pasted in snapshot albums. To others, again, they are textiles with designs applied in color, such as chintzes or cotton and silk dress goods. Prints, especially when prefaced by the word "public," are sometimes used to mean newspapers and magazines. In a specialized sense, however, fine prints usually denote the etchings, woodcuts, and lithographs which artists make for esthetic or other reasons. They are usually called fine prints to distinguish them from prints in general. All of the above meanings are strictly correct, for as a matter of fact, "print" stands for anything that is printed. That the word has so many and so varied connotations, merely emphasizes the extent that prints have permeated and become part of our daily life. Indeed it would be amusing to speculate on how barren life today would become were all prints removed. All books and newspapers, all of photography including the movies, most of the intellectual life, science, philosophy, social science, most of music except that played by ear or from manuscript, and most of graphic art would disappear.

The graphic arts, which include fine prints, illustrated books, and photography, are a great cultural force in our lives; indeed they rank as one of the three principal spheres of art activity in general, the other two being the art of personal adornment, costume, etcetera, and the arts that cluster around the home or around public buildings (including churches), painting, sculpture, furniture, and all the applied arts. To put it in a catch phrase, art is focused at three essential points—the Body, the Building, and the Book. Practically every branch of art can find its expression and use within these three categories. Since the Middle Ages, with the development of the democratic idea, the graphic arts, summarized in the last great B, the Book, have become a major art. It is only in recent times, however, that the real importance of prints has been recognized, when it was discovered how closely their development coincided with the rise and development of the bourgeois or middle class. When the graphic arts will have become so widespread as to touch and speak to every man, woman, and child in the community, then it may be said that they truly have become the art of the people.

Just as people in speaking of prints often mean quite different things, so also, when referring to fine prints in the specialized sense, they like them for various and sundry reasons. There is no doubt that there are many different incentives to own prints, some of which have little to do with art or esthetic standards. There is, for example, the incentive to own religious images or icons, which was most powerful during the Middle Ages. Sometimes a person likes a print because it recalls pleasant memories of a holiday spent abroad or of a hunting or fishing trip. Sometimes a person collects prints because it is the thing to do. (There used to be a saying current that no wedding was legal unless a print by a certain etcher was present among the gifts to the happy couple.) Sometimes, again, because a person sees a picture in the possession of another whose taste he values. Sometimes, following Veblen's theory of conspicuous consumption, because a person desires to show that he can

12

afford expensive things. Sometimes, a person buys a picture because he thinks, or has been told, that it is a good investment, and will enhance in value, just as stocks and bonds sometimes do. But, sometimes a person owns a print just because it appeals to his esthetic sense: because he gets a unique pleasure from a particular pattern of black and white, or a delicious bit of fine draughtsmanship. Or because he is moved in a special way by the intensity or grandeur of a visual idea. Or because he is amused by a portrayal, whether benevolent or malicious, of some aspect of the *Comedie Humaine*. Because, in short, some element in the picture haunts his memory like a phrase of poetry or a strain of music.

Finally the critics by their varied approaches contribute their testimony to the conclusion that art is not any one thing but a vastly intricate complex as elusive as the secret of life itself. Most critics, sitting in judgment on the art of the past and present with one or another of their measuring rods, remind one of the fable of the seven blind men and the elephant. Each one of them was sure that he was right in his report about the elephant, and strangely enough he was right—they were all right. A work of art, like a fact of life, has a certain being of its own—it just *is*. If it be great and vital enough, it will have a long life, and each generation will look at it anew and interpret its virtues and defects according to the prevailing taste of its time.

Just as the connoisseur of food is interested in cook books, in how the delectable dishes are prepared, so the print lover is interested in the technique of the graphic arts, the "cookery" of fine prints. Therefore it might be well to explain briefly how prints are made. There are three general methods of reproducing designs: the first the "relief" method usually employed on wood; the second the "intaglio" or "incised" method on metal such as copper or zinc, or for very brief periods on iron or steel; the third the "planographic or chemical" method on stone or zinc or aluminum. The relief method or woodcut is the oldest in point of time. The technique is relatively simple. The artist takes a block of wood, cut along the length of the tree and planed smooth, and proceeds to cut away all those portions of his design that he does not intend to print black. When he has finished cutting on the wood,

13

his drawing stands complete in relief with the rest of the block cut down to a depth of about one eighth of an inch. The artist then inks the surface of the block, lays a sheet of paper over it, runs it through a press, and the composition appears complete on the paper. The earliest woodcuts were printed not in a press but by rubbing with a spoon-like instrument on the back of the paper in the way that all Japanese prints are made. In early times too there generally was a division of labor, the design being drawn on the wood by the artist and the cutting away being done by a professional woodcutter.

There is a variation and development of woodcut technique called wood engraving. In this instance the artist works on a block cut from the cross-section of a tree (thus avoiding the difficulties of cutting against the grain) and uses among others a burin or engraving tool which makes a white line against a background of black. There is some confusion and difference of opinion as to the exact meaning of woodcut and wood engraving. Some hold that the difference lies in the artist's fundamental conception of his picture: in a woodcut he conceives of the picture in terms of black lines against a background of white; in a wood engraving in terms of white lines against a background of black. It sometimes happens that the artist uses both methods in the same picture, and then it becomes difficult to say which predominates. The other school holds that the difference between the two lies in the technique. Woodcuts are printed from blocks sawed along the grain and cut with knives and gouges; whereas wood engravings are printed from end-grain blocks cut with a burin. This classification at least has the virtue of not being ambiguous; the artist cannot combine end-grain and along-the-grain on the same block. But it is not always easy to tell what kind of wood was used just by looking at a print. Dürer's woodblocks and Japanese prints are typical woodcuts. Bewick's blocks and Urs Graf's *Standard-Bearer* are examples of wood engraving. An early development of wood engraving is seen in the prints in the "dotted manner" or *manière criblée*. In these white line engravings, the solid blacks are often broken up by means of little white dots executed with a punch. Most of them were printed from metal blocks, such as copper, tin, bronze, or lead. Indeed the distinction between the two great processes of relief and intaglio lies not so much in the material as in the way of printing. Eric Gill has printed etchings, or rather engravings, from wood blocks, and William Blake etched copper plates for his "Songs of Innocence and Experience" in such a way that they could be printed as woodblocks. Still another variation of woodcut technique is seen in the "chiaroscuro" prints perfected at the beginning of the sixteenth century. This form of color printing involves the use of several blocks, a black and white key block, and one or more tone blocks in which the high-lights are cut out in order to increase the range of tonal relations.

The class of intaglio print includes metal engraving, etching, drypoint, mezzotint, stipple engraving, aquatint, and soft ground etching. In engravings the lines are incised into copper or other soft metal by means of a burin or graving tool. The technique of etching was perfected early in the sixteenth century in order to lighten the labor of cutting into the metal with the burin. It was discovered that it was possible to dig out the lines by chemical means instead of by the sweat of one's brow. Therefore over the polished surface of the metal, a thin coating of an acid-resisting ground (consisting largely of wax) is laid; the artist makes a drawing upon the plate with a needle and thus lays bare the surface of the copper. The plate is then laid in a bath of acid (commonly nitric) which attacks the metal wherever it is exposed. It is this method of "etching" lines in metal that gives the process its name. One great advantage of etching over engraving is the greater freedom it gives in the drawing of the lines, since all manner of wayward and curved lines can be laid, which are exceedingly difficult to execute with the burin. Furthermore by "stopping out" some of the lines with an acid-resisting varnish and again inserting in the acid bath, it is possible to vary the biting and consequently the depth and quality of the line.

The printing principle of an engraving or etching is exactly the reverse of a woodcut. In a woodcut the lines stand out in relief and become the surface which is inked and printed. In an etching or engraving the lines are incised in the metal; the ink is forced into these lines and the surface of the metal is wiped clean. When a dampened sheet of paper is laid on the plate and the whole run through a press under

15

considerable pressure, the paper is forced into the lines and picks up the ink therein; and the whole design is printed on the paper and becomes an impression, or proof as it is sometimes called, of an original etching. In an impression of an etching or engraving, the lines are ever so slightly raised above the surface of the paper, as can be proved by running the finger very lightly over the proof (though this action will grieve the true print lover!). This fact and the noticeable impression which the edge of the copper plate works upon the paper, called the plate mark, are among the features which help to distinguish an etching or engraving from the woodcut processes. Etching is primarily a line technique, that is to say the etcher builds up his design by means of lines bitten at various depths. To amplify the technical means at the etcher's command, the Frenchman, Le Prince, invented in the late eighteenth century, the process known as aquatint. The technique is complicated but the principle is simple. By its use the etcher is enabled to draw not only with lines but also with washes or areas of tone with varying degrees of dark and light, thus adding a certain richness and variety of tonal color to his linear composition. Since both are etched with acid, it is easy to combine pure etching and aquatint.

There is still another intaglio method designed to reproduce tones and not lines, namely mezzotint. A copper plate is covered with a multitude of tiny indentations made with a special instrument called a rocker. The plate if it were inked at this stage would print uniformly black. The engraver by means of special instruments scrapes away and burnishes out at will the minute indentations to establish his high lights, and working from dark to light, gradually creates a complete pattern of light and dark tones. It is a process particularly adapted to reproducing oil paintings, and was used almost exclusively for that purpose. It is printed like an engraving but does not yield as many impressions. Another technique, used largely to reproduce drawings and paintings, is stipple engraving or, similarly, engraving in the crayon manner. It is a variation of etching in which the design is built up by minute dots produced by means of a roulette and similar instruments. It can reproduce the texture and grain of a crayon drawing with great fidelity, but owing to its softness and lack of definition (even the lines are made up of tiny dots like a modern halftone) it found its widest use in sentimental and "fancy" subjects. Still another variation is soft ground etching. A special and rather sticky ground is laid on the copper plate and upon this is laid a sheet of paper or silk or other textile. The lines are drawn over this, and when this is lifted off, the ground sticks to it wherever it was drawn upon. The plate is then bitten in the regular way. By this means a considerable variation in the textures of line work can be produced. It is sometimes used in conjunction with aquatint since its rather crumbly line is in keeping with the grained surface of aquatint.

There is another modification of engraving called drypoint. Where the lines of an engraving are cut into the metal with a burin, in drypoint they are scratched into the surface with a steel needle or diamond point. In the process a furrow or shaving of metal is raised beside the line, called the burr, which catches and holds more ink than the ordinary engraved line and imparts the rich and velvety black characteristic of the drypoint line. This burr soon wears down and few good impressions can be pulled unless the plate is steel-faced. The technique was known in early times, Dürer and the Master of the Amsterdam Cabinet having both made drypoints, but Rembrandt was the first to use the medium with a full realization of its possibilities. Drypoint is often used in conjunction with etching to give added richness and color to a composition.

The third great graphic method is lithography. It makes use of still another principle of printing. Its lines are neither incised in metal nor raised in relief on wood. It is called surface or chemical printing, and was invented around the beginning of the nineteenth century by a German, Aloys Senefelder. The process is based upon the well-known antipathy of grease and water. The artist draws with a greasy crayon on a slab of special limestone (found only in Bavaria) which has been grained to a requisite degree of fineness. When the artist has finished his drawing, the stone is turned over to a lithographer for printing. By a series of chemical steps which it will not be necessary to elaborate here, the greasy content becomes fixed in the stone. The stone is then moistened with a sponge. Wherever there is a greasy spot or mark the water will be repelled, but everywhere else the stone will absorb water and become damp. The stone is now ready for printing. A greasy ink

17

is rolled over the surface. Wherever there is a greasy mark the ink will take, wherever the stone is damp and clear the greasy ink will not take. A sheet of paper is placed on the stone and the whole run through the press, with the result that an exact replica of the drawing appears on the paper. A certain kind of zinc plate can be used in place of the lithographic stone with equal success. Lithography is an exceedingly flexible medium with an enormous range of effects; lines with crayon or pen, washes, stamp work, tonal values of all kinds can be rendered with fidelity and subtlety. For this reason many modern artists use lithography in preference to the other graphic media.

One final word on the use of the word, "original." Since it is used in two different senses, confusion sometimes ensues. It is used as an adjective in contradiction to "reproductive." An original etching is one which the artist has conceived and executed himself. A reproductive etching is one in which the etcher has copied another artist's design or painting. This distinction has lost much of its force in the last fifty years since photography has taken over the reproductive function of prints. In any case the distinction is invidious because some so-called reproductive engravings, by Raimondi after Raphael for example, are infinitely superior to a multitude of original etchings by mediocre artists. When used as a noun, original refers specifically to a print. Some people have the mistaken notion that all prints are copies of some hidden and mysterious original. Every single impression of a woodcut, etching, or lithograph is an "original," the final and complete embodiment of the artist's intention, of which the plate, the paper and the ink are the preliminary steps. The miracle of the process is that there are not one but many originals—the incarnation of the democratic ideal.

The pictures which make up the main portion of this book, form an anthology, as it were, of six centuries of fine prints. Out of the millions of prints that have been made in the course of time, some five hundred have been selected here. It is hoped that they are typical and representative of the manifold activities of the graphic arts. No special claim is put forth for any originality in the ideas expressed in this book: they are part of the current idiom of scholarship today. In making the

18

selection an attempt has been made to maintain a balance between two different attitudes: that of the historian who searches for what is typical, average, and expressive of the time, and that of the artist who is interested in what is unusual, heightened, and timeless. In some rare instances, it is believed, these seemingly divergent aims have been united in one and the same print, that is at once timeless and nobly expressive of its time. Furthermore the attempt has been made, as far as it is possible in the brief space allotted, to project prints against the background of history, to synchronize their production with that of the other arts and sciences, with the events of war and statecraft, economic and social life; in short to try to see them as their contemporaries saw them as well as in the perspective of time. There is a give-and-take between the artist and his age: he leaves an impress on his contemporaries, and contemporary influences leave their impress on him. All this is mirrored dramatically in his works, more especially in such a medium as the print, which, being widespread and popular, reflects more accurately contemporary conditions. Two great factors have molded the actions of all men, economic conditions and ideology, stomach and mind. These inevitable strands of warp and woof are as evident in the tapestry of art as they are in the other activities of life. Art is one of the noblest of man's endeavors, but it is not mysterious; it is still essentially human, the product of his hand and brain.

Some of the qualities of this human approach to art have been indicated in Vincent Sheean's beautiful appreciation of Persian art:

It seemed to me that I understood those works of Persian art. I did not *know* them, as an expert knows such things, with an instant recognition of the details of excellence, a comprehension that went from type to individual and back again. In fact I knew nothing about them. But their form and color, I believed, spoke clearly to me. I knew why the artists of the great centuries on the plateau of Iran worked in this way and no other: I understood their dialect. It was the gentle dialect of the desert garden, the speech of privacy and repose. The soft glowing splendor of the golden carpet from the mosque at Qum, the lovely light that came out of the great rose carpet from Rome, must have been put there by artists whose essential nature did not differ from that of (say) Pollaiuolo or Poussin or

Renoir or Sir Christopher Wren. The impulse to create in beautiful form would have been in all cases the same, but the specific shape in each was determined by a set of circumstances the artist could not control, against which, as often as not, he spent his life protesting. The conditions of daily life produced the conditions of the art that undertook (at least in the great centuries) to embellish or enhance it. The life of the oasis, when it was lived by sensitive, sedentary, indolent, and passionate people of the Irani race, compelled its art works to assume the mood of refuge, of rest, under forms predetermined by the oasis itself, the actual instrument of man's struggle with surrounding nature—so that the garden determined both the architecture and the carpet, and the works produced by artists under such conditions of life coalesced, when they were assembled together, to give the impression of style.

If this was true—and it seemed to me incontestable—then the problems of style and form in general in the whole range of creation had to take a secondary place like the elaborate considerations of scholarship, which could never rise to greater dignity than that of a footnote. These works were something more than the toys of rich men, the objects of a dilettante's fascination, or the theme chosen by bourgeois intellectuals to display the cultivated subtleties of their minds. These were actual instruments in the long battle of mankind to make life more tolerable, and were in their consequent shapes and styles determined by race, climate, the forms of society, the economic shape and style of the world in which the artist lived.

The whole weight of what Cézanne called *l'art des musées* came to life with a bound, when it was seen, not as an accumulation of certain beautiful tricks that some men had been able to do better than others, but as an organic part of the life of man, a supremely useful instrument in the adaptation of nature and control of society for his greater happiness.

2 . The End of Gothic

DURING the fifteenth century—as far as it is mirrored in the history of prints—one great epoch ended and another began. In the northern countries, France, Germany, and Flanders, the Gothic era ended and the Renaissance began; in Italy the Renaissance was in full bloom. In one sense, however, the classifications of Late Gothic and High Renaissance are relatively minor distinctions: the very idea of making prints, a cheap multiplication of originals, like the idea of printing from movable types, was an event of the greatest cultural importance, and one that marked the transition between the medieval and the modern point of view. "The Gothic sun," as Victor Hugo said, "set behind the colossal press at Mainz." It was during the fifteenth century that both woodcuts and copper engravings in any quantity began to be made and printed and sold.

It is interesting to speculate why the idea of making prints should have been carried to a practical conclusion at that particular period in the annals of European history. It was not that the idea or the technique of engraving was a new one. There exist incised drawings by primitive man on mammoth tusks capable, when inked, of producing prints in our sense of the word. Likewise the Greeks sometimes engraved designs on the back of their bronze or silver mirrors which could easily serve as printing plates. And there are examples of Romanesque art such as the famous Chandelier of the Emperor Barbarossa at Aix-la-Chapelle of the twelfth century, parts of which contain metal plates with incised designs, as if made to order for the production of engravings. About a century ago when this chandelier was taken down to be cleaned, some one conceived the idea of inking the plates and striking off a small number of impressions from them. One of these prints, the *Nativity*, in circular form is reproduced in this book (illustration 142). The result might easily be

21

taken for a true engraving in Romanesque style some three centuries before the earliest known engraving. Likewise, the technique of designing and cutting a wood block had already been perfected for the printing of textiles. There exist Coptic textiles of the sixth century which are stamped with wood blocks (illustration 107). Printed textiles were common in the Middle Ages. Cennino Cennini describes the technique in his *Book of Art* at the end of the fourteenth century.

One of the chief reasons why prints were not produced in the twelfth century was the fact that there was no cheap and efficient reproducing medium such as paper. Paper, to be sure, was known in Europe at the time. The earliest extant document on paper in Europe is a deed by King Roger of Sicily written in Arabic and Latin and dated 1109. Paper is officially recorded as having been invented in China in the year 105. It remained a Chinese secret until its manufacture in Samarkand in 757 and in Bagdad in 793 through knowledge gained from Chinese prisoners. This knowledge was later transmitted to the Saracens in Spain in 1150. The first paper-mill in France was established at Hérault in 1189, in Italy at Fabriano in 1276, in Germany at Nuremberg in 1391. Much of the paper used in Europe, however, was still imported from the Saracen mills in Spain and Damascus, and it was not until the middle of the fifteenth century that paper was in general use in Europe. "There were few in Europe who could read," as Carter points out, "and the demand for a cheaper writing material, until the advent of printing, was small. It was the coming of paper that made the invention of printing possible, yet it was the invention of printing that made the use of paper general."

Thus it is to be seen that a plentiful supply of a cheap reproducing material such as paper was a conditioning factor in any widespread production of woodcuts and engravings. There was, however, still another factor to be considered, namely the demand on the part of the people. In the early Middle Ages the standard of living was very low. In this age of scarcity there was little demand for such marginal luxuries as pictures or the written word. In so far as a demand for pictures existed it was satisfied by the church, which was the meeting place and treasure-house of the whole community. Most of the people were scattered on the land; very little of the population was concentrated in towns. Furthermore there was little trade. Each community was a self-contained economic unit. It produced, with considerable effort, all that it required for subsistence; there was no surplus. It is difficult for us in this day and age to visualize such a state of society. There were no books or newspapers, no ready-made clothes, and few utensils, no shops or stores, few artisans who practiced their trade exclusively. There was practically no money: almost all trade was effected by barter. There was very little travel. The roads were bad, and there were many knights and nobles who made common practice of out-and-out brigandage, or, with some show of legality, of the exaction of tolls. A great many of the people could not travel at all since they were bound to the land as serfs or tenants. The standard of living in the manors and castles was more sumptuous but not much higher.

It is small wonder then that in such a milieu there was small demand and no place for "art in the home." There were, however, several major historical developments which eventually succeeded in breaking up the stagnation of the feudal or manorial system. One of these was the Crusades; by increasing travel they introduced new ideas and cultivated a taste for the comforts and luxuries of the Orient. Another was the rise of Free Cities, which either retained or acquired exemption from feudal obligations incumbent on the peasantry. Concomitant with the growth of Free Cities was a vast extension of trade both with the Orient and with various parts of Europe. The Italian cities, Genoa, Pisa, Amalfi, and chiefly Venice, grew rich through the Crusades and the oriental trade. The cities of Flanders, chiefly Bruges, were the meeting place of the northern and southern maritime trade, and at the same time the center of the woolen-weaving industry of Europe. Augsburg, Nuremberg, Ulm, Basel, Mainz, Frankfurt, and Cologne were cities that waxed prosperous along the overland trade routes from Venice to the north. All of these engaged in manufacture and trade—activities of the middleman as opposed to the agrarian and producer-consumer economy of feudalism. Their merchant and artisan guilds became wealthy and powerful, and their citizens acquired a taste for art and other luxuries. Albrecht

23

Dürer, in his diary of his journey to the Netherlands in 1520, recounts how he was received in Bruges in the height of its prosperity:

Then they prepared a banquet for me, and I went thence with them to their guild hall; there were many honorable men gathered together, goldsmiths, painters, and merchants, and they made me sup with them and they gave me presents and sought my acquaintance and did me great honor.

And thus he describes a festival in Antwerp:

The Sunday after the Feast of the Assumption I saw the great procession of Our Lady's Church at Antwerp, where the whole town was gathered together, with all the trades and professions, and each was dressed in his best according to his rank; every guild and profession had its sign by which it might be recognized. Between the companies were carried great costly gold pole-candlesticks and their long old Frankish silver trumpets; and there were many pipers and drummers in the German fashion; all were loudly and noisily blown and beaten. I saw the procession pass along the street, spread far apart so that they took up much space crossways, but close behind one another: goldsmiths, painters, stonecutters, broiderers, sculptors, joiners, carpenters, sailors, fishermen, butchers, leather-workers, clothmakers, bakers, tailors, shoemakers, and all kinds of craftsmen and workmen who work for their livelihood. There were likewise shopkeepers and merchants with their assistants of all sorts. After them came the marksmen with their guns, bows, and cross-bows; then the horsemen and foot soldiers; then came a fine troop of very gallant men, nobly and splendidly costumed.

It was in such free and vigorous city life that the practice of printmaking in the North took hold and spread rapidly. Prints, being produced in relatively large quantities, require, if not trading, at least an organized distribution over a wide area. Furthermore a prosperous middle class, which made up the urban population, was then and for many centuries to come the best customer for prints. The peasant and laborer never had any margin above subsistence to buy more than an occasional religious image. And the nobles and the court circles, notably the Burgundian court of the fifteenth century and the rulers of the Italian cities, bestowed their greatest patronage on painting, sculpture, miniature painting, and architecture.

Of the two great genres of printmaking the woodblock was the

24

first to be developed. Its actual beginnings are lost in the obscurity and anonymity which surround most popular art. Popular art, the obvious and omnipresent thing, the cheap common object, is generally quite literally worn out in use; little value is attached to it at the time and it is preserved only by some happy chance. Those prints which have come down through the ages have sometimes been found in out-of-the-way places, pasted inside the bindings of old books, or pasted on doors and walls like wall paper. Occasionally they are found pasted on the insides of little trunks or traveling cases (illustration 133). These boxes, as Hind suggests, were probably used by lawyers or merchants for their documents or accounts, or by priests to carry their breviaries and other requisites on their journeys. It is obvious that with such great lacunae in the record, the history of the woodcut in its origins is hard to determine. It is probable, however, that the idea of printing impressions on paper to supply a demand for a cheap multiplication of designs first gained currency around the beginning of the fifteenth century. And demand there was, on two separate counts. One was for playing cards. Although there are no examples of woodcut playing cards extant before about 1450, cards by their nature being apt to be worn out, there is every reason to suppose that there was a flourishing production of playing cards from the beginning of the century in Germany and Italy. An example dating from the second half of the fifteenth century and signed by J. de Dale of Lyon is reproduced as illustration 56. The more primitive cuts were in outline only and were designed to be colored either by hand or through stencils. An early representation of card playing, with a glimpse of the cards themselves, is given in illustration 6, from a book printed in Augsburg in 1472 by Gunther Zainer.

The second great demand for prints was for religious images, pictures of the saints, illustrations of the life of the Virgin or of Christ. Some of the early woodcuts were probably produced in monasteries by the monks themselves. The monasteries enjoyed immunity from guild restrictions, and at the beginning there undoubtedly was opposition by the guilds of artists and illuminators to a technique which threatened their livelihood. To a certain extent printmaking in these early times labored under the stigma of being a counterfeit or illegitimate art. The

25

great bulk of the work, however, was either made by regular artists by direct commission from monasteries or produced with an eye to the religious market at the great centers of print production, such as the cities of Ulm, Augsburg, Bamberg, Nuremberg, Cologne, Dijon, Avignon, Bruges, Salzburg, etcetera. The religious orders and the churches, in any case, were among the chief customers for such prints. Hind quotes Luther's complaint against the Pope, in his pamphlet, *An den christlichen Adel deutscher Nation:* that he granted the revenues of a convent to some cardinal, who would leave a single monk in charge, one of whose chief duties was to sell pictures to pilgrims. The artists and printers also sold directly to the people at their shops or at the fairs. Dürer, when in Venice, wrote back to his friend, Pirkheimer: "Now I commend myself to you, and tell my mother to be ready to sell at the Crown Fair."

A characteristic example of primitive woodcut is reproduced herewith as illustration 19. The Buxheim *St. Christopher* was for a long time famous as the first example of a woodcut actually bearing a date, namely 1423, though further research has discovered an earlier print, the Brussels *Madonna* bearing the date 1418. It was discovered in the binding of a book in the Carthusian monastery of Buxheim and is probably of Bavarian origin. It is a dramatic rendering of the Christopher legend and is full of simple and naive charm. In addition to the date below there is a Latin inscription which may be translated as follows: "On whatsoever day thou hast seen Christopher's face, on that day, to be sure, thou shalt not die an evil death." This inscription furnishes a clue to the extraordinary popularity of images of St. Christopher: the sight of him was talismanic and insured if not against death, at least against an unshrived and unsanctified death—according to popular superstition. It is interesting to discover in a painting of the Annunciation by Robert Campin, the Master of Flémalle, in the Brussels Museum, a print of St. Christopher hanging (with charming disregard for historical sequence) over the chimney. It illustrates the way in which these prints, unmatted and unframed, were used in the home, and also demonstrates why so few of them have survived. The anachronism of displaying a print of St. Christopher in a room where the Archangel Gabriel is foretelling to

26

the Virgin the miraculous birth of Christ is characteristic of the age. This disregard of the unities of time or place is mirrored in our print of St. Christopher itself: various incidents in the life and miracle of St. Christopher are telescoped into one picture. The intention of the artist was not realistic but symbolic. The realistic touches that do appear in the picture are in the nature of corroborative or decorative detail. This approach to the solution of an artistic problem has been widely used by artists of all ages, including the twentieth century. The *St. Onuphrius* (illustration 132) and the *Nativity*, already mentioned (illustration 133), both in the Metropolitan Museum, are examples of single woodcuts of the second half of the fifteenth century. St. Onuphrius was a patron saint of weavers, possibly because he wove his own clothes of leaves during his fifty years' sojourn in the Thebaid. Still another *"Einblattdruck"* is reproduced, more realistic and satiric in subject matter, and executed on metal in the dotted print manner. It probably dates from about 1480 of German provenance. The subject is a satire on *Gossip during the Celebration of Mass* (illustration 18). The technique of *manière criblée* undoubtedly grew out of the metal worker's use of punches of various sizes and shapes to build up a design, often of great richness and delicacy. The subject is unusual and is executed with great spirit.

The so-called block-books form an interesting phase in the development of the woodcut. In block-books text and pictures were combined in one impression, and the lettering was cut out of the same block as the picture. At one time the importance of these books was greatly exaggerated when it was thought that they formed a connecting link between the graphic arts and the printing of books. Subsequent research has demonstrated, however, that the perfection of the art of printing proceeded quite independently of the block-books. As works of art they have relatively little merit, with the possible exception of the *Ars Moriendi* and the *Canticum Canticorum* (illustration 29). They were nevertheless very popular in their day and many successive editions have been recorded.

Not so many years after the invention of printing, the printers saw the possibility of using woodcuts for illustrating their books and thus competing more advantageously with the illuminated manuscript. From about 1470 on, woodcut books began to appear with increasing frequency in all the leading centers of book production. William Morris has written with appreciation of these early books:

The invention of printing books and the use of woodblocks for book ornament in place of hand-painting, though it belongs to the period of the degradation of medieval art, gave an opportunity to the Germans to regain the place which they had lost in the art of book decoration during the thirteenth and fourteenth centuries. This opportunity they took with vigor and success, and by means of it put forth works which showed the best and most essential qualities of their race. Unhappily, even at the time of the first woodcut book, the beginning of the end was on them; about thirty years afterwards they received the Renaissance with singular eagerness and rapidity, and became, from the artistic point of view, a nation of rhetorical pedants. . . . It may surprise some of our readers, though I should hope not the greatest part of them, to hear that I claim the title of works of art, both for these picture-ornamented books as books, and also for the pictures themselves. Their two main merits are first their decorative and next their story-telling quality; and it seems to me that these two qualities include what is necessary and essential in book pictures.

It would not be possible in so brief a space to make a complete survey of illustrated incunabula, and a few typical examples will easily do service for the whole. From Ulm three examples have been chosen: Johann Zainer's edition of Boccaccio's *De Claris Mulieribus* of 1473 (illustration 7) cited by Morris as a special favorite of his; Lienhart Holle's edition of *Bidpai* of 1483 (illustration 20), a collection of Oriental fables also known as the *Panchatantra*, compiled by Anthonius von Pforr from a Latin version based upon a Hebrew version in turn based upon an Arabic translation of the original Sanskrit; the third Dinckmut's edition of Terence's *Eunuch* of 1486 (illustration 22). In the last mentioned woodcuts, the houses and windows have been conventionalized into a delightful pattern of black and white. It is interesting to compare this early print with a recent print by Niles Spencer where the modern artist has also made a lively abstract pattern by conventionalizing house forms (illustration 446). Another revelation of the medieval conception

28

of Terence and the theater is given in illustration 21, after a woodcut from a Lyons edition of 1493. The designer has presented a view of the theater as a whole including the audience, and below has portrayed the "*Fornices*" or "Stews" with the daughters of joy plying their trade.

Two examples of Netherlands presses are given: the *Chevalier Delibéré* (illustration 23) printed in Gouda in 1485, a ponderous panegyric on the exploits of Charles the Bold; and the cut of *Sir Hercules Fighting Three Lions* (illustration 30) from the *Histoire van Trojen* printed by Bellaert in Haarlem in 1485. This woodcut, with its highly decorative pattern of black and white, is conceived in a sort of heraldic style with artistic conventions familiar to all students of heraldry. It is interesting to note that the hero wears the plate armor which replaced the old fashioned knee-length coat-of-mail around the beginning of the century. It was this style of armor that brought about the use of a separate upper and nether garment, shirt and hose or trousers, which has remained characteristic of male attire ever since.

The introduction of printing and the expansion of the forces which led to the Reformation focused much attention and interest on the Bible. Not only were various editions of the Latin Vulgate printed, but many translations into Dutch, French, Italian, Czech, German (notably Luther's of 1522) were made and printed during the fifteenth and sixteenth centuries. The authority of God's Word in the vulgar tongue (as interpreted by each individual conscience) was invoked to controvert the authority of the Catholic Church in matters of salvation. One of the articles of the Schmalkaldic League, a league of Protestant principalities, specified that "the articles of faith shall be based upon God's Word and that of no one else, not even an angel's." Many of these popular Bibles were illustrated with woodcuts, some of only archaeological interest, others famous for their beauty and design. Three characteristic examples are reproduced herewith as illustrations 5 and 8 and 50. The first is the *Adam and Eve and the Expulsion from Paradise* from the Cologne Bible printed about 1479 by Quentel. It was the most ambitious undertaking made up to that time and the blocks had considerable influence on other artists; Koberger borrowed them (a not uncommon procedure of the day) to use in his edition of the Bible at Nuremberg in

1483, and both Dürer and Holbein borrowed and transformed some of the designs in their own series of Bible illustrations. The other woodcut is from the Bible printed in Lübeck by Steffen Arndes in 1494. There are certain realistic touches and a certain interest in the psychological interplay of the characters—the embarrassment of Joseph's brothers in the presence, as they suppose, of a high Egyptian dignitary—that strike a somewhat new note in German illustration. Most early German illustration is schematic, a sign-post, as Kristeller called it, a symbol rather than an illustration in the true sense of the word. They presented the bare bones of a subject but seldom clothed it in flesh and blood. The pictures were subordinate to the text and served as a quick method of locating a particular chapter or subject. In the *Nuremberg Chronicle*, for example, one and the same portrait cut was used to represent Thales, Paris, Anastasius, Odofredus, and Dante. The Lübeck Bible illustrations foreshadowed the time, soon to come, when the artist's illustrations would have an importance and validity equal to that of the text. Another famous book which initiates a more modern attitude is Breydenbach's *Voyage to the Holy Land*, Mainz 1486 (illustration 28). It is the first illustrated book in which the designer's name is mentioned—Erhart Reuwich. The author took the artist along on his journey, and he made many drawings, translated into woodcuts, of city views and sketches of foreign peoples, Turks, Saracens, Jews, etcetera. There is also a page of animals including a camel, monkey, giraffe, crocodile, and, believe it or not, a unicorn; underneath is an inscription saying, "These animals are accurately drawn as we saw them in the Holy Land." In spite of such occasional lapses, the book is not only lively and entertaining but surprisingly accurate. It is the first work of travel and geography that is based not on Aristotle or Ptolemy but on independent observation, and it inaugurates a long line of views and maps in printed form that were to extend man's knowledge of the globe.

Not only Bibles but other religious books were adorned with woodcuts, Missals, Psalters, and Books of Hours. A cut depicting the *Celebration of the Mass* from the Paris Missal of 1481 printed by Jehan du Pré, is shown in illustration 15. It is the earliest illustrated book printed in Paris, and it set the style of French illustration for some time to come.

30

It contains more sensuous imagery than most of the German work; more of the élan of the actual scene is carried over into the picture. With it all, the artist has succeeded in illustrating literally, after the fashion of the Middle Ages, the image of the priest lifting up his soul to God. Another charming example of French engraving is the *Bible en Françoys* printed for Vérard about 1505. Its *Adam and Eve* (illustration 50) affords an interesting contrast to the similar subject from the Cologne Bible. The emphasis of the German work is on the moral question, whereas that of the French work is on a naive delight in the wonders of a terrestrial paradise. Among the most beautiful and touching productions in the whole history of prints were the *Horae* or Books of Hours, printed in Paris in the two decades just preceding and succeeding the turn of the sixteenth century. These *Horae* were prayer books chiefly for the laity, designed as cheap substitutes for the manuscript *Horae* which had been current for hundreds of years. They usually contained the Kalendar, extracts from the Gospels, the Canonical Hours or daily offices of the church, various other offices including the Office of the Dead, the Litanies, and the Penitential Psalms, and the whole furnished with a host of charming designs and pictures, following out the Latin proverb, "*Pictura est laicorum scriptura.*" There might be large cuts of the Visitation, Nativity, Adoration of the Shepherds, and the Magi, Flight into Egypt, Dives and Lazarus, David and Bathsheba, and similar subjects traditionally associated with certain portions of the text. And there would be borders made up of small cuts of Gothic designs, scenes from the life of the Virgin and of Christ, the story of Susanna or Joseph and his Brethren, images of saints, the procession of the *Danse Macabre*, the occupations of the months, glimpses of huntsmen and stags and dogs, of lovers and fools, of griffins and mermaids—a veritable kaleidoscope of imagery, austerely religious or enchantingly secular, to strike the fancy and delight the eye. The essence of the Middle Ages is distilled in these pages, the faint perfume of incense, the quiet and the coolness of churches, the perennial magic of an ancient legend sweetly told, a gallimaufry of sublime and grotesque. A page from the *Horae* printed in 1498 by Philippe Pigouchet for the bookseller Simon Vostre is reproduced as illustration 16. The dramatic story of Dives and Lazarus is set

31

within a frame of beautiful Gothic ornament and this in turn is surrounded by a border of small cuts depicting the Cumaean Sibyl, the Marriage of Joachim and Anna, and three scenes of the Dance of Death, the Pope, the Emperor, and the Cardinal. These books of hours were very popular at the time, about six hundred editions by various French publishers having been preserved and recorded, in addition to countless others that have been lost. They were one of the last fine flowerings of the Gothic spirit, and their popularity was short-lived. The impact of the Renaissance created an entirely new style of ornament and design, which is reflected in the *Horae* designed by Geoffrey Tory and printed by Simon de Colines in 1525 (illustration 60). Tory, famous humanist, typographer, and designer of type and woodcuts, author of *Champfleury*, was thoroughly imbued with the ideals of the Italian Renaissance. But these ideals were not in the long run sympathetic to a mode of expression so essentially medieval as the books of hours, and they eventually ceased to have any influence in the lives of the people. Though this later *Horae* does not suggest the religious feeling of the fifteenth century book, from a typographical standpoint it is a beautiful work, the Renaissance ornament and open line work harmonizing perfectly with the light roman type face.

The Dance of Death was a theme that haunted the medieval mind. And well it might, for the vision of sudden and inevitable death was a vivid and terrible reality in the later Middle Ages. There had been plagues in Europe before, but in 1348 the Black Death or bubonic plague swept through the whole of Europe in successive epidemics with an overwhelming loss of life. It is estimated that in England over half the population lost their lives; in Venice two-fifths of the people died; in certain districts of France only one-tenth of the population survived. There were two reactions possible toward this catastrophe: one licentious, "eat, drink and be merry, for tomorrow we die," and the other ascetic, "memento mori." Both attitudes had their reflection in the art of the time, though the austere attitude predominated. An example of the first attitude is Boccaccio's *Decameron*, which as every one knows were the tales told to pass the time away by a group of people who had retired to escape the plague. (This work is here represented by illustra-

32

tion 3, from the Venice edition of 1491.) The *Danse Macabre*, a typical expression of the more austere attitude, was immensely popular for several centuries to come. Not only was it literally performed as a Dance of Death, a sort of Mystery Play, but the sequence was painted on the walls of churches, cemeteries, and covered bridges, and appeared in innumerable prints and books. Perhaps the idea of death as the great leveler, before whom all ranks and privileges were abolished, unconsciously nourished certain democratic notions that were growing at the time. Typical of the earlier *Danses Macabres*, and indeed based upon the lost frescoes in the cemetery of Les Innocents at Paris, is the *Danse Macabre des Hommes* which Pierre le Rouge printed for Guyot Marchant in 1485 (illustration 34). Here the Doctor and the Lover are confronted with their dead selves in the shape of grinning corpses and skeletons. The series is completed by representatives of all walks and ranks of men, and was followed later by the equivalent panorama for women. In Holbein's woodcut series of the Dance of Death (illustration 31) first published by Trechsel at Lyon in 1538, the obvious dance form has been discarded in favor of a more subtle and imaginative juxtaposition of death and victim. The illustrations, dramatic in conception, masterly in drawing, and beautifully executed in wood by Hans Lützelberger, are justly famous in the annals of printmaking. It was perhaps the last great sequence of the Dance of Death and was copied many times. Other artists have touched upon the theme, but usually in single examples rather than in a connected series.

As an example of the woodcut in relation to science, a cut from Bartholomaeus Anglicus' book, *El Libro de Proprietatibus Rerum en Romance*, printed in Spanish at Toulouse in 1494 is reproduced (illustration 27). Although the work is perhaps not as important as the Mainz *Gart der Gesuntheit*, the Mainz *Hortus Sanitatis*, and other herbals and compendiums of natural history, nevertheless it reflects accurately enough the unscientific state of science at the time, and its illustrations with their naive and decorative stylizations, have a charm that transcends their scientific interest. They were probably designed by a Spanish artist. Another example of a book printed in Spain, representing King Jaime I of Aragon and the Cortes of Leida (illustration 17) was taken from the

33

book *Usatges de Barcelona e Constitucións de Cataluña,* printed in Barcelona in 1495. The print, of striking decorative character, was undoubtedly printed from metal instead of wood, and cut in the dotted or *manière criblée.* Spanish art, essentially aristocratic in character, never took kindly to such democratic forms as books and prints, and little of interest was produced in Spain until Goya's time.

One further example of the relation of prints to science is a woodcut map (illustration 179) taken from Hartmann Schedel's *Weltchronik,* familiarly known as the *Nuremberg Chronicle* of 1493. Its significance in relation to voyages and explorations will be discussed later; it is here cited in relation to the book as a whole. The work was a ponderous and popular encyclopedia of world history and geography, profusely illustrated with 1809 cuts of decidedly mediocre quality, few of them being distinguished either in design, in cutting, or in the arrangement on the page. Sydney Cockerell has analyzed the woodcuts, and discovered that there are in reality only 645, the other 1164 being repeats, doing service for portraits and city views without much regard for historical or scientific accuracy. The whole was designed to impress rather by its quantity than its quality. It sold bound for two Rhenish florins and is an early example of mass production made possible by the fact that the printer Koberger had agents in Paris, Lyon, and Toulouse for the sale of his books. A transition was taking place between the printer or the craftsman who sold books at his printing-shop and possibly at some of the local and more important distant fairs, and the publisher with a regular selling organization and international affiliations. The capitalist nature of Koberger's undertaking is further emphasized by the fact that two rich men of Nuremberg, Sebald Schreyer and Sebastian Cammermeister, advanced money to be used in publishing enterprises including the *Nuremberg Chronicle.* Koberger at one time employed twenty-four presses and over one hundred workmen. Koberger's was far from being an isolated example of capitalistic enterprise, since similar ventures have been recorded in Italy, Basel, and elsewhere.

We must now return to an earlier period and trace the origin and development of the second great class of reproductive technique, line engraving on metal. The most important of those artists who, possibly

34

inspired by the successful example of reduplication through woodcuts, first thought of engraving on copper for the purpose of multiplying his designs on paper, was an unknown whom scholarship has designated as the Master of the Playing Cards, so called from one of his outstanding works. That he was an artist of some power and sensibility is evident from such engravings as the *Handkerchief of Veronica*, the *Virgin and the Serpent*, and the set of playing cards one of which, the Cyclamen Queen, is reproduced as illustration 124. According to Geisberg he was active in the neighborhood of Basel from 1430 to 1445. His work stands out from a large group of rather mediocre work which has been associated by modern scholarship with such nebulous personalities as the Master of the Nuremberg Passion, the Master of Balaam (who engraved a fine portrait of St. Bernardino of Sienna and a quaint St. Eligus, patron saint of goldsmiths, seated in a goldsmith's workshop), the Master of the Gardens of Love (from two prints of Gardens of Love interesting for their reflection of the manners of the Burgundian court), Master of the Banderolles and the like. A print by one of these, the Master of the Power of Women, is reproduced as illustration 137, not so much for its artistic merit, for it is the creation of a derivative artist who copied much from the Master of the Playing Cards and other sources, but because it is typical of a genre which had a vogue at all times in popular art—satire. The print is a satire on the power of woman. The obvious symbolism is confirmed by the verse that is flaunted on a banderolle: "A donkey I ride when I choose; a cuckoo is my pet; with it I catch many fools and monkeys." Another variant of the theme is the feminine *Fight for the Trousers*, which has a strangely modern sound, yet which can be traced in prints from the fifteenth century down to the *imagerie populaire* of the early nineteenth century. Still another theme is the antithesis of love and gold: old man and young girl, youth and old woman. Four-fifths of the engraving of the fifteenth century, however, had religious subjects.

The next important personality in engraving is Master E. S., who is supposed to have flourished from about 1440 to 1467 in the neighborhood of the Lake of Constance. Three hundred and seventeen different prints by this goldsmith engraver have come down to us. In spite of the fact that we have never been able to discover his name (the E. S. being a monogram found on some of his prints) a definite personality speaks through his work. His types of men and especially women have an easily discernible style, a mingling of sweetness and naiveté. One feels, somehow, the presence of a real human being, albeit vague and shadowy, behind these rare engravings, the figure of a man with likes and dislikes, a certain ideal of womanly beauty, some quiet touches of humor, a simple religious feeling combined with quite a sensuous appreciation of the lusts of the flesh (there are extant a half dozen rather free subjects engraved by him). He composed a whole alphabet of grotesque figures, a procession of saints, knights, ladies, gross-looking monks, grotesque animals, and the like. One of them, the letter N, made up of mounted knights and villains, is reproduced as illustration 143. It is doubtful whether he realized the significance that might be read into the positions of the men of such different stations of life. An important and typical example of his religious work is the large *Madonna of Einsiedeln* of 1466 (illustration 130). At the Swiss monastery of Einsiedeln was a famous shrine of the Virgin much visited by pilgrims. "Pilgrimages," as Douglas Percy Bliss has charmingly put it, "were a form of medieval holidaying, combining spiritual benefits with enjoyment. With the sweet showers of April, says the most famous of all pilgrims, Wives of Bath, Prioresses, and Millers all get restive—'Than longen folk to goon on pilgrimages.' And just as Chaucer's Pardoner, who had been at Rome, bore a pewter vernicle upon his hat and when he had got to Canterbury would pin an ampulla beside it, so if you went to a shrine or convent in Germany at a later date, you would buy a print or even, at some places, a block-book." On the print the Virgin and Child are seen enthroned between an angel and St. Meinrad, and in front are kneeling a male and female pilgrim with their staffs and hats and robes. Above, as if by a personal appearance from a balcony, are revealed the Trinity and the whole heavenly host. Altogether a most delightful picture. Other charming prints are the *Hortus Conclusus*, the *Virgin with Child Bathing*, and the *Nativity*, in which last the artist has suggested psychological reverberations in the characters of Joseph and Mary, simi-

36

lar in mood to the famous *Cherry Tree Carol*. Dürer later used a similar theme in his woodcut of the *Holy Family with the Three Hares*.

The technique of Master E. S. is typical of the goldsmith's approach, based entirely on line, and showing a loving preoccupation with ornament. His work is among the earliest bearing a signature or monogram. It has been suggested that this monogram might be more in the nature of a hallmark (following the practice of goldsmiths), a guaranty of honest and masterly workmanship rather than a signature in the modern sense of the word. It may thus represent a transition stage between the complete anonymity of the Middle Ages or of oriental countries like India, and the thorough capitalization of the individual artist's personality beginning with the Renaissance in Western art. In the medieval, and to a large extent in the oriental conception of art, the artist's personality was completely submerged in his work; whereas in Western art, with the growth of capitalist society and the development of the artist as a trader, the artist's name became a valuable asset, and his work, issued under his trademark, became almost a special brand of merchandise. Under such a scheme questions of forgery and plagiarism become important, in the Middle Ages they were not. Artists copied and recopied each other's work without feeling that they were committing a crime; there were certain traditional ways of depicting things which were transmitted from artist to artist and generation to generation. Van Meckenem as we shall see, acquired many of the coppers of Master E. S., retouched them, and put his own mark on some of them.

Only a few of the prints of Master E. S. were signed, and those late in his life; every one of the 115 engravings by Martin Schongauer, of the third generation of early German engravers, was signed with a monogram and distinctive mark. He was born around 1445 at Colmar. The son of a well-to-do goldsmith, he matriculated at the University of Leipzig in 1465. He must have given up scholarly pursuits to follow the career of artist. Although he was a painter, he still worked largely in the goldsmith tradition, and is better known for his engravings than his paintings. He was famous in his day: the young Dürer came to study in his workshop, only to find that he had come too late, for Schongauer died in 1491. Later, Vasari cites a number of his engrav-

37

ings and concludes as follows: "In another he did St. Anthony beaten by devils and carried into the air by a swarm of them, of the most curious forms imaginable, a sheet which so pleased Michelangelo when young that he began to color it." But he is still essentially the medieval artist, occasionally depicting devils and fantastic monsters like the *Griffin* (illustration 145). In complicated compositions such as the *Death of the Virgin*, or *Christ Carrying the Cross*, he is not quite so successful, since he lacks the dramatic sense to subordinate detail for the sake of pictorial emphasis; he still has the goldsmith's conception of a flat linear pattern. He is at his best in the simpler compositions such as *Christ and the Magdalen*, the *Virgin and Child in the Courtyard*, *St. Michael* and other Saints and Madonnas, where his innate delicacy and refinement find untrammeled expression. In this class, too, falls his lovely *Nativity* (illustration 128), carried out in an exalted mood of adoration and beauty. It has all the grace, the enchanting unworldliness of a fairy story.

It was more or less traditional to conceive of the Nativity in terms of fantasy and imagination. It was likewise more or less customary to treat the Birth of the Virgin realistically with a wealth of literal detail. A typical example by Israhel van Meckenem is reproduced as illustration 129. The theme was similarly treated by Dürer in his woodcut series of the *Life of the Virgin*. We see the newly born infant about to be bathed by a neighborly housewife who is testing the temperature of the water with her foot; we see roast chicken and drink being offered to the exhausted mother; we see the cradle and other utensils at hand —an interesting glimpse into the daily life of the fifteenth century. Van Meckenem is one of the most baffling artists in the history of engraving, as well as the most prolific of the fifteenth century, about 570 examples having been ascribed to his hand. He produced some of the most banal and mediocre engravings ever made, yet at times he was capable of work of considerable merit. We know what manner of man he was, since he has left a striking portrait of himself and his wife (illustration 134), not a particularly spiritual face, but a cheerful industrious type with a sense of humor and a keen eye for business. He must have been one of the earliest commercially professional engravers. He copied works by E. S., Schongauer, Master of the Amsterdam Cabinet, Wenzel von

Olmütz, Hans Holbein the Elder, and Dürer. He acquired the original plates of Master E. S. on his death in 1467 (he had been his pupil in 1466 and 1467) and a number by the Netherlands Master F. V. B.; he retouched them and did a thriving business selling prints. He is one of the first engravers whose work shows any great variation in the number of states—a fact which has endeared him to many modern collectors. He was born some time before 1450 and lived most of his life at Bocholt in Flanders. He died there in 1503. Among the best of his work, interesting chiefly as reflections of the life of the time, may be counted the large *Dance at the Court of Herod*, the *Death of Lucretia*, a series of genre subjects such as *A Woman Spinning and a Visitor* and the *Enraged Wife*, and a group of engravings of ornament.

Engravings of ornament were in the fifteenth century, and continued to be for several centuries to come, an important class of non-religious engravings. These engravings of ornament were designs to be followed, or models to be copied, by fellow artists and craftsmen, such as woodcarvers and carpenters, masons and stonecarvers, goldsmiths and metal workers, embroiderers, weavers, and other textile workers, decorative painters and the like. Master E. S., Schongauer, and many other fifteenth century artists made ornament prints. Two representative examples of Gothic ornament are reproduced. The first a pattern with figures on the theme of the *Fight for the Trousers* by Master E. S. (illustration 141). The second a model for a Baldachin or shrine (illustration 140), by that unknown but highly individual artist, Master I. A. M. with the Weaver's Shuttle, who flourished at Zwolle in Holland about 1485 and who engraved a most moving *Lamentation over the Body of Christ* and a striking *Adoration of the Magi*.

Two more examples complete the survey of Gothic engravings. Both are by artists who were not in any broad sense professional engravers, but rather painters or sculptors who made a few plates. Thus they may be said to inaugurate a long and interesting line of graphic productions in which their authors brought to their task a freshness and breadth of view often lacking in the pure craftsman's approach. The first is the charming *Madonna with the Apple* (illustration 125) by the famous Nuremberg sculptor, Veit Stoss (1447-1553). The second is by an artist about whom little is known, and who is variously designated as the Master of the Amsterdam Cabinet (where some eighty of his total eighty-nine engravings are conserved, many of them in unique impressions) or as the *Meister des Hausbuchs* from a book containing some of his drawings at Wolfegg. He probably was active somewhere in the Middle Rhine from about 1475 to 1490. Little else is known about this personality who speaks so charmingly and attractively from his prints. He can hardly be classed as a professional engraver, since, owing to the extreme scarcity of his prints (many existing in only one impression), it is evident that he made comparatively little effort to multiply and sell his designs. Furthermore his technique was not that of the regular goldsmith engraver: it was more like a drypoint line (scratched into the metal) which would not hold up under many impressions. His approach is rather that of a painter having an eye for the figure as a whole and the interplay of light and color. But especially attractive are the freshness of his conception and the lovely lyric spirit that pervades his work. Seldom has the enchantment of love, the sweet and quiet delight of lovers in each other's company, been more charmingly depicted than in his print (illustration 127). Equally outstanding in their way are his *Death and the Young Man*, the *Three Knights Confronted with Their Dead Selves*, the *Crucifixion*, *Two Men Talking*, and a delightfully realistic picture of a dog scratching himself, one of the first in that genre of prints. Altogether, the work of the Master of the Amsterdam Cabinet is one of the dewy and fragrant pages in the history of the graphic arts.

Henry Adams wrote:

The Gothic is singular in this: one seems easily at home in the Renaissance; one is not too strange in the Byzantine; as for the Roman, it is ourselves; and we could walk blindfolded through every chink and cranny of the Greek mind; all these styles seem modern, when we come close to them; but the Gothic gets away. No two men think alike about it, and no woman agrees with either man. The Church itself never agreed about it, and the architects agree even less than the priests. To most minds it casts too many shadows; it wraps itself in mystery; and when people talk of mystery, they commonly mean fear.

It is true that the Gothic era seems more alien to our modern temper than most of the other periods. To be sure the Gothic as reflected in the graphic arts represented the latest period, its decadence so to speak. The great glory of the Gothic was the Cathedral and the painting and sculpture that went into it. It was an age of faith and a Universal Church —which our age emphatically is not. It is difficult for us, brought up as we are from earliest childhood with the notion of a rational physical universe, to accept such impossible contradictions as simultaneous existence in two places, miraculous changes without natural causes, anachronisms based upon ignorance of historical development and the like. The Gothic was a credulous age of beautiful legend and little science, of touching faith and macabre humor, of unworldliness and chivalry and starving serfs, of uncertain life and violent death. The medieval artist sought to express an idea, not to imitate nature. As St. Thomas Aquinas said: "Art imitates nature [not in its form but] in its processes, *ars naturem imitat in sua operatione*." It was symbolic in form, and lacking in sensuous and realistic elements. When Worringer spoke of "the ceaseless melody of Northern line," he was referring particularly to architecture, but the phrase also has a certain aptness in regard to engraving. The Gothic line is calligraphic, that is to say it has a rhythm and melody of its own. The folds of drapery for example, as depicted in a print or drawing, may not be at all naturalistic or revealing of the figure beneath; they may be arbitrary and abstract; but they have intrinsic beauty and vitality nevertheless. After all, graphic art, which expresses everything, color, form, atmosphere, largely by black and white lines, is in itself an abstract and arbitrary art.

In conclusion it might be well to summarize the conditions which brought about the development of the graphic arts. In the first place there was the desire for religious images inculcated by organized religion. At the end of the Middle Ages the worship of a multitude of saints and above all of the Virgin Mary, reached its fullest development. Religion had been humanized. Every occupation and profession had its patron saint who was endowed with special virtues (as we have seen for example in St. Christopher). A canonized saint was a comforter in tribulation and a mediator between a sinner and a remote Godhead.

41

Thus the saints and their attributes figured largely in the thoughts and feelings of the people. In a sense they personified them, as the feeling of tenderness and sweetness and mother love is personified in the Virgin and Child, as sorrow and affliction are personified in the drama of the Passion, as fear and terror are personified in the *Danse Macabre* and the Vision of the Last Judgment. Thus were the desire and the need for images provided, while economic conditions—a larger and larger number of people coming to enjoy a slight margin above a subsistence level—provided the means to satisfy the desire. Organized religion has at almost all times furnished a stimulus to the practice of the arts. It was likewise so, as we shall see in another chapter, when the spread of Tantric Buddhism in China produced the demand for religious images and charms which had magical properties, and thus brought about the perfection of woodcutting and printing throughout the Chinese Empire as early as the eighth century. In addition to the religious stimulus, the graphic arts had other organic roots in the lives of the people. There were playing cards and prints of gallantry that ministered to the play instinct. There were prints of satire and caricature, those lightning rods that channeled the fury and resentment of the oppressed. Portraiture, a deep-seated desire in man, made a halting beginning in the fifteenth century, but was destined later to be one of the chief functions of prints. There were prints illustrating science and exploration. And finally there were prints of ornament, the trade secrets which the artists circulated among themselves. All these prints were purposive; there was no thought as yet of art for art's sake.

3. The Renaissance

THE dramatic transition from Gothic to Renaissance can be personified in the life and works of one man—Albrecht Dürer. He began in the Gothic tradition and died a painter and engraver of the Renaissance, acclaimed in Germany, Flanders, and even in Italy, the home of the Renaissance. Distinguished as he is as an artist, he is even greater as a dramatic figure, as a man in whom the tremendous forces of his age had their play and interplay, all the more so because he has left such a voluminous documentation of his thoughts and feelings. Many of the qualities which we particularly associate with the Renaissance—intellectual interests, passion for the antique, self-conscious interest in fame, pride in individual achievement, proficiency in diverse professions ("the man of virtu"), devotion to science as well as to art, a preoccupation with proportion and perspective—found their expression in his many-sided personality.

He was born in Nuremberg in 1471, the son of a goldsmith. Of himself Dürer wrote:

And my father took special pleasure in me, because he saw that I was diligent to learn. So he sent me to school, and when I had learned to read and write he took me away from it, and taught me the goldsmith's craft. But when I could work neatly, my liking drew me rather to painting than to goldsmith's work, so I laid it before my father; but he was not well pleased, regretting the time lost while I had been learning to be a goldsmith. Still he let it be as I wished, and in 1486 on St. Andrew's Day my father bound me apprentice to Michael Wolgemut, to serve him three years long. During that time God gave me diligence, so that I learned well, but I had much to suffer from his lads.

Having served his term with Wolgemut (who had supplied designs to Koberger for the *Schatzbehalter* and the *Nuremberg Chronicle*) and thus become steeped in the Gothic tradition not only from him but from his goldsmith father, he spent four years wandering about as a journeyman. It is not known what places he visited, but it is reasonably certain that he spent some time at Basle designing woodcuts for the publishers, notably two series of illustrations for the *Ritter vom Thurn* and for Sebastian Brant's *Ship of Fools*, both satiric commentaries on the foibles of mankind. One of these about the fool who miscalculates his costs in building a house and finds his workmen walking out on the job, is reproduced herewith (illustration 24). There is little to distinguish these works from a number of Gothic illustrations except possibly a certain competence of drawing and gusto of observation. It is generally assumed that from the fall of 1494 to the spring of 1495 he made a trip to Venice. Before this, while still in Nuremberg, he had seen (interesting side-light on the international trade in prints) and copied in pen and ink two engravings by Mantegna and one by a North Italian engraver of the *Death of Orpheus*. At any rate from about this time a new note came into his work, a stronger painter-like feeling (thinking in terms of color, and painting in watercolors), a preoccupation with tactile form instead of the calligraphic line characteristic of the Gothic North. And in the woodcuts and the copper engravings (in which he seems to be largely self-taught) he gradually began to perfect the style associated with his name. In the series of fifteen large woodcut illustrations of the *Apocalypse*, issued in 1498, this style may already be seen in its completeness. When a print like the *Four Riders of the Apocalypse* (illustration 25) is compared with a similar subject from, say, the Cologne Bible, the measure of his achievement is obvious. The print is conceived as a complete picture with the bounds of a rectangle, the figures and the details are disposed within that space with the most telling dramatic effect. There is a sense of movement and of color; the figures are drawn in the round with some regard for realistic tactile values. Dürer managed to perfect a system of representation, a combination of the calligraphic and ideographic elements of Gothic art and the more painter-like pictorial qualities of the Renaissance, which became the prevailing idiom in Germany and the Netherlands for a century to come. Of course in comparison with the work of Parmigiano or Rembrandt, Dürer's style

44

as a whole seems Gothic. Nevertheless it will always remain an exemplar of a striking and effective mode of graphic expression.

About 1500 he met in Nuremberg the painter Jacopo de' Barbari, and wrote of him thus:

I can find no one who hath written aught about how to form a canon of human proportions, save one man, Jacopo by name, born at Venice, and a charming painter. He showed me the figures of a man and woman, which he had drawn according to a canon of proportions; and now I would rather be shown what he meant than behold a new kingdom. If I had this canon, I would put it into print in his honor, for the use of all men. Then, however, I was still young and had not heard of such things before. Howbeit I was very fond of art, so I set myself to discover how such a canon might be wrought out. For this aforesaid Jacopo, as I clearly saw, would not explain to me the principles upon which he went. Accordingly I set to work on my own idea and read Vitruvius, who writes somewhat about the human figure. Thus it was from, or out of, these two men aforesaid that I took my start, and thence, from day to day, have I followed up my search according to my own notions.

From that time on indeed he gathered, with more zeal perhaps than style, the notes, measurements, and researches, that eventually were published in his book *On Human Proportions*. Meanwhile in 1504, making use of his studies in the ideal figure, he engraved his famous *Adam and Eve* (illustration 147), which he proudly signed "Albert Dürer of Nuremberg made this 1504." In it he expressed his dream of an ideal Adam and Eve, prototype of Man and Woman, and his nostalgia for the antique, Apollo and Venus transformed into the First Pair—the Adam indeed is based upon the Apollo Belvedere. This print typifies the emancipation of the North from a medieval contempt for the flesh, a sensuous interest and a freedom in the handling of the nude, characteristic of Renaissance artists. A half century before such a picture would have been unthinkable, except in Italy, which had the advantage of a more or less unbroken tradition from the antique. Not only were the medieval artists restricted in depicting the nude and semi-nude to such subjects as the Last Judgment, Adam and Eve, the Crucifixion, a few saints like St. Sebastian, and biblical stories like David and Bathsheba,

45

but there was also little opportunity to draw from the nude. Professional models were unknown. For male models the artists often used themselves or their apprentices, for female models their wives and mistresses and occasionally prostitutes and the attendants in the public baths (which had none too respectable a reputation even as late as Casanova's time). Drawings exist by Pisanello, Dürer, Dirick Vellert, and others, of bath attendants, and Dürer made a woodcut of a Men's Bath. Professional models first came into use in Carracci's Academy. During the Renaissance there was a general feeling that the male body was superior in beauty and proportion to the female. Michelangelo used male models for a number of his Sibyls. And Dürer in his engraving worked with more *esprit* on his Adam than on his Eve. He, however, retained an interest in the nude of both sexes till the end. In 1520 he was at Antwerp and witnessed the triumphal entry of Charles V.

He afterwards described to Melanchthon the splendid spectacles he had beheld, and how, in what were mythological groups, the most beautiful maidens figured almost naked, and covered only with a thin transparent veil. The young Emperor did not honor them with a single glance, but Dürer himself was very glad to get near, not less for the purpose of seeing the tableaux, than to have the opportunity of observing closely the perfect figures of the young girls. As he said, "Being a painter, I looked about me a little more boldly."

Meanwhile he led in Nuremberg a busy and industrious existence, doing portrait commissions, engraving sacred and profane subjects, Madonna pictures and the like. One of the most beautiful and charming of these is the *Virgin and Child with the Monkey* of about 1498 (illustration 148) with its lovely landscape background of the Weierhaus, which was copied by Giulio Campagnola in his engraving of Ganymede. Dürer's fame had spread far into Italy; many of his prints were sold and copied there. So much so that he was moved to make a second journey to Venice to protest against the wholesale forgery of his prints by Marcantonio Raimondi (no less than seventy-eight in all).

Marcantonio [wrote Vasari] began by imitating the things of Albert, studying all the prints which he had bought, which for their novelty and

46

beauty, were sought by everyone. Having engraved on copper, all the Passion and Life of Christ in thirty-six sheets, with the A.D. with which Albert signed his works, Marcantonio succeeded in making them so like that no one could tell the difference, who did not know; and they were sold and bought as Albert's works. On being informed of this, one of the counterfeits being sent to Flanders [Vasari was vague about geography outside of Italy], Albert flew into such a rage that he left Flanders and came to Venice, and complained of Marcantonio to the Signoria. But all he obtained was that Marcantonio should no longer use his signature.

Dürer's letters to his friend Pirkheimer give a picture of his life in Italy. He exerted himself (perhaps in vain) to show that he was a great painter as well as a great draughtsman and engraver. He encountered the jealousy of the Italian painters; Bellini alone wished him well. He found everything expensive. Yet he wrote, "How I shall freeze after this sun! Here I am a gentleman, at home only a parasite." He made a pilgrimage to Mantua to visit Andrea Mantegna whom he greatly admired. "But," as Camerarius wrote, "before he could reach Mantua Andrea was dead, and Dürer used to say that this was the saddest event in all his life." An interesting side-light on Dürer's relations with Raphael is given on a Raphael drawing which has the following inscription in Dürer's handwriting: "Rafahel de' Urbin, who is held in such high esteem by the Pope, he made these naked figures and sent them to Albrecht Dürer at Nuremberg to show him his hand." Raphael had, we are told by Lodovico Dolce, drawings, engravings, and woodcuts of Dürer's hanging in his studio; and Vasari quoted Raphael as saying, "If Dürer had been acquainted with the antique he would have surpassed us all."

There is not space to recount all of Dürer's contacts with the writers and humanists, Erasmus, Melanchthon, Luther, Hans Sachs, Conrad Celtes, Stabius, Camerarius; with the great merchants, the Imhofs and Fuggers and Paumgartners; with the Court of the Emperor Maximilian. Dürer's portrait of Pirkheimer, patrician, humanist, and councilor of Nuremberg, and his life-long friend, will have to typify his contacts with the learned world. Pirkheimer was a ponderous, pompous, irascible individual—what we would today call a stuffed shirt—and the engraving

47

(illustration 151) does give a suggestion of this, though it lacks any sense of style. The textures are built up in a rather dull and literal way, and Dürer indulges in the somewhat flashy trick of showing the reflection of a window in the subject's eyes. But Dürer was no flatterer. The Gothic North has a fairly honorable reputation in this regard, being on the whole more interested in "character" than in elegance. Later, Titian, Van Dyck, and the French portrait engravers marked the beginning of the elegant style which eventually developed into the official or fashionable portrait, an art of flattery pure and simple. Dürer's engraved portrait of Erasmus was no likeness at all. Erasmus when he saw it, politely excused its deficiency by saying that no doubt he had changed somewhat in the years since the drawing was made. The truth of the matter, however, probably was that the artist engraved the portrait some five or six years after he had made the preliminary drawings and he had simply "gone cold" on the subject. He had hoped to compensate for this by over-elaborating all the accessories. Whether Pirkheimer liked his portrait or not is not known. He had the plate in his possession and no doubt had proofs printed as one would of a photograph today. It later passed into the hands of the Imhof family (Pirkheimer's daughter married an Imhof), and was sold by Hans Imhof in 1636 to the Earl of Arundel for forty Reichsthaler.

Dürer designed or engraved several great series besides the *Apocalypse*, such as the Large Woodcut Passion (12 blocks), the Little Woodcut Passion (37 blocks) (illustration 26), the *Life of the Virgin* (20 blocks), all three published by Dürer himself in 1511 (though some of the individual blocks were completed before that), and the Copper Plate Passion (16 plates). These and a number of single blocks and plates proved a considerable source of income to him. When he made his journey to the Netherlands in 1520, he took a large quantity of prints with him which he sold, exchanged, or gave away, as we learn from his detailed diary. He even sold to a dealer at wholesale prices:

Sebald Fischer bought of me at Antwerp sixteen small Passions [woodcut] for four florins [about $2.50 per set], thirty-two of the large books [sets of the Apocalypse and Large Passion] for eight florins [about $2.50

per set], also six engraved Passions [on copper] for three florins [about $5.00 per set].

He exchanged prints with other artists: "I gave eight florins' worth of my prints for a whole set of Lucas' [van Leyden's] engravings." Again: "I gave to Tommaso of Bologna a whole set of prints to send for me to Rome to another painter, who will send me Raphael's work [engraved by Marcantonio] in return." Occasionally he jotted down retail prices: "I sold a woodcut Passion for twelve stivers [about $5.00], besides an Adam and Eve [copper engraving] for four stivers [about $1.65].

One of the most famous of the later engravings is the *Melancholia* (illustration 150), more or less uniform with two other famous engravings, the *St. Jerome in his Cell*, and the *Knight, Death, and the Devil*. It is possible that Dürer intended to illustrate in a series the various temperaments of man such as the phlegmatic, choleric, and melancholic. The idea of melancholy is capable of extended and diverse elaboration as readers of Burton's *Anatomy of Melancholy* well know. Much has been written about the significance of Dürer's strange plate, but nobody has succeeded in producing a satisfying interpretation. Sturge Moore has come perhaps as close as any one:

The pose and build of Melancholy must have been those of many a matron in Nuremberg. It is not till we come to the face that we find traits that correspond with the obvious symbolism of the wings and wreath, or the serious richness of the black and white effect of the composition; but that face holds our attention as not even the Sibylla Delphica can—not by beauty, not by conscious inspiration, but by the spell of unanswerable thought, by the power to brood, by the patience that can and dare go unresolved for many years. Everything is begun about her; she cannot see unto the end; she is powerful, she is capable in many works, she has borne children, she rests from her labors, and her thought wanders, sleeps, or dreams. The spirit of the North, with its industry, its cool-headed calculation, its abundance in contrivance, its elaboration of duty and accumulation of possessions—there she sits, absorbed, unsatisfied.

In the early years of the sixteenth century there was talk among the German engravers of a new technique that would mitigate the labor

49

of engraving on metal. It was called etching and was probably derived from the armorer's craft. The first known etching was a portrait of Konrad von der Rosen by Daniel Hopfer (see a later etching of his, illustration 157). The first etching with a date is the *Woman Bathing Her Feet* by Urs Graf, 1513. Dürer tried his hand at the new technique, and made in all, six etchings, two of which, the *Christ on the Mount of Olives* of 1515 and the *Cannon* of 1518, are reproduced herewith (illustrations 149 and 156). These early etchings were made on iron with red lead as a ground, and the lines were all of one uniform thickness in the biting. The *Christ on the Mount of Olives* is one of the noblest of Dürer's works. The storm-tossed tree mirrors the psychological drama of Christ's Agony, and the whole is conceived and executed with a fury and spontaneity rare in his work. The *Cannon* represents a showpiece called the Nuremberg Serpent, popular at the moment, and was made in etching as a quick means of supplying a transient demand. The Turks for whom, as pictured, the cannon was a warning and a threat, were the great bugaboo of the time. The first siege of Vienna by the Turks occurred in 1529. The landscape in the background is quite charming in spite of its lack of subtlety, and the print is prized not only because it is one of the earliest etchings but also because it is one of the earliest examples of the growing interest in landscape.

Augustin Hirschvogel made a number of etchings of pure landscape, that is to say, without any figure interest (illustration 155). They are notable because they show a variation in the quality of line accomplished, possibly by more than one biting of the plate, but more likely by the use of needles of varying thickness. Other early etchings of pure landscape were made by Albrecht Altdorfer and Hans Sebald Lautensack. The full development of the landscape print, however, was to come with the Dutch etchers of the seventeenth century, and with Bruegel and Rubens in engraving and Titian in woodcut.

Dürer died in Nuremberg in 1528 after a life of unremitting application to his craft. He was a great draughtsman and technician. If we sometimes miss in his work the fire of a great emotion, we nevertheless must be impressed by his insatiable pre-occupation with the representation of all natural objects. It may be questioned whether his scientific

50

interests, the canon of proportion, the mathematics and mensuration, the military engineering, all the things he wrote about in his books, did not affect his art adversely. Leonardo's scientific interests were even greater than Dürer's, and they may have affected the quantity but certainly not the quality of his art. The matter goes deeper: Dürer pinned his faith too much on externals. "To paint," he wrote, "is to be able to portray upon a flat surface any visible thing what so ever that may be chosen." He was, par excellence, the extravert artist. The world was too much with him. His power of description and analysis stood in the way of a vitalizing synthesis. He attempted to storm Heaven with a pedlar's pack of literal details. That he searched all his life for some elusive secret of art is in itself revealing. Yet withal he is a most engaging figure, in Melanchthon's words, "a wise man, whose genius as a painter, were it ever so brilliant, would be the least of his gifts." His pride and his humility, his wisdom of life, his childlike delight in all natural objects, his systematizing capacity and technical skill, and his recording instinct make him one of the most fascinating men of art that the world has ever known.

One of the most famous of Dürer's friends was Lucas van Leyden, born at Leyden in 1494. Dürer exchanged prints with him and drew his portrait during his visit to the Netherlands. Lucas was a precocious artist, having engraved his first plate, *Mahomet and Sergius*, at the age of fourteen. He engraved many religious subjects, but like Schongauer and Dürer, also executed several genre scenes or illustrations of popular life. One of the most delightful of these is *The Milkmaid* of 1510 (illustration 158). He also designed a number of distinguished woodcuts. One of his masterpieces is the portrait of the Emperor Maximilian of 1520 (illustration 154). In addition to its masterly characterization and draughtsmanship, the plate has a technical interest. It is one of the earliest examples of a combination of etching and engraving. The earliest etchings had been made on iron which could be engraved with difficulty. By using copper instead of iron, it was possible to combine etching and engraving on the same plate. Lucas van Leyden's plate inaugurated that technical procedure of etching the preliminary work and finishing up with the graver, that reached its culmination in the engravings of the eighteenth and early nineteenth centuries. In his later work Lucas assimilated the technique of Marcantonio, and with it gave up Dutch raciness for a rather empty Renaissance allegorical style. He died at the early age of thirty-nine. Another Flemish artist whom Dürer mentions in his diary is Dirick Vellert, painter, glass-worker, engraver. He made about nineteen engravings and etchings, many of them small in size. One of the most charming of these, the *Faun on a Wine Barrel*, 1522, is reproduced as illustration 172.

The Emperor Maximilian, "the last of the Knights," was a great patron of the arts. Inspired perhaps by the *Chevalier Delibéré*, he commissioned a number of elaborately illustrated works designed to glorify his person and his exploits, often imaginary—*Genealogy*, the *Theuerdank*, the *Weisskunig*, the *Freydal*, the *Triumphal Arch*, and the *Triumphal Procession*. Dürer, Burgkmair, Altdorfer, Springinklee, Schäufelein, and others were employed on these works. Most of it is pedantic and heraldic, interesting chiefly to the historian; some of it indeed was left unpublished at the death of Maximilian. An interesting but perhaps not very typical example is given in illustration 38. Most of the figures of the *Triumphal Procession* were mythological and allegorical, but toward its end are a group of figures designed by Burgkmair which have a touch of reality. The scene might easily represent a highway of the time with its rumbling wagons, horsemen, and straggling foot passengers. Hans Burgkmair was a typical court painter, witty, elegant, courtly, competent to undertake any subject upon request. After the death of Maximilian he went back again to work for the Augsburg book publishers.

Lucas Cranach was also a court painter (he entered the service of the Elector of Saxony about 1505). His later work suffers from the dilution so often attendant upon official renditions, but at its best it is charming, sensuous, elegant, and saturated with real feeling for nature. Through his residence in Wittenberg he came in close contact with Luther and other leaders of the Reformation. He designed woodcuts for the first edition of Luther's German Bible in 1522, and also engraved on copper the vivid portrait of 1521 (illustration 152), which fixes for eternity the warm, fanatic, yet human personality of the miner's son who defied Rome and established the written form of the German vernacular.

The sixteenth century was a warlike one. According to Sombart there were only twenty-five years which did not witness a war somewhere in Europe. Soldiers were everywhere, including a new kind of soldier, the mercenary. Erasmus wrote that the German disorders were "partly due to the natural fierceness of the race, partly to the division into so many separate States, and partly to the tendency of the people to serve as mercenaries." The insolent swaggering type and his female counterpart have been pictured by many German artists: Dürer, Virgil Solis, Burgkmair, Huber, Nicholas Manuel, Beham, Holbein, and Cranach (illustration 37). But most typical of all were the woodcuts of Urs Graf, who was himself a Landsknecht and fought in the murderous battle of Marignano. He led a violent and undisciplined life, was repeatedly brought before the authorities "because of his licentious life that he openly and shamelessly leads with strumpets," and once was made to promise that "he would no longer push, beat, crush, or pinch his lawfully wedded wife, the daughter of an honorable tanner, who married against the will of her parents." Much of this wild and wayward energy, of this bluster and swagger, of this excess of animal spirits, is carried over into his prints, *The Soldiers and Death* (illustration 36) and the *Standard Bearer of the Arms of Unterwalden* of 1521 (illustration 51). This last is a wood engraving, conceived as a white line engraving, and is an interesting anticipation of the method which Bewick later made famous.

Hans Holbein is famous as the painter of the court of Henry VIII, but he is equally outstanding for his work for the Basel publishers, Froben and others, for the drawings illustrating his friend Erasmus' *Praise of Folly*, and for his woodcut designs for the Bible and the *Dance of Death* both of 1538 (illustrations 32 and 31). In these last he carried the method of Dürer to its classic perfection, the completest expression of the German Renaissance.

In strong contrast to his classic feeling of balance and restraint, is the demonic energy of Hans Baldung, surnamed Grien. Comparatively little is known of his life. He was born in 1476 near Strassburg; he was

53

a friend and possibly a pupil of Dürer; he later fell under the spell of that strange genius Grünewald, he probably died at Strassburg around 1540. His fame has suffered strange mutations. In his lifetime he achieved considerable acclaim and reputation; Baldung's prints were the only ones outside of his own that Dürer took with him for trade on his Netherlands journey. But in the seventeenth and eighteenth centuries his name and work were practically forgotten. In the early nineteenth century his name was again discovered, and at one time even Grünewald's masterpiece, the *Isenheimer Altar*, was ascribed to him. The twentieth century has resurrected his works and accorded them high praise. Indeed in such works as *Adam and Eve*, the *Fall of Man*, the *Conversion of St. Paul*, the *Ascension of Christ*, the *Nativity*, the *Lamentation*, the *Witches*, the *Horses*, and the *Groom Bewitched*, there is an emotional intensity of conception, an originality and appropriateness of composition, a passionate and sensuous expression, and above all a wild and haunting power that are peculiarly appealing to the modern temper. Consider for example that most vivid drama of the flesh—the color and sensuousness of it—in the *Fall of Man* (illustration 54); the magic unearthly beauty of the *Nativity* (illustration 52); the breath-taking power of the composition, the tenderness of feeling—Christ not triumphant but crushed, utterly crushed, by the evil forces of this world, carried to the pitying arms of God the Father—in the woodcut of the *Ascension* (illustration 53). Or the demonic overtones, the bold recession of planes, in the *Groom Bewitched* (illustration 55); the swirling lines of force in the *Witches* (illustration 169); or the wild and elemental energy of the *Horses in the Wood* (illustration 40). And finally the dynamic balance of forces, the thrusts and parallelisms of the lines in that dramatic illustration of the Fifth Commandment, *Thou Shalt Not Kill* (illustration 35). Baldung was a fiery partisan of the Reformation but he also seems to have been one of a circle, with Brunfels, Indagine, and Johannes Has, interested in chiromancy, astrology, and magic. He made several woodcuts and drawings of witches, notably the famous chiaroscuro already mentioned. The belief in witches which had been growing for centuries was crystallized and officially encouraged by the growth in power of the Inquisition and the publication of the *Malleus Malificarum*,

54

or *Inquisitor's Manual* in 1489. The belief in and punishment for witch-craft continued through the seventeenth century.

There was another group of artists most of whom had had some contact with Dürer either as pupil or as indirect influence. From the small size of most of their prints, they are generally called the Little Masters. Three of them, Georg Pencz and the two brothers, Barthel and Hans Sebald Beham, got themselves in trouble for atheistic utterances and sympathies for the Peasant Revolt, and were banished from Nuremberg. An interesting reflection of this is seen in H. S. Beham's *Drummer and Standard Bearer* with an inscription "In the Peasant War 1525" (illustration 173). Barthel Beham's print, the *Bookplate of Baumgartner* (illustration 175) is not perhaps typical of his work (he was by far the more pictorially creative of the two brothers) but it is interesting as an early example of a class of print which has continued its popularity to the present day. The Little Masters were very much interested in applied art of all kinds, and much of their work consists of prints of ornament, models for other arts, such as goldsmith's work, costume, etcetera. Heinrich Aldegrever was one of the most talented of them, and produced some of the best Renaissance ornament in Germany, as well as some elegant costume studies of patricians, wedding dancers, and the like. The engraving, *Ornament with Lettering* (illustration 177) has been chosen to represent his work because it touches upon a field which had great interest especially during the sixteenth century. It was the period when the forms of letters were being established and new variations were being experimented with. First there were the theoreticians on the shaping of Roman letters, Fra Luca Pacioli in 1509, Sigismondo de' Fanti in 1514, Dürer in his *Treatise on Mensuration*, 1525, Tory in his *Champfleury*, 1529. The growth of the trade and culture of the middle class produced a demand for correct models for various types of script, legal, notarial, chancellary, documentary, ornate, as used in various countries and languages. The first practical book of this kind was by Ludovico Vicentino, the official scribe at the Papal Court, in Rome, 1522 (illustration 61). Similar books were produced in Italy, France, Spain, Holland, Germany, and England during the sixteenth, seventeenth, and eighteenth centuries, by Tagliente, Palatino,

55

Yciar, van de Velde, and many others. Another interesting phase of applied art were the costume books and the model books for lace and embroidery. The *Corona delle Nobili et Virtuose Donne*, published at Venice in 1591 (illustration 63), may serve as representative of the pattern books published by Gastel, Sibmacher, Quentel, Pellegrino, Vavassore, Pagan, Osthaus, Vinciolo, Parasole, Franco, and others. The *Corona* was issued by Cesare Vecellio, a cousin of Titian, and he also published in 1590 a famous work on costume, the first indeed with any pretense to historical or scientific accuracy, though similar works had been issued previously by Vico, de Bruyn, Boissard, Weigel, and Amman. Venice occupied during the sixteenth century, as Max von Boehn points out, a position as an emporium of luxury and fashionable amusement similar to that of Paris during the eighteenth and nineteenth centuries.

Another aspect of applied art is treated in the model for a highly ornamented bed, 1533 (illustration 62), by the Swiss German wood-carver, architect, and woodcutter, Peter Flöttner. He designed, and un-doubtedly cut with his own hand (as evidenced by the woodcutting tools which he introduced in many of his pictures as his trade mark) a considerable number of woodcuts of architectural ornament and models for intarsia or inlay work. He also designed a set of playing cards one of which is reproduced as illustration 58. Many books of herbals were issued to satisfy popular demand. One of the most noteworthy was the *Herbarum Vivae Eicones* by Otto von Brunfels (whose portrait Hans Baldung cut in wood, illustration 46) published at Strassburg in 1530. The woodcuts of the plants, the most accurate of their time, were de-signed by Hans Weiditz (illustration 57). The works of this master, whose name and personality were rediscovered only in recent times, are among the most appealing and charming in the history of prints. He illustrated several popular moralizing works compiled from Petrarch and Cicero, extolling all the good old bourgeois virtues of thrift, pru-dence, moderation, piety, and the like. He was a born story-teller, and he illustrated these dull books with such zest and charm, above all with such a wealth of observation, that they have become a treasure-house of the manners and customs of the Augsburg of his day. He had what the

56

historian loves above all else—a talent for the obvious. He rarely shows any great gift for design, but he more than makes up for this lack by his talent as a narrator and observer. Two characteristic woodcuts are reproduced herewith, one from a popular story *The Tragedy of Calixtus and Melibea*, Augsburg, 1520 (illustration 42), and the other from Petrarch's *Consolation in Fortune and Misfortune*, Augsburg, 1532 (illustration 43), illustrating the story of the man who was so proud of his wife's unadorned beauty that he showed her off to a friend. Incidentally it reveals the norm of female beauty that was prevalent in Augsburg at the time.

One more of the Little Masters still remains to be considered, the most important of the group—Albrecht Altdorfer, who flourished at Regensburg on the Danube as a painter, engraver, architect, and city councilor, from about 1505 till his death in 1538. There is something very personal and appealing in his style, filled with homely feeling and endowed with a simple love of nature. There is something a bit amateurish about his engravings, as if he did them for his own pleasure: his draughtsmanship at times leaves something to be desired. In 1515 he executed (for it is believed that he cut many of his own blocks) a series of forty small woodcuts of the Passion which have truly the distinction of being *multum in parvo*. They display an imagination, a dramatic power, and a depth of feeling that have been seldom surpassed. In the example here reproduced, the *Death of the Virgin* (illustration 33), consider how the weight of the composition presses down upon the dying woman. The lovely and serene *Holy Family at the Fountain* of 1520 is also reproduced (illustration 41). Notable among his copper engravings are the *Crucifixion*, the *Virgin and Child in a Landscape*. As an example of his burin work in a sweet and tender vein the *Virgin and Child at the Cradle* is reproduced as illustration 171.

With the consideration of Altdorfer the survey of German graphic art of the Renaissance now comes to a close. At its best it was of brief duration: by the middle of the century there were no important German artists. Thereafter German art merits no serious consideration for several centuries to come. Some critics, among them William Morris, have ascribed this to the injurious influence of the Italian Renaissance upon so alien a culture as that of the Gothic North. Although it is true that the Renaissance, and likewise the Reformation, produced first a quickening and later a depressing effect on German art, there were nevertheless other factors which contributed strongly to its downfall. The political, social, and economic conditions in Germany at the middle and end of the century were not conducive to the cultivation of art. The country was in a state of anarchy, torn by the religious factionalism of Catholic against Protestant which culminated in the disastrous Thirty Years War of the seventeenth century, broken up into a multitude of avaricious, cruel and warlike principalities, checked by practically no central authority. Travel was unsafe. The trade which had flourished so auspiciously in the previous century had been impaired by two events of far-reaching importance: the Portuguese development of a sea trade route around Africa to India, and the closing of the overland caravan routes by the conquests of the Suliman Turks which ruined the Venetian monopoly of oriental trade. With the decline of the Venetian trade and the rise of Dutch naval commerce, the Hansa merchants and the Free Cities along the overland German trade route suffered a disastrous decline. In addition, the vast influx of silver and gold from the Spanish colonies caused a serious depreciation in the value of the precious metal mined in Germany. From these considerations it is easy to see that German art suffered a blight from which it did not recover for several centuries.

The Italians, set in the midst of natural loveliness and among the ruins of ancient art, had never wholly lost the sense of beauty; they may have paid but slight attention to what was about them, but they lived lifelong in the daily sight of fair scenes and beautiful forms, which impressed their senses and molded their nature, so that, when with the revival of letters they felt the native impulse of humanity toward the higher life stirring once more in their hearts, they found themselves endued with powers of perception and appreciation beyond any other people in the world. These powers were not the peculiar possession of a well-born class; the centuries had bred them unobserved into the nature of the race, into the physical constitution of the people. The artisan, no less than the prince, took delight in the dawn of art, and welcomed it with equal worship. Nor was this artistic instinct the only common acquisition; the enthusiasm for letters was likewise widely shared so that some of the best manuscripts of the classics have come down to modern times from the hands of humble Florentine workmen. Italy, indeed, was the first country where democratic civilization had place; here the contempt of the Northern lord for the peasant and the mechanic had never been widespread, partly because mercantile life was early held to be honorable, and partly because of peculiar social conditions. The long, uninterrupted intercourse with the remains of Roman civilization in the unbarbarized East, the contact with Saracenic civilization in the South, the culture of the court of the Two Sicilies, and the invariably leveling influence of commerce, had made Italy the most cosmopolitan of European countries; the sharp and warlike rivalry of small but intensely patriotic states, and the necessity they lay under of utilizing for their own preservation whatever individual energy might arise among them, perhaps most of all the powerful example of the omnipresent Church in which the son of a swineherd might take the Papal Throne, had contributed to make it comparatively easy to pass from lower to higher social ranks; the aristocratic structure remained but the distinction of classes was obscured, and the excellence of the individual's faculties, the energy and scope of his powers, were recognized as the real dignities which were worthy of respect. In this recognition of the individual, and this common taste for art and letters, lay the conditions of new and vigorous intellectual life; they resulted in the great age of Italy. It was this in the main that made possible the popular fervor for the things of the mind in the Italian Renaissance, to which nothing else in the world's history is comparable but the popular enthusiasm of the modern Revolution for liberty. Dante gave his country a native language, the Humanists gave it the literature of Rome, the Hellenists the literature of Greece; poets sang and artists painted with a loftiness and dignity of imagination, a sweetness and delicacy of sentiment, and energy and reach of thought, a music of verse and harmony of line and color, still unsurpassed. The gifts which these men brought were not for a few, but for the many who shared in this mastering, absorbing interest in the things of the mind, in beauty and wisdom, which was the vital spirit of the Italian Renaissance.

Thus did George Edward Woodberry summarize the background of the Italian Renaissance, from which sprang, about the middle of the fifteenth century, the art of engraving apparently quite independently of Germany. Just as in the northern countries, its development was bound up with the goldsmith. Modern scholarship has distinguished two schools or workshops of goldsmiths in Florence where the new art probably had its origin. The first workshop, traditionally associated with the name of Maso Finiguerra (to whom indeed Vasari mistakenly attributes the invention of engraving), produced prints in the "Fine Manner." The distinguishing characteristic of this technique was a system of crosshatching by fine lines giving somewhat the effect of a wash drawing. One of the outstanding works of this school is a series of *The Planets* with their attributes and influences on daily life. The *Planet Mercury*, patron of commerce and art (illustration 122) presents a delightful picture of the flourishing state of the arts in Florence. In the foreground a sculptor is carving a portrait bust. To the left is a goldsmith's shop with an artist making an engraving, and a customer bargaining for a handsome goblet. Above on a scaffolding an artist is painting a fresco while his assistant is grinding colors. In the background is an astrologer with an astrolabe. To the right scholarly pursuits are illustrated. In the foreground a richly dressed youth is feasting in the company of the innkeeper. Truly a paradise for artists and scholars. Similar in technique is a class of goldsmiths' work, known as nielli. These were small plates, usually of silver, in which a decorative design had been engraved and filled with a kind of enamel of contrasting color. The artist sometimes kept a record of his design by inking the plate and making a proof on paper or other material; from this—another transition step in the art of printmaking—he got the idea of making plates for the specific purpose of printing off designs. Two little niello prints by Peregrino of the Bolognese School, which together with Florence produced the most nielli, are reproduced as illustrations 138 and 139. Another charming group in the Fine Manner are the so-called Otto Prints, from the name of an early owner (illustration 144). They were round ornamental engravings and were perhaps designed for decorative purposes just as we might paste designs on a candy box.

The second large group of Florentine engravings are in the "Broad Manner." They are differentiated from the Fine Manner engravings by the use of parallel lines of shading, giving somewhat the effect of a pen and ink drawing. Two examples of the Broad Manner are shown in the *Libyan Sibyl* from the series of the *Prophets and Sibyls* (illustration 120) and the *Assumption of the Virgin* (illustration 123). The latter, one of the finest and also largest of the early Italian engravings, was undoubtedly based upon a design by Botticelli. The composition is noble and distinguished, and the engraving manages to translate some of the linear movement, rugged characterization, and lyric beauty that is associated with Botticelli in his last period.

One of the most important productions of the North Italian School is the set of so-called *Tarocchi Cards* of Mantegna which, as Hind points out, are neither cards nor Tarocchi nor by Mantegna. They are a series of fifty instructive prints divided into five series classified as *Ranks and Conditions of Men, Apollo and the Muses, Arts and Sciences, Genii and Virtues,* and *Planets and Spheres.* The *Primum Mobile,* or *Angel of the Ninth Sphere,* of the last-named series is reproduced as illustration 121. The engravings were probably made at Ferrara around 1465. Dürer made a copy of this print on his first journey to Italy; the drawing is preserved in the British Museum. The greatest artist of the North Italian School, however, was Andrea Mantegna. He was born of humble parentage near Padua about 1430. He studied at the studio of Squarcione, a mediocre painter and dealer in antiquities, whose shop was the meeting place of the scholars and humanists of Padua. It was in this atmosphere that he developed the admiration for the works and culture of Roman civilization which became the ruling passion of his life. In Vasari's words, "Andrea always maintained that the good antique statues were more perfect and beautiful than anything in nature." He lived in an ideal world of his own imagination, the world of Rome in which moved figures of incomparable nobility, dignity, and grandeur. And he set out to embody his dreams with all the tactile feeling, the sculpturesque power, the knowledge of nature and of representation, all the resources of a supremely creative temperament. His engravings, so seemingly dry and austere, are in truth loaded with emotion: every line is saturated with feeling. Never has tenderness and brooding protection been more superbly expressed than in the *Virgin and Child* (illustration 131). For breath-taking grandeur *The Risen Christ be-*

61

tween St. Andrew and Longinus has never been surpassed; for the expression of sorrow and lofty sense of tragedy, his three *Entombments* (illustration 126). Consider also those re-creations of the antique, the *Battle of the Sea Gods*, and the *Bacchanal with Silenus* and the *Bacchanal with a Wine Press* (illustration 118); with what solidity and tactile reality these types are rendered concrete. There they are—brought into being by Mantegna to live forever like the figures on Keats' urn—types of revelry, types of tenderness, types of grandeur, types of sorrow and tribulation. The concrete embodiment of types is creation of a high order, much higher in fact than realistic representation of natural objects, because it requires a much greater concentration of mental and emotional faculties. So, in spite of the smallness of his *œuvre*, seven engravings in all and the score that are associated as engravings of his school, Mantegna ranks as one of the supremely great artists in the history of prints.

Mantegna established a reputation with some twenty prints, but Pollaiuolo became famous for only one, the *Battle of the Naked Men* (illustration 119). Antonio del Pollaiuolo was born in Florence about 1432 and was one of the most famous goldsmiths, sculptors, and painters of his time. "Antonio's treatment of the nude," says Vasari, "is more modern than that of any of the masters who preceded him, and he dissected many bodies to examine their anatomy, being the first to represent the proper action of the muscles." Berenson's famous appreciation of this engraving, one of the world's greatest masterpieces, is well known:

What is it that makes us return to this sheet with ever renewed, ever increased pleasure? Surely it is not the hideous faces of most of the figures and their scarcely less hideous bodies. Nor is it the pattern as decorative design, which is of great beauty indeed, but not at all in proportion to the spell exerted upon us. Least of all is it—for most of us—an interest in the technique or history of engraving. No, the pleasure we take in these savagely battling forms arises from their power to directly communicate life, to immensely heighten our sense of vitality. Look at the combatant prostrate on the ground and his assailant bending over, each intent on stabbing the other. See how the prostrate man plants his foot on the thigh of his enemy, and note the tremendous energy he exerts to keep off the foe, who, turning

62

as upon a pivot, with his grip on the other's head, exerts no less force to keep the advantage gained. The significance of all these muscular strains and pressures is so rendered that we cannot help realizing them; we imagine ourselves imitating all the movements, and exerting the force required for them—and all without the least effort on our side. If all this without moving a muscle, what should we feel if we too had exerted ourselves! And thus while under the spell of this illusion—this hyperaesthesia not bought with drugs, and not paid for with cheques drawn on our vitality—we feel as if the elixir of life, not our own sluggish blood, were coursing through our veins.

There is a charming profile *Portrait of a Lady* (illustration 135) of a style made famous by the paintings of Domenico Veneziano, Verrocchio, Pollaiuolo, and others. This engraving was formerly classified among the early anonymous prints in the Fine Manner, but Hind in his recent big *Catalogue of Early Italian Engravings* attributes it to the School of Pollaiuolo. In any case, with its emphasis on ornament and linear values, it is the work of a goldsmith rather than a painter. There is another profile *Portrait of a Lady* (illustration 136) which is sometimes ascribed to Leonardo da Vinci. That the great experimenter might have tried his hand at a new art technique is not improbable; and the slipped stroke on the forehead, as Hind points out, might be evidence of an unpracticed hand. Other critics, however, have felt that the engraving was much too professional for a one and only plate.

Some of the charm and enchantment of the School of Giorgione are carried over in the engravings of Giulio Campagnola, born at Padua about 1482. The son of the writer, Girolamo Campagnola, Giulio was precocious and many-sided in his development: painter, engraver, poet, musician, scholar, and designer of type. About 1507 he went to Venice and may have had some direct contact with Giorgione. He died after 1515. Of the sixteen plates which he engraved, some are quite banal, being copies after Dürer and others; but there are about a half dozen that are among the most exquisite prints of the period, the *Shepherds in a Landscape*, the *Stag at Rest*, the *Astrologer*, the *Young Shepherd*, the *St. John the Baptist*, and *Christ and the Woman of Samaria*. It is hard to analyze wherein the magic of an engraving like the *Christ and the Woman of*

63

Samaria (illustration 160) lies, but it is equally obvious that the enchantment exists. Perhaps it lies in the perfect identification of matter and form (in Walter Pater's words) or in the mood of serene and pure beauty that it so elusively suggests. The *St. John the Baptist* (illustration 164)—the landscape Giorgionesque, the figure deriving its nobility from Mantegna—likewise manages to convey a definite emotion in purely pictorial terms. Campagnola's work is distinguished not for intensity or strength but for sensibility and grace. Some of his works like the *Young Shepherd*, the *Stag at Rest*, or the *St. John*, are executed with an exquisite placement of every detail, including the lettering of the name. In this embodiment of sensibility and good taste as a creative principle, Campagnola is the exemplar of a long line of artists reaching to the present day. His technique is noteworthy also for its use of dots and flick-work combined with more or less amounts of regular graver work to blend and soften his effects. It is an interesting anticipation of stipple engraving, not so much in its method as in its final result.

The allegories and mythological conceits dear to the Renaissance and Humanist temperament were depicted by a number of secondary yet charming engravers such as Robetta (illustration 181), Master I. B. with the Bird, Nicoletto da Modena, Jacopo Francia, Benedetto Montagna, and others. The man who was destined to make engraving into a professional system was Marcantonio Raimondi. He was born in Bologna about 1480 and studied with the goldsmith-painter, Francesco Francia. In due course he left his native city to seek his fortune in the big world. He was a facile engraver and had a great talent for assimilation. In Venice, most cosmopolitan of cities, he discovered the work of Dürer and as we have already heard, copied much of it. "Arrived at Rome," in Vasari's words, "he made a beautiful copper engraving of a drawing of Raphael, representing Lucretia killing herself, executed with such beauty and diligence that, when it was shown to Raphael, the artist was disposed to issue some prints himself from his own designs." This was the beginning of a long and fruitful partnership between artist and engraver in the dissemination of designs, which had enormous influence on art for centuries to come. It established a practice of reproductive engraving which was to last until the perfection of photographic repro-

64

ductions. It was in the form of reproductive engraving that a large portion of art was made accessible to other practicing artists. Not only did Marcantonio, in collaboration with Raphael establish the practice but he also, through his pupils, laid down a system of technique. As Ivins points out, "Marcantonio combined the German linear scheme for representation of textures and rotundity with the Italian feeling for volumes, and in so doing gave engraving its pictorial enfranchisement." Two of the greatest examples of these two artists' collaboration are the *Judgment of Paris* and the *Massacre of the Innocents* (illustrations 161 and 162). They are marvels of space composition, rhythmic movement and balance, linear design and felicitous handling of the figure. The engraving of *Two Fauns* (illustration 146), based upon the antique, shows the extent to which Renaissance decoration deviated from medieval ornament. After the death of Raphael, Marcantonio's work suffered a strong deterioration, and this decline was completed by his financial ruin in the sack of Rome in 1527. He fled to Bologna and died a broken man.

Another engraver who collaborated with Raphael in still another form of reproductive engraving was Ugo da Carpi. Vasari credits da Carpi with the invention of chiaroscuro wood engraving or the use of several blocks in color for the reproduction of drawings. It has been discovered, however, that the Germans, Burgkmair, 1508, Cranach, 1509 (illustration 170), Baldung Grien (illustration 169), Altdorfer, Wechtlin, and others had perfected the process either previously or contemporaneously with the Italian. The methods of the two schools were nevertheless slightly different. The Germans in general worked up the black and white key block to its completion so that it could function as a woodcut independently (many such proofs exist) and then added color blocks to heighten the effect. Whereas the Italians conceived the whole in terms of color and made less use of detailed black and white accents. In the *Miraculous Draught of Fishes* by da Carpi after the drawing by Raphael (illustration 168) the details are treated so broadly and so completely in terms of color, that the key block would have no meaning independently of the other blocks. Another example, the *Saturn*, by da Carpi after Parmigiano, is reproduced as illustration 167. Other prac-

65

titioners of the art in Italy were Andreani, Vicentino, and Antonio da Trento.

Mention of the woodcut leads us back half a century to trace the development of the art in Italy. Single woodcuts of the fifteenth century were not so frequent in Italy as in Germany, though woodcut playing cards are mentioned as a flourishing industry at Venice as early as 1441. The illustrated book, however, soon developed into one of the most important achievements of the Renaissance in Italy. The first illustrated book in Italy was the *Meditations of Cardinal Turrecremata* printed in Rome in 1467 (illustration 1). The cuts were probably made by a German craftsman, but the interesting thing about them was the printed statement that they were reproductions of frescoes appearing in the Church of Marie de Minerva in Rome, and thus the earliest extant example of the use of engraving for reproducing artists' paintings and designs, the practice which Raphael and Marcantonio first put on a successful business basis.

The second illustrated book in Italy was Valturius, *De Re Militari*, printed at Verona in 1472. The designs of this early and important book on military engineering have been attributed to the medallist, Matteo de Pastis or to Valturius himself (illustration 2). As an example of the pictorial treatment of another of the arts, the *Organist* from Gafurius, *Theorica Musicae*, printed in Milan in 1492, is reproduced as illustration 13. In Ferrara in 1497 was published an illustrated book with the same title though not with the same contents as the Ulm *De Claris Mulieribus* of 1473. The picture, which serves as a portrait of both Paula Gonzaga and of Marcella Romana (illustration 9), is in striking contrast to the earlier *Sappho*, and shows how divergent were Gothic and Renaissance ideals.

The two great centers of book production in Italy were Venice and Florence. The illustrators of Venice perfected a kind of engraving in outline not only intrinsically charming and graceful but also perfectly in keeping with the roman type face. The *Decameron* of 1492 has already been mentioned (illustration 3). One of the most distinguished examples of Venetian illustration is Ketham's *Fascicolo di Medicina* of 1493 (illustration 14). This noble and dignified work gives us a glimpse

66

of the medical practice of the time: we see the doctor visiting the patient ill with the plague, being careful not to come too close for fear of infection. Perhaps the most famous Venetian book was the *Hypnerotomachia Poliphili*, or the *Strife of Love in a Dreame*, as an Elizabethan translated it. It was printed by Aldus in 1499 at the expense of Leonardus Crassus (illustration 4). The text by Colonna is a mélange of humanist and classical conceits, and the book is now remembered only for the beauty of its woodcuts and the harmony of its type and illustrations. The work has been a model to many subsequent illustrators, notably Ricketts and Maillol in modern times.

In Florence, among other things, were published a large group of illustrated books which bear the same relation to the Renaissance, in their perfection of a popular art, that the French Books of Hours bear to the Gothic spirit: the essence of the Renaissance is distilled in their pages. These woodcuts, like the cuts of the *Horae*, possess a distinctive and easily recognizable style. And curiously enough, the period of their greatest production coincided almost exactly with that of the French books, that is to say the ten years before and the thirty years after the beginning of the sixteenth century. Like them, too, the names of the artists or engravers are not known. Many of the Florentine cuts appeared in little booklets, manifestations of popular art, *Rappresentazione* or sacred mystery plays, sermons, poems, little novels—an enormous range of subject matter. The daily life of Florence is re-created before our eyes. Hundreds of scenes, the facts, the gestures, the characters of everyday life are transformed into decorative pictures of lasting charm. We see a group singing before an image in church, we see the swain bringing his sweetheart a flower (illustration 48), we see the citizen at the shoemaker's shop or at the fishmonger buying fish during Lent (illustration 11), we see young bucks carousing. We see dramatic incidents from the lives of the saints, we see Savonarola preaching in church (illustration 10), nay we almost hear him as he holds his audience spellbound by his eloquence:

Women, you rejoice in being beautiful. Be beautiful, it is woman's greatest delight. But tell me in what does beauty consist? In colors? No. In contours? No. It is in the harmony between them. And how is that harmony revealed? By light. Beauty is light. You see happy spirits; their beauty consists in light. You know, God is light: He is beauty also. The more truly that creatures participate in the beauty of God and approach it, the more beautiful they become. . . .

We see illustrations to poems, Dante's *Divina Commedia* (illustration 49), Pulci's *Morganti Maggiore*, Boccaccio's *Ninfale Fiesolano* (illustration 12), a charming pastoral bit. And this whole panorama is depicted with such charming decorative effect, such color and vivacity, such zest and *joie de vivre*, such unerring balance between particular and universal, that they have never been surpassed in the history of prints.

Single sheet woodcuts were not made in great quantities in the sixteenth century in Italy except for a few in Venice. Here Titian was the dominant influence. The five sheets of the *Triumph of Faith*, dated 1508, and the twelve sheets of *Pharaoh's Army Submerged in the Red Sea*, of 1549, are epoch-making works, grand both in size and significance. These works are too huge for reduction on a small scale, and two other works by Titian (illustrations 45 and 39) have been chosen for reproduction, both cut by Nicolo Boldrini, the *Venus and Amor*, and the *Landscape with the Woman Milking a Cow*. They are faithful translations into wood of the characteristics of Titian's drawing, and one of them shows Titian's pastoral interest and method of treating pure landscape, which probably influenced Bruegel and Rubens when they came to take up the same theme. Titian's portraits were famous for their penetration of character, their decorative fullness and nobility of style. Typical of these is Titian's portrait of his friend, the great poet, Ariosto, cut in wood by Francesco de Nanto and published in an edition of his *Orlando Furioso*, Ferrara, 1532 (illustration 47). Incidentally Ariosto mentions Titian in his poem. The great Venetian died in 1576 at the age of ninety-nine, rich in honors and achievement, one of the first professional artists in the modern sense of the word.

A distinguished portrait of Titian was engraved by Agostino Carracci (illustration 153), one of three brothers who founded the Eclectic School of Bologna, and who also were among the first to introduce the Academy system of teaching to replace the older master-apprentice

68

method. The Carracci, dominant in the second half of the sixteenth century, represented the eclectic and somewhat decadent tendency which followed the great outburst of the Renaissance. Two other painters whose work anticipated and led up to some of the qualities associated with Baroque art were Parmigiano and Baroccio. Francesco Mazzuoli, called Parmigiano, was the first Italian who practiced etching. His etchings, dating from about 1520 onwards, have the spontaneity and charm, the refinement and feminine grace of his drawings (illustration 166). He was one of the first of the Mannerists. Federigo Baroccio (1528–1612) made about four etchings, notably the large *Annunciation* (illustration 165). This plate is rather theatrical in style but executed with considerable subtlety of biting. Baroccio was to have considerable influence on the religious painting of Boucher and other artists of the eighteenth century.

The early illustrated books had been decorated with woodcuts. But at the end of the sixteenth century woodcut illustrations were being replaced by intaglio or copperplate engravings. There were several reasons for this. Copper engraving became more fashionable than woodcuts. But there also was a growing differentiation in the purpose of the book: between the book as a cheap popular work and the book as an object of luxury. In the fifteenth century the differentiation had been between the cheap printed book and the sumptuous illuminated manuscript. Now, the differentiation was made between the cheap woodcut book and the expensive copperplate book. There was no doubt that the copperplate book was more expensive to produce: it required more than one printing, the plates took longer to print and could not yield as many impressions as a woodblock. Thus the illustrated book became intaglio in character and luxurious and expensive in production. The woodcut went underground, as it were, and continued an unbroken tradition from the fifteenth century to the nineteenth century in the chapbooks, broadsheets, *images populaires*, and fugitive prints of the people. Of course in certain kinds of scientific work such as maps or architectural illustrations, where the greater precision of copper engraving was desirable, there were reasons other than economic for the change. By the middle of the sixteenth century the technical difficulties in the

69

way of using intaglio illustrations had been more or less overcome. Three books may be used to typify the new tendency. The first, catering to an aristocratic luxurious class, is Gualterotti's *Description of the Royal Fête at the Marriage of Christina of Lorraine with Don Ferdinando de' Medici, Grand Duke of Tuscany*, published at Florence in 1589. It was a sort of souvenir book of the ceremonies describing all the pageants, mimic battles, balls, triumphal arches, allegories, etcetera, that were part of the festivities. There were sixty-seven paintings made of the various incidents by a number of court painters, and for the book they were etched with great zest and vigor by some unknown hand. The illustration chosen (182) apparently represents the actual wedding ceremony, and was painted by Giovanni Balducci, called Cosci. The etching is carried out with a breadth and power, an incisive line and flair for style that is truly a delight to the eye. It contains a trace of mannerism but there is still a lot of sap in the manner. Incidentally, at this same wedding a number of musical *intermezzi*, precursors of opera, were produced. One of them, *The Harmony of the Spheres*, was composed by Emilio del Cavaliere, who later produced the first oratorio.

The second example is midway between the scientific and the sumptuous book: *Della Trasportazione dell' Obelisco Vaticano*, published at Rome in 1589 (illustration 178). This work, written by Domenico Fontana, the well-known architect of Pope Sixtus V, describes the engineering feat of transporting the obelisk to its present location in the Piazza of St. Pietro, and is illustrated with a number of engravings by Natalis Bonifaccio after Fontana's designs. The plates were executed with gusto and a fine balance between scientific and pictorial interest. The artistic treatment of scaffolding, building construction, "the wonder of work," has been generally assumed to be of modern origin. Although the scientific aspect is stressed, it is probable that it was considered more as a sumptuous gift book given out by the Pope and his friends. The third example is more specifically of scientific interest, a page from the great Atlas of Ortelius, the *Map of America* of 1589 (illustration 180), printed by the famous Antwerp printer, Plantin, of whom we shall hear further in connection with Rubens. It is interesting to contrast this map with the Nuremberg map of the

70

world in 1493 and trace the growth of man's geographical knowledge. In 1492 Columbus discovered America; in 1497 Cabot discovered Newfoundland; in 1498 Vasco de Gama sailed to India around Africa; in 1499 Amerigo Vespucci discovered Venezuela; in 1513 Balboa discovered the Pacific at Panama; in 1514 the Portuguese were in China and in 1542 in Japan; in 1520 Magellan sailed around the world; from 1539 to 1577 the explorations of de Soto, Coronado, Cartier, Frobisher, and Drake took place. Ortelius was one of the first cartographers to issue maps that were based on actual scientific observations. Yet withal the map is beautifully designed, with a fine sense of placement of the decorative cartouches and other accessories. The ship in the Pacific represents Magellan sailing around the world. Ortelius drew at a time when the truth about geography was still beautiful. Later on it was to become strictly utilitarian.

About this time in Antwerp and later at Brussels there lived a man who was one of the world's greatest artists, Peter Bruegel. He was born about 1525 and studied with Pieter Koeck van Aelst, whose daughter he afterwards married. He undoubtedly derived inspiration in his macabre aspects from Hieronymus Bosch. In 1551 he was enrolled in the artists' Guild of St. Luke at Antwerp, and was furnishing designs to the print publisher, Jerome Cock. Most of our knowledge of his life comes from the almost contemporary account of Karel van Mander.

With [his friend and patron] Franckert, Bruegel often went on trips among the peasants, to their weddings and fairs [illustration 186]. The two dressed like peasants, brought presents like the other guests, and acted as if they belonged to the families or acquaintances of the bride or groom. Here Bruegel delighted in observing the manners of the peasants in eating, drinking, dancing, jumping, making love, and engaging in various drolleries, all of which he knew how to copy very comically and skillfully. . . . He was astonishingly sure of his composition and drew most ably and beautifully with the pen. . . . Bruegel was a quiet man who did not talk much, but was jovial in company, and he loved to frighten people, often his own pupils with all kinds of ghostly sounds and pranks that he played. . . . He painted a *Massacre of the Innocents*, in which there is much to see that is done true to life—a whole family, for instance, begging for the life of

71

a peasant child whom a murderous soldier has seized in order to kill it; the grief and the swooning of the mother and other events appear realistic. . . . Many of Bruegel's strange compositions and comical subjects one may see in his copper engravings. But he has made many skillful and beautiful drawings; he supplied them with inscriptions which, at the time, were too biting and too sharp, and which he had burned by his wife during his last illness, because of remorse, or fear that the most disagreeble consequences might grow out of them. In his will he left his wife a picture of a Magpie on a Gallows. By the magpie he meant the gossips whom he delivered to the gallows. In addition, he had painted a picture in which Truth triumphs. According to his own statement, this was the best thing painted by him.

Bruegel had a deep and abiding love for humanity, for the peasant and common man, for life in its essentials. But it was not a patronizing attitude, something he could exploit cynically or commercially for his own ends. It grew out of his innate sympathy for all the manifestations of life, high and low, the eternal verities of man and woman. He also had a great love for nature, its trees and rocks, its rivers and mountains, its fertile plains, as his many landscapes show (illustration 183). But he was also a great intellect, one of the world's greatest pictorial designers in line and color in space; like Bach, whom he resembled in many respects, a master of noble and intricate contrapuntal effects. Above all he was a philosopher who meditated on first and last things, who was capable of those profound syntheses of human experience which he clothed in archetypes of the most convincing realism. He gave his allegiance to no faction but to humanity as a whole. He pursued his way serenely in troublous times with an enduring faith in Truth and Man. And parlous times they were: the presence of sudden and cruel death, bitter religious strife, rapine and wanton destruction, the horrible oppression of the Spanish rulers and soldiery. That he felt all these things is evident from the inscriptions he destroyed and from the nostalgia that permeates his *Luilekkerland* (illustration 185), the "Land of Cocaigne," the "Rock-Candy Mountains," that land of milk and honey where sorrow and effort and care are banished. But he also faced the facts with unflinching realism in the *Massacre of the Innocents* or in that magnificent synthesis of *Justice* (illustration 184) where are

72

assembled all the tortures of the Inquisition. He never took sides in the narrow sense. Is this the role of the artist? At any rate it is one solution of the artist's problem. It must be remembered that the issues were not as clear at the time as they are to us in perspective; even the oppressed were disorganized and torn with opposing factions, and he died before the Spanish Fury had reached its climax. He never took sides, but he always believed that his greatest painting was the *Triumph of Truth*.

France contributed relatively little to the history of prints during the sixteenth century. The chief school of the first half of the century was the School of Fontainebleau, largely an importation from Italy, and in the second half-century France was rent with civil strife. One strange and mysterious figure stands out, however, among the early engravers of France—Jean Duvet. This goldsmith-engraver was born about 1485, probably at Dijon, and died after 1561 at Langres. He executed some goldsmith's work as a present from the town of Langres to Francis I, and was honored with the title of Goldsmith to the King. He made some sixty engravings including a series of the *Apocalypse* and the *History of the Unicorn*, an allegory bearing some relation to the amours of Henri II and Diane de Poitiers. But this summary recital of his life and work give no hint of the particular quality of his genius. He was a mystic, one of those extraordinary figures whose prints are moving not by what they say but by what they imply. As with many mystics his expression is often turgid and confused, often his very language and forms are derivative—mystics are indifferent to such matters, since mundane expression bears the same relation to the inner light as a candle does to the sun. But through these naive and clumsy engravings shine breath-taking illumination and fiery emotion. His conception is so much greater than his execution that he sometimes leaves his plates unfinished in despair. His plates of the *Apocalypse* with their swirling forms and phantasmagoric appearances, seem more akin to the spirit of that great mystical document than Dürer's somewhat more prosaic version, from which many of the details are borrowed. In a serener, more joyous vein is the *Marriage of Adam and Eve* (illustration 163). It is interesting to compare this with Dürer's *Adam and Eve* for a further contrast between the mystic and the man of the world.

Jean Cousin, painter, sculptor, engraver, architect, glass-worker, mathematician, and writer, made a small number of engravings, notably an *Entombment* (illustration 159) distinguished for its moving arrangement of figures against a background of classical landscape. His *Book of Perspective* of 1560 with its charming and precise woodcuts bears witness to the great interest that existed in that branch of science. But the first French work, indeed the first printed work on perspective in any language, was issued at Toul in 1505 by Jean Pélerin. Pélerin, or Viator, was Canon of the Cathedral, had been in the service of the historian Philippe de Commines, and wrote books on Ptolemy as well as on devotional subjects. It is not known how he achieved the miracle of working out to perfection the complete system of perspective, but he did and illustrated it with a series of woodcut diagrams of a room (illustration 59), bridges, a courtyard, Notre Dame Cathedral, etcetera. The book was popular and went through several editions, and was pirated in a Nuremberg edition of 1509. The work was dedicated to artists and in the dedication he mentions some that he considered worthy in his day. They are, as far as they can be identified, as follows: Mantegna, Leonardo, Raphael, Michelangelo, Perugino, Bellini, Lucas van Leyden, Cranach, Dürer, Baldung Grien, Hugo van der Goes, Schäufelein, and Fouquet.

This concludes the survey of the Renaissance as expressed in prints. The astonishing thing about the Italian Renaissance was the extent to which all the people participated in it. There are always a few cultivated and creative people in every age, but when these qualities are spread among all the people, it becomes a great period. Artists and craftsmen of great talent sprang up on every hand; but there were also a great demand and encouragement for their work. Time and time again one comes across passages in Vasari like this: "Agnolo Doni was then in Florence, and though sparing in other things, spent willingly upon paintings and sculpture, of which he was very fond." Or the following: "All of which brought Marcantonio such fame that his things were more valued than those of the Flemings for their good design, and the merchants found them very profitable." It was in Italy that the print-seller–publisher first developed. There were Il Baviera (Raphael's agent),

74

Nicolo Nelli, Antonio Salamanca, Antoine Lafrery, C. Duchetti, Jerome Cock of Antwerp, and others. Even the commonest books and pamphlets were beautiful. But in the mutations of man's fate, this widespread cultivation of the beautiful did not last for long. We marvel at the calmness and casualness with which Vasari mentions the sack of Rome in 1527. Italy had been broken up into many rival cities and principalities, and the Hapsburg vied with the rulers of France for their domination and control. Italy was undoubtedly the most civilized country of Europe, civilized not only in the sense of culture and refinement but also in the sense of commerce and manufacture. Italy gave much to Germany and Flanders and especially to France through the encouragement of its rulers from Francis I to Catherine de' Medici. With the development of these countries, Italy's prestige and its trade gradually declined. The dominant power in the second half of the sixteenth century was Spain with all the wealth of the Americas at its command (illustration 212), and its policy was reactionary and monarchical, definitely opposed to the relatively democratic cultures of Italy, England, and Flanders.

4. Seventeenth Century

THE seventeenth century has sometimes been called the century of the Baroque. And although an art period or style cannot be precisely delimited by centuries, many of the artists of the time display qualities that are associated with this style. The Baroque developed from the Renaissance and to a certain extent was a reaction against it. It was the age of the counter-Reformation, a re-affirmation of faith and dogma, initiated largely by the Jesuits against the individualist interpretations of the Protestant Reformation. It has been claimed that the Baroque had a relation to the Gothic in its stress upon emotional elements. It is true that both Gothic and Baroque were ages of faith; but in the one case it was naive faith, a primary and creative impulse, in the second case it was a faith in established dogma, a secondary or derivative impulse. The Baroque would have been impossible without the Renaissance. A definite convention, a dogma had been firmly established—a convention that embraced not only religious but also social and artistic forms, absolute monarchy, forms of building and painting, forms of social life—and the Baroque was the individual's reaction to this. The dogmas were not challenged: they were taken for granted; and with that foundation they were either expanded into a swelling system as with Rubens, or embroidered with grotesque themes as with Callot. The Baroque was a product of leisure and luxury, a slackening of the terrific outburst of energy of the Renaissance. The fires had died down; what remained were the flickerings of fantasy. The artists of the Renaissance expressed their ideas in attitudes and gestures energetically and beautifully appropriate to the occasion, the natural outgrowth of the action expressed. In the Baroque the gesture became important for its own sake; the artists played with it, they heightened it or exaggerated it, played variations on it, till it became largely devoid

76

of logical meaning. The gesture became a mannerism, a form often employed purely for compositional effect. They were bored with austere or tragic effects; they craved novelty and ingenious invention. The positive, the affirming, the best side of the Baroque was expressed by Rubens.

Peter Paul Rubens, the Prince of Painters, lived and breathed in the grand manner. His work is one grand *largesse;* which was not with him a mannered attitude only: out of his fecundity, his incomparable zest, he endowed his forms with swelling pulsating life. He was a man of action: he painted pictures as a general would direct an army or a prince would rule a principality. He had vast organizing skill: he organized his pictures into masterly compositions, he organized his pupils and assistants to execute them; on both his instrument and his creation he put his own impress. He did not innovate, he summed up. He did not create new forms, he used the material at hand, he worked in the spirit of the age. He lived as Fromentin said, *"en plein lumière,"* in full light—never a shadow of scepticism or doubt. Born in 1577, he started his career as a court page; he died in 1640 the most renowned painter of his time. He studied with three masters and went to Italy to complete his education. At thirty-three he was a successful man with a beloved wife and children and an imposing house filled with art treasures. He became a diplomat, working consistently to maintain peace between Protestant Holland and Catholic Belgium. He was the courteous friend of Philip II of Spain, the companion of the art-loving Charles I, the painter of the *Triumphs of Marie de' Medici,* the confidant and trusted agent of the Infanta Isabella of Belgium. He engaged in vast correspondence in Latin, Spanish, Italian, and Flemish on many matters of diplomacy, business, antiquities, collecting, but never any speculation on art. We have a contemporary account of his daily life by the Dane, Otto Sperling:

We paid a visit to the very celebrated and eminent painter, Rubens, whom we found at work, and, while he went on with his painting, listening to a reading from Tacitus and dictating a letter. We kept silent for fear of disturbing him; but he spoke to us without stopping his work or the reading or the dictation, and answered our questions as if to give us proof of his powerful faculties. Then he ordered a servant to conduct us round

77

his magnificent palace and show us his antiquities and the Greek and Roman statues of which he owns a great quantity.

It is natural that such an expansive and practical nature should, like Raphael, see the advantage of publishing engravings of his work under his own auspices. He set about to train and employ a school of engravers of whom Soutman, Vorsterman, Pontius, and the two Bolswerts were the most famous. In the Bibliothèque Nationale in Paris, there exist proofs of their engravings containing corrections and emendations in Rubens' hand. It is doubtful whether he ever himself handled the burin. One etching, however, is ascribed to him with considerable certainty— the superb *St. Catherine* with its monumental swelling forms (illustration 222). The more than eight hundred engravings that were made after his works did much to spread Rubens' fame throughout Europe. As an example of landscape with genre interest the *Village Dance* engraved by Bolswert is reproduced as illustration 204. As an example of a religious subject, *The Temptation of Christ* from the plafond of the Jesuit Church in Antwerp, cut in wood by Christophel Jegher, is reproduced as illustration 64. In the archives of Plantin-Moretus museum in Antwerp is preserved Moretus' account referring to the printing of this very woodcut on September 2 and 8, 1633, "*item, doibt pour l'impression de 2000 images de bois avec le papier etc. Florins 72*" (item, to printing 2000 proofs of woodcut with paper 72 florins).

Anthony van Dyck was Rubens' most talented pupil. Before he settled permanently in England as court painter to Charles I in 1632, he began an ambitious undertaking known as the *Iconography* or collection of one hundred portraits of the famous men of his day. He executed eighteen of these in etching, of which five remained unchanged (*Peter Bruegel the Younger, Erasmus, Snellinx, Suttermans* and *Josse de Momper* [illustration 201]), six others were later supplied with engraved backgrounds (*Jan Bruegel, Franken, van Noort, Pontius, Vorsterman,* and *de Wael*) and the balance completely reworked by professional engravers. He initiated a new style of portraiture, the freely etched portrait, concentrating on certain features of the face with open lines and dots, and leaving the body and background lightly sketched in. But the prevailing taste of his day was for the more formal portrait and the balance of the *Iconography* was executed by the engravers of the Rubens school after his own drawings. It was not until several centuries later that the etchings themselves were appreciated. Van Dyck perfected a method for setting down the external features of a sitter without prying too deep into his essential character, which made him the eminently successful and fashionable portrait painter that he was. Even in his early days before the formula had mastered him completely, and when he was portraying his friends and fellow-painters, he could not resist endowing them all with a flattering dignity and nobility. It is known that van Dyck painted Charles I forty times and his Queen Henrietta thirty times. After the Countess Sophie of the Palatinate had been presented to the Queen and her attendants she recorded her naive astonishment at the discrepancy between fact and fiction: she had had such a different impression of the court from van Dyck's portraits.

Van Dyck died in 1641 just before the Great Rebellion in England. Another foreign etcher, Wenzel Hollar, allied himself with the Cavalier cause and fought in some of its battles. He was born in Prague in 1607 and studied with Mathias Merian. In 1637 he came to England under the patronage of the Earl of Arundel who employed him to reproduce treasures in his collection. Born in a noble family which had lost everything in the Bohemian wars, Hollar took up etching as his life profession: he made about 2700 plates, characterized by sobriety, precision, and great technical skill. He married a lady-in-waiting at the Court and was very much interested in depicting costume, as for instance in the famous series of the *Theatrum Mulierum* of 1643. Characteristic is the *Winter* (illustration 220) of the set of the *Seasons*. The background shows a view of Cornhill and the Old Exchange in London. Underneath are four lines of verse in the spirit of the court of Charles:

> "The cold, not cruelty makes her weare
> In Winter, furrs and Wild beasts haire
> For a smoother skinn at night.
> Embraceth her with more delight."

After the Restoration he fell into poverty and worked for the book and print publishers at twelve pence per hour. According to his friend,

Francis Place, "he had a method of working not common. He did all by the hour, in which he was very exact, for if anybody came in, and kept him from his business, he always laid the hourglass on one side, till they were gone." He died in extreme poverty in 1677.

As a foil to the almost feminine daintiness of Hollar one might put forward the masculine exuberance of Hendrick Goltzius. Born in 1558 of a long line of artists, he early developed an artistic temperament, and many stories are told of his pranks, of his posing as a cheese merchant before the engraver, Sadeler, of making engravings in the style of Dürer and Lucas van Leyden which fooled many would-be connoisseurs, of making his servant pose as the master while he in the role of servant listened to unguarded comments about the master. In his engraving he perfected the system of the swelling line, or minute variations in the thickness of each engraved line, which enabled him to render surface textures and color with more facility. This carried engraving further in the direction of a purely reproductive or copying technique in contrast to the systems of Dürer and Marcantonio which were more in the nature of translations of one medium into the conventions of another. Nevertheless his technical proficiency brought him great fame, and he was specially invited to Paris to do the portrait of Henri IV (illustration 236). He was one of the few seventeenth century artists who also made chiaroscuros and woodcuts, of which the *Landscape* (illustration 65) is a charming example. In his figure work he carried the Baroque tendency of mannered gesture, of swelling out and puffing up forms to the limit, as may be seen in the typical engraving of the *Statue of Hercules in the Farnese Palace in Rome* (illustration 219). With its glimpse of the visitors gazing in admiration at the statue, it affords a delightful suggestion of the *tourisme* of the time. John Evelyn in his diary thus records his visit in 1644:

In the first place, our sights-man (for so they name certain persons here who get their living by leading strangers about to see the city) went to the Palace Farnese, a magnificent square structure built by Michael Angelo. . . . Descending into the court, we with astonishment contemplated those two incomparable statues of Hercules and Flora, so much celebrated by Pliny.

80

Italy and its many art treasures were still the goal of artists and cultured tourists. The names of two great French etchers of the early seventeenth century were intimately associated with Italy: Callot and Claude Gellée of Lorraine.

Callot [wrote Meaume] when a child of thirteen ran away from his home at Nancy, meaning to journey to Rome and study art. It was in the spring of 1606 the young fugitive departed on foot, almost without money, and quite without influence, relying entirely on his face and his good luck. He was soon obliged to join a troupe of gypsies who were going to Florence. There he was recognized by merchants from Nancy and was taken home to his parents. He ran away a second time and was again brought home, this time by his brother. In 1608 Callot's parents finally permitted him to go to Rome where he studied under Thomassin.

In 1611 he left Rome for Florence (according to legend on account of a gallant adventure with his master's wife) and entered the service of Cosmo II de' Medici. Eleven years later he returned to his native Lorraine where he remained with brief outside excursions till his death in 1635. Callot was a great etcher and perfected the technique of repeated bitings to secure effects of great delicacy and subtlety. He was also a great Baroque artist in his predilection for the grotesque (the *Temptation of St. Anthony* and the series of *Gobbi*), for masks and pageants (in *Florence* and *Nancy*), for mannered religious engravings (the series of *The Saints, The Passion,* and *The Prodigal Son*) and in his research in the characters of the *Commedia dell'Arte*. Faithful reflections, too, of the movements of his time were his numerous war pictures, the *Military Exercises,* the three huge *Sieges of Breda,* the *Island of Ré,* and *La Rochelle,* and the larger and smaller *Disasters of War*. It is said that after the invasion of Lorraine in 1633, Louis XIII asked him to commemorate the siege of Nancy in another huge battle piece, but Callot refused to "do anything against the honor of my prince and my country." At any rate he had seen enough of the horrors of war during the French invasion in 1632 and 1633 to execute his two bitter series of *Les Misères de la Guerre* while his memory was still vivid. They are the first of a series of terrific indictments of war that have been drawn up by artists. No

81

greater contrast could be imagined than between the brutality of the subject and the exquisite delicacy of the treatment (illustrations 210 and 211). Not only were the savage lusts of murder and plunder depicted but also the equally devastating starvation and poverty. The social system of the age was rich in contrasts, and Callot has faithfully recorded its full range, from the *Garden at Nancy* (illustration 209) and the *Costumes of the Nobility* to the studies of *Beggars* (illustration 208), card sharpers, and wandering gypsy life (illustration 213). But in no respect was he so much a child of his age as in his picturing of the *Commedia dell'Arte* (illustration 217). The *Commedia* was the quintessence of the Baroque: it was improvised, often extravagant and satiric, anti-intellectual and anti-rational, stressing emotional values, raising the caprice to an art form, playing variations on an accepted theme, a comedy of attitudes and gestures. In the *Commedia dell'Arte* certain types (Harlequin, Columbine, Isabelle, Scaramouche, Pulcinella, Pantaloon, Brighella, Mezzetino, Scapin, Sganarelle, Cantarina, Inamorata, Soubrette, Pierrot, El Capitan, The Doctor) with attributes known to everyone played their parts in dramatic situations which again were familiar to all. The dialogue was not written down or fixed, but was improvised by the actors following patterns that were well established. Thus the emphasis and charm of the art form lay not in the significance or meaning of the drama, but in its expression, in the gestures and pantomime of the actors, and in the wit, the satire, the *double entendre* of their speech. The *Commedia* flourished chiefly in the Latin countries during the seventeenth and eighteenth centuries.

According to legend Callot's contemporary, Claude, was a pastry cook's apprentice who longed for Arcadia and found it. Claude Gellée, called Lorrain, was born in the Vosges in 1600. Left an orphan at twelve he wandered about Italy, Germany, Switzerland, and Lorraine, pursued by many adventures and misadventures, falling sick, being several times robbed, and picking up here and there a knowledge of the technique of art. In 1627 he settled down in Rome where he lived a quiet and uneventful life. He did not associate with the French academicians in Rome, or perhaps they would not associate with him, though he occasionally went on painting excursions with Poussin; he was no courtier, said Sandrart, and he had but few intimates like Swanevelt, Bombaccio, Andries Both, and Sandrart. He never married; all his passion went into his work, the task of rendering visible his dream of Arcadia, where all is peace and beauty and order. Sandrart wrote:

He applied himself with great earnestness and industry to perfect himself in his art and learn the secrets of nature. Day after day he would spend in the Campagna, from sunrise till long after nightfall, noting the tints of the dawn and the splendor of the setting sun. . . . As a master of aerial perspective, he well knew how to blend the sharp division of colors to make them appear like nature's. And at his studio he would sit long hours in reverie till there came to him those grand conceptions which grew in his mind so saturated with images of life and nature.

Claude made about twenty-seven etchings. He was no great technician and some of his plates suffer from foul biting and poor printing. But the best of them are among the masterpieces of the art. Claude was the first great impressionist in etching. He knew how to suggest the play of light on objects, and shimmering quivering atmosphere. His plates are sometimes heroically composed like the *Sunrise*, the *Seaport with Tower*, the *Herd in a Storm*, or the *Rape of Europa* (illustration 203) or touched with soft arcadian charm like the *Bouvier*, the *Dance under the Trees*, the *Dance by the Waterside* (illustration 205). The etching of *The Brigands* strikes an unpleasantly realistic note unusual in his work, yet even this is infused with so soft and pastoral an atmosphere as to make it seem like an illustration of Daphnis and Chloe. Fortunately success came to him later in life (he never could have carved it out for himself) and he died in peace at the age of eighty-two—a simple, naive, unlettered man who dreamed a sweet and beautiful dream.

There was another foreign artist living in Rome whose works display creative power and imagination but whose life ended tragically at thirty-two after years in a debtor's prison—the German painter, Adam Elsheimer. Both Rubens and Rembrandt admired his work. His small paintings of religious and mythological subjects have a strange and moving quality, which has been successfully carried over into black and white by his friend, the amateur engraver, Count Goudt, who also seems to have suffered a mysterious and tragic fate. Goudt engraved seven plates, all after Elsheimer, among them the large *Tobit and the Angel* with its lovely sky, the *Aurora* with an equally lovely sky, the mysterious *Mocking of Ceres*, the *Flight into Egypt* copied by Seghers, and finally the *Philemon and Baucis* (illustration 198). This last engraving, so beautiful in composition and magical in its chiaroscuro, illustrates the legend of Philemon and Baucis as told in the eighth book of Ovid's *Metamorphoses*. It is one of the most beautiful stories of hospitality ever told. Jupiter and Mercury disguised as travelers wandered into a Phrygian village. Asking for hospitality they were turned away at every door until at last they came to the humble dwelling of Philemon and Baucis. Here they were received with genuine hospitality by the aged couple. They bustled about to minister to their comfort and set before the weary travelers what provisions they could muster from their slender store. During the repast the old folks were astonished to see that the wine, as fast as it was poured out, renewed itself in the pitcher. Struck with terror, they recognized their heavenly guests and implored forgiveness for their poor entertainment. And they replied, "We are gods; this inhospitable village shall pay the penalty of its impiety; you alone shall go unpunished." They destroyed the village and transformed the humble dwelling into a beautiful temple, and Jove in a benignant mood asked the mortals what boon they might wish of him. And, counseling with Baucis, Philemon replied, "Grant us to be priests and guardians of this your temple; and since here we have passed our lives in love and concord, we wish that one and the same hour may take us both from life, that I may not live to see her grave, nor be laid in my own by her." And their prayer was granted.

Another great personality in print history with an equally tragic maladjustment to his surroundings was the Dutchman, Hercules Seghers. He was born about 1590 and died about 1640 as the result, it is said, of an accident while trying to drown his sorrows in drink. "He approached his art," related his contemporary, van Hoogstraaten, "with incomparable zeal." The outstanding mark of his work is its emotional quality, its intensive identification with nature. Like a Chinese mystic he became one with rocks and brooks in forbidding Alpine valleys

84

(illustration 195), with moss-laden firs, with crumbling ruins, with sunny fertile plains, with tiny ships battling alone on a desperate sea. Nature became the *mise-en-scène* for the tortured drama of his soul. There was something in him that was akin to his countryman van Gogh, something of his passionate absorption, something of his rhythmic vibrant manner of drawing. He was no doubt a bit unbalanced: he felt too keenly, he went too deeply into things. The baffled public would have none of his work; they did not know what it was all about. At that moment they preferred realism to imagination, with the result that his life was one continuous struggle against poverty and despair. Today we look at the little that has been preserved of his work with more favorable eyes. Take for example that masterpiece, *The Three Books* (illustration 196), existing only in two impressions, both printed with brownish black ink on yellow colored linen with the background painted black; how simple it is, how beautiful in composition, with what emotional overtones of brooding and mystery. Seghers was a great experimenter; he apparently conceived many of his etchings in terms of color. He worked with various colored inks on various colored papers and even on linen, and often colored the prints still further by hand. He was one of the first of the Dutch artists to take up etching and especially to fall under the spell of wild mountain scenery. Some sixty etchings have come down to us, many of them existing only in one or two impressions. But we value him today not so much for his technical experiments as for his spirit, for the imagination and the emotional *timbre* with which his work is so richly endowed. And we couple his name—not in equality but in kinship—with that of Rembrandt, who admired his work and owned some of his pictures.

Rembrandt was the greatest etcher who ever lived. No one had a greater range and greater mastery within that range than he. Religious subjects, portraits, landscapes, nude studies, still life—in all of these he created masterpieces. In the field of genre alone he did not produce much, unless we consider his studies of beggars, the *Hog*, and his *Jews in the Synagogue*, as genre pictures. We learn little from him of the externals of life as lived in Amsterdam, but we learn much about humanity, the essentials of life which do not change from age to age. He

85

was the visionary, the man apart, who moved above or below contemporary life. To the Holland of the seventeenth century he was an enigma; it took the world several centuries to catch up with him. Rembrandt Harmenz van Ryn, the miller's son, was born in Leyden in 1606. His parents were ambitious that he become a scholar, and he entered the University of Leyden in 1620. But he had no call for letters and he left within a year to enter a painter's studio. After studying with three different masters, he set up for himself, and in 1628 he received his first pupil, Gerard Dou. In 1631 he moved to Amsterdam. Three years later he married Saskia van Ulenburch, a woman of some wealth and position. He was successful; he sold his pictures and obtained portrait commissions; his studio was crowded with pupils. He bought a house and filled it with treasures, jewels and rich robes for his Saskia, with sculpture and oriental carpets, Dutch and Italian paintings, engravings by Lucas van Leyden and others. This period of prosperity was checked by two events, the death of his wife and the debacle of the *Night Watch* in 1642. Thereupon his material affairs went into a decline which culminated in his bankruptcy in 1656. He always had been generous and impractical, he always had been a passionate and extravagant collector of art works. But this would not account for all the debts and money spent. It may easily be, as Carrington suggests, that after the death of Saskia, he got into the clutches of a female golddigger who worked him for all he was worth. This part of his life is exceedingly obscure. His last years were solaced by the affection and care of his serving maid, Hendrickje Stoffels (to the scandal of pious folk!). Forgotten or ignored by the burghers of Amsterdam, he was driven more and more to himself. Hendrickje died in 1664 and his son Titus in 1668. In 1669 Rembrandt himself died, possessing, as the formal inventory records: *"alleenlijck sijne cleederen van linnen en wollen en't schildergereetschap"*—only certain linen and woolen garments and his painting materials.

Rembrandt's first etchings are dated 1628. His early work, with a few notable exceptions, is not especially distinguished. He was learning his metier, his language. Rembrandt had great capacity for self-development; he could profit by his mistakes in art, however badly he

86

managed in practical life. The process went slowly, for he was building up an independent art form: he raised etching into a major art. It was he who gave to etching the significance and direction it was subsequently to take. The following are but a few of the artists (quoted by Lumsden) who show his influence: Bauer, Bone, Bracquemond, Cameron, Forain, Geddes, Goya, Haden, Jacque, John, Jongkind, Legros, McBey, Ostade, Potter, Tiepolo, and Whistler. He explored the medium and showed the way. He gave to etching the freedom and spontaneity and subtlety of drawing; and because his drawing was distinguished, dramatic, and noble he proved that an etching could be as lofty a work of art as a painting or statue. Most prints before Rembrandt had been translations as it were from another medium; he composed directly in the language of etching itself. In him we see the beginning of the modern attitude.

His early work consisted largely of studies of single figures: beggars (illustration 207), portraits of his father and mother (illustration 188), studies of "picturesque" types, expression studies, mostly of himself, in every attitude, grimace, and costume. Many of these were obviously experimental, for the sake of his own training or for teaching purposes. There were also some compositions that were fumbling and petty, without the grandeur of his later work. The *Self-Portrait Leaning on a Stone Sill* (illustration 187) perhaps inspired by Raphael's portrait of Castiglione, and made in the height of his prosperity in 1639, shows that he could beat van Dyck at his own game. But Rembrandt went on to make the supremely self-revealing *Self-Portrait Drawing at a Window* in 1648, which van Dyck never could have done. With the skill and freedom of expression acquired in these early experiments, fortified by the development of his inner nature, he went on to execute the great portraits where the inner character, the breathing essence of the sitter, is revealed in the outward form, the *Jan Sylvius* of 1646, the *Clement de Jonghe* of 1651, the *Older and the Younger Haaring* of 1655, the *Tholinx and Lutma* of 1656.

The illness and death of Saskia seemed to have driven him from the haunts of man into the arms of nature. He had already made a few landscapes, inspired possibly by the example of his friend Seghers: the

87

View of Amsterdam, the *Cottage with Hay Barn,* and the *Mill.* And in 1643 he etched the *Three Trees* (illustration 192). If, as Ivins penetratingly remarks, Bruegel is the Bach of landscape, then Rembrandt is its Beethoven. Rembrandt in these and his other etched landscapes, *Six's Bridge, Landscape with Square Tower, Goldweighers' Field,* and *Landscape with Sportsman,* displays the emotional power and the transmutation of natural forms into perfect artistic expression that is characteristic only of genius. How marvelously the freshness of the passing shower has been suggested in the *Three Trees;* how enchantingly the pattern of light and dark and rhythmic line is arranged in the *Landscape with Farm Buildings and Tower* (illustration 191). Most landscape prints before Rembrandt were composed or heroic landscapes; he took the intimate themes familiar to all and turned them into songs of lasting beauty.

Like most emotionally creative types, Rembrandt had a strong dramatic sense, and this was the quality that vitalized his mythological and religious pictures. Take the *Dr. Faustus,* for example (illustration 189), in his study gazing at the magic disk, the intensity and suspense, the way the painter emphasizes, dramatizes by means of line, by means of light. His approach to the religious picture is unique and personal; he serves no religious dogma. He retells the sacred story in human terms. He makes the characters live with incomparable art and dramatic effect: with tenderness in the *Rest on the Flight, lightly etched,* or in the *Holy Family with Cat* (note the reminiscence of Mantegna in the Virgin and Child); with humor in *Abraham Entertaining the Angels,* and *Christ among the Doctors;* with pathos in the *Blindness of Tobit,* the *Christ Carried to the Tomb,* the *Entombment in the Vaulted Chamber,* and the *Descent from the Cross by Torchlight;* with splendor in the *Presentation in the Temple;* with epic monumentality in the *Three Crosses, Christ Healing the Sick,* and *Abraham's Sacrifice.* One of the most satisfying and completely realized of his religious works is the *Christ Preaching* (illustration 194). The composition is exceptionally beautiful, and the range of characters delineated is almost as great as that of the *Hundred Guilder Print,* and expressed in more purely linear terms. The vista into the courtyard beyond, shows what Rembrandt could do

88

in rendering buildings. In all these representations there is no touch of the theater: all is pure drama, the perfect fusion of stirring theme and expressive form.

There has been much difference of opinion about Rembrandt's nudes. To many they are inexpressibly ugly and realistic. But in such early plates as the *Naked Woman on a Mound* (the Adam and Eve is, I am convinced, just a parody), Rembrandt was not interested in drawing a so-called pretty figure; he wanted to learn how to etch flesh, and he took what models he could find. It was not always easy to find handsome models, as Raphael records in 1515 in a letter to Baldessare Castiglione (who evidently had made some complimentary remarks about the model for the *Galatea*):

As far as the Galatea is concerned I would consider myself a great master if only half of the things you said about it were true. I recognize in your words the high regard you have for me. However I must tell you that whenever I have to paint a beautiful woman, it is necessary that I see a number of beauties (with the stipulation that you be present to choose the most beautiful!). Since, however, there is a dearth of such accomplished connoisseurs of women, as well as of beautiful women themselves, I depend upon a certain ideal and idea that I have in my mind. If this be an artistic advantage I know not, nevertheless I strive to attain it.

The question of the esthetic qualities of nudes, especially of the female sex, is a very complex one; when people say that a particular nude drawing is not artistic they often mean something else. It is questionable whether Rembrandt ever intended to emphasize the sexual attractiveness of a nude (as for example Zorn did) although the painting of *Danaë* in the Hermitage is quite as sensuous as Goya's *Maja*. In his later etchings of the nude, the *Woman beside the Stove*, the *Woman Bathing with a Hat beside Her*, the *Woman with the Arrow* (illustration 190), he aimed to present just Woman, the wholeness of a human being in an intimate pose. In these later etchings he came closer to that fusion of universal (Raphael's idea and ideal) and particular (convincing detail) which is the mark of great art.

Rembrandt's influence on succeeding generations has not been in

89

every respect beneficial. His early etchings of picturesque types were the starting point of a flood of mediocre and sentimental and patronizing exploitations of the theme. His many experimental sketches, probably made with no thought of wide publication, became the excuse for countless trivialities by subsequent artists. In his endeavor to make etching an important and independent mode of creative expression, he sometimes forced the medium far beyond the limits of appropriateness, as in the *Portrait of Jan Six*, the various night pieces and even the *Hundred Guilder Print*. It is to be regretted that he was not familiar with the technique of mezzotint and lithograph. Nevertheless he was one of the titans of art, a visionary who lived most truly in the world of his imagination. Fortune smiled on him for a while and then turned her back to him. It would have been better perhaps if she had not noticed him at all. He posed as a man of the world, yet he never was, and the world soon found him out. Like Claude he was no courtier; he consorted with humble folk and beggars and doctors and preachers. His influence on his immediate contemporaries was negligible. Amsterdam in the seventeenth century was a tough place to live for one not of this world. Like his friends, Roghman and Seghers, and like his contemporary, Spinoza, whom he never met, Rembrandt died neglected and in want.

Now that we have sketched some of the outstanding personalities of the seventeenth century we shall take up the broader aspects of its schools and tendencies. The most flourishing and homogeneous movement of the first half of the seventeenth century was the Dutch School. The Dutch had emerged victorious from their desperate struggle against the domination of Spain. Their independence had intensified their national consciousness. They were vigorous, industrious, and enterprising. They became a great trading nation and entered upon a period of unparalleled prosperity. They were practically supreme on the sea. They had vast colonial possessions; they carried the world's goods in their vessels. Their cities were the commodity markets of Europe; they were the first to institute the practice of auction sales. They took the lead in the development of the banking system which originated in the seventeenth century: through the extension of bills of exchange and the practice of leaving money and gold on deposit with the goldsmiths for safe keeping and carrying on commercial transactions by means of checks and credit, they became the bankers of the world. All of which is by way of saying that they became rich and prosperous. And so they bought art. John Evelyn relates in his diary for 1641:

We arrived late at Rotterdam, where was their annual mart or fair, so furnished with pictures (especially landscapes and drolleries, as they call those clownish representations), that I was amazed. Some of these I bought and sent to England. The reason of this store of pictures, and their cheapness, proceeds from their want of land to employ their stock, so that it is an ordinary thing to find a common farmer to lay out two or three thousand pounds in this commodity. Their houses are full of them, and they vend them at their fairs to very great gains.

There was monetary inflation and so they invested their money in art. It was a special kind of art. As they acquired and rejoiced in tangible possessions, so they demanded of art that it be a representation of tangible objects, familiar scenes in daily life or landscape. No doubt other factors beside the economic entered into this predilection. It was a secular and not a religious art, because the tradition of religious art had been broken, not only by iconoclasm and the destruction of Catholic art during the wars, but also by the Protestant-Puritan attitude toward religious art in general. The general tone was bourgeois and middle-class because there was no outstanding court to set the fashion. It was realistic, literal, and factual; it was technically accomplished, but not inspired by any tremendous depths of feeling. It is easy now to see why Seghers and Rembrandt did not fit into the scheme. Nevertheless within its limits it was an art of great distinction and charm, and the world is richer for the picture it gives of the Holland of the seventeenth century.

The work as a whole can be classified into several general groups. The first is the picture of daily life, the genre scene, which the Dutch may be said to have invented. One of the outstanding artists in this field was the painter and etcher, Adriaen van Ostade (1610–1685). He etched fifty plates, not all equal in merit, but at their best displaying fine draughtsmanship and compositional effect and considerable feeling. Two characteristic examples are reproduced, the *Family* of 1647 (illustration 199) and the *Fisherman* (illustration 228). His tradition was carried on in the work of his pupils, Bega and Dusart. Contrasting with Ostade's representations of peasants and artisans, is Willem Buttewych's etching of the patrician *Lovers* (illustration 200) executed in an elegant, stylized, almost caricatured manner. The next group are the landscape etchers, the van de Veldes, Roeland Roghman, Pieter Molyn, Jan van Goyen, Allardt van Everdingen, and others. Two examples may be taken as representative, the *Linden Tree by the Inn* (illustration 225) by Anthony Waterloo, typical of the average run of Dutch landscape and the *Cornfield* (illustration 226) by Jacob van Ruysdael chosen because of his importance in the landscape tradition. His studies of trees and other natural forms strike a quite modern note. There were some etchers who specialized in pictures of the sea, and of these Renier Nooms, called Zeeman (so much admired by Meryon), and Ludolph Backhuysen were outstanding. Zeeman knew how to portray moods of calm with great delicacy and atmosphere, and Backhuysen in his *Distant View of Amsterdam* (illustration 227) has admirably rendered a breezy day and a choppy sea. Then there were the etchers of animals and pastoral life, Claes Berchem, Karel du Jardin, and above all Paul Potter (illustration 206). Another and slightly overlapping group are the Italianizers like Breenbergh, Jan Both, and Swanevelt, who had been to Italy and sought to impose the arcadian tradition of Claude upon the realism of Holland.

The journeyings of these later Dutchmen bring us back to Italy again. Italian art of the settecento lacked the force of the preceding centuries. There is undoubted sweetness and charm in the etchings of Guido Reni and his pupil Cantarini (illustration 223) and Giovanni Barbieri, called Guercino (illustration 221). But they represent the gradual ebbing away of the religious tradition. Castiglione in his etchings was influenced by both van Dyck and Rembrandt. The Venetian, Carpioni, did a few charming plates. José Ribera, Lo Spagnoletto, Spanish born, but living in Naples, represented the naturalistic school of Caravaggio, in his few but very accomplished etchings (illustration 197). Salvator Rosa, also of Naples, had a wild and adventurous enough life. Poet, painter, musician, he took part in the insurrection of Masaniello

92

against the Spanish rule, and lived for a while with bandits. His etchings (illustration 224) have the mannerism and show of force of the Baroque style but in their delineation of wild and rugged scenery they anticipate to a certain extent a favorite theme of the Romantic School.

In France during the first half of the seventeenth century, the foundation was laid for the reign of Louis XIV, which for its patronage of arts and letters Voltaire called "the most enlightened age the world has ever seen." The build-up was favored by the policies of the Queen Mother Marie de' Medici, Cardinal Richelieu, founder of the French Academy, and Cardinal Mazarin, patron of art, music, and the theater. It was firmly established by Louis XIV and his minister Colbert upon his accession in 1661. Colbert believed "that it was by the standard of monuments that one measured kings." The Academy of Painters was founded; artists and craftsmen were encouraged with pensions and given lodging in the apartments of the Louvre and the Gobelins. The Gobelins, a state institution, was the center not only of the finest tapestry manufactured in Europe but also of the manufacture of furniture, metal work, and jewelry. It was also a training school for artists, and in this way a high standard of craftsmanship was maintained. An interesting glimpse of its activities is given in Le Clerc's engraving (illustration 234) where Colbert is seen inspecting some new tapestries. The seventeenth century witnessed a vast extension of luxury which found its reflection in ornament prints, models for jewelry (illustrations 229 and 230), lace, leather work, metal work (illustration 232), vases, furniture, and wall decoration (illustration 233). Formal gardens, with grottoes, etc. (illustrations 235 and 209) were laid out in greater and greater numbers. Ornament itself, in keeping with the Baroque style, tended to become exaggerated, grotesque, bursting with swelling bands and fantastic cartouches (illustration 231). All these exuberant elements were organized and somewhat restrained into a standardized and coherent system of great taste and decorative value by the artists and craftsmen under Louis XIV.

For a faithful picture of comfortable French life during the Regency and early part of the reign of Louis XIV, one must turn to the etchings of Abraham Bosse. He was typically the artist of the upper middle class, and he depicted their manners and customs with peculiar fidelity, so-

93

briety, and vividness (illustrations 215 and 216). The upper middle class are in general the backbone of the culture of a nation. It is they, through their opportunities for higher education, who supply the learned professions, law, medicine, and theology. They stand midway between the frivolousness of the court and the indigence of the proletariat. It is they who buy books and pictures, who patronize the theater, who cultivate music. A charming picture of a musical gathering is given in Bosse's engraving, *Hearing*, from the series of the *Five Senses*. In the sixteenth and seventeenth centuries music was still a language familiar to many cultivated amateurs. Many of the charming compositions of the contrapuntal schools, part songs, madrigals, motets and the like, were performed in company with accomplished musicianship. The century also witnessed the development of stringed instruments (Stradivarius, etcetera), and also a form of dramatic music which eventually became opera. Another picture of the time is given in the contrast between the two accouchement scenes portrayed by Bosse and by Callot in his *Gypsies*. Bosse made about 1400 engravings and is also famous for his text book on the art of etching and engraving. Bosse and Hollar have much in common.

The portrait of Molière in the role of Sganarelle in his own play *L'Ecole des Maris* (illustration 218) is a reminder of the great development of the drama in the seventeenth century, not only in France with Corneille, Racine, and Molière, but also in England with Shakespeare and the other Elizabethan dramatists, and in Spain with Calderon and Lope de Vega.

The portrait received great impetus in the seventeenth century, and in France there grew up a school of portrait engraving that has never been surpassed. The earliest practitioner was Claude Mellan who developed Goltzius' linear system into an instrument of great power, as may be seen in the portrait of Fabri de Peiresc (illustration 202), Rubens' great friend and correspondent. Jean Morin engraved some colorful portraits. But Robert Nanteuil was the chief glory of the school. He was quartered in the Gobelins, and Louis XIV also granted in his favor the famous Edict of St. Jean-de-Luz which declared that engraving henceforth was to rank as a liberal and not as a mechanical art. He

94

engraved over two hundred portraits, including eleven of *"le Grand Monarque"* (illustration 238), and a host of great men of the time, Richelieu, Mazarin, Cardinal de Retz, Jacques Amelot, Colbert, Fouquet, Loret, C. M. le Tellier, Gassendi, John Evelyn, etcetera. He usually received about 2000 livres per plate (about $400). He set the style of portraiture which was followed by his pupils and associates, Masson, Edelinck, Poilly, Pitau, van Schuppen, and others. He perfected the frame which gave the portrait its formal decorative quality. A consummate draughtsman, he concentrated, as Thomas points out, on the expression of character by the head. There is nothing spontaneous about these portrait engravings: every detail is studied and calculated. It is the opposite extreme of the candid camera shot: it is the "set portrait," where the sitter looks and appears as he would like to be, noble, dignified, in the grand manner. Mlle. de Scudéry wrote a quatrain which sums it up:

> "Nanteuil en faisant son image
> A de son art divin signalé le pouvoir.
> Je hais mes traits dans mon miroir,
> Je les aime dans son ouvrage."

(Nanteuil in his pictures has shown the power of his divine art. I hate my features in the mirror, I love them in his work.) Pepys in his *Diary* for January 1668-69 records: "My wife showed me many excellent prints of Nantueill's and others, which W. Batelier hath, at my desire, brought me out of France, to my great content." As the prevailing taste changed, from the sober delineation of character to a greater ostentation and display, so the portrait changed from the head to the full-length figure in gorgeous array of silks and satins. Drevet's *Bossuet* or Bervic's *Louis XVI* are characteristic of this tendency. However, Drevet's portrait of Robert de Cotte was chosen for reproduction (239) because of its subject interest. The architect De Cotte, together with Oppenordt, may be said to have originated the Rococo style, which was to be dominant in France and Germany in the eighteenth century. De Cotte, pupil of Mansart, the architect of Versailles, finished the Grand Trianon at Versailles and built the Hôtel de Vrillière in Paris. The French school of portrait engraving was the most distinguished in Europe; it drew many foreign artists, notably the Fleming Edelinck, to Paris. Comparatively little portraiture of merit was made during the century outside of the engraved portraits of Paris or the etched portraits of Rembrandt and van Dyck. An exception must be recorded, however, in the charming portrait engravings of Ottavio Leoni of Rome. The portrait of the astronomer Galileo, who got in trouble with the Inquisition, is reproduced in illustration 237. The portrait of the Duke of Olivares, often ascribed to Velasquez, is probably by Leoni.

The seventeenth century witnessed a further widening of the breach between rich and poor. The extensive wars of this and the preceding centuries contributed greatly to the spread of capitalism by nourishing that one great form of luxury, the army. Not only was a military career a direct avenue to riches through the opportunities for plunder and exaction of indemnities (Wallenstein when he was assassinated was worth nine million gulden) but the army encouraged lucrative capitalist enterprises through the contract system and large-scale production of food, clothing, guns, and ammunition. Wealth was becoming more and more concentrated in the hands of a few, while the great mass of the people were being ground down in abject poverty. Holland was the exception to this rule, but there it was the middle class which was acquiring wealth. Elsewhere the Court, the Church and the rich were the chief supporters of art. Rubens' chief patrons were the Church, the extravagant Charles I and his favorites, and Philip of Spain whose income came from the gold of America. The seventeenth century saw the emergence of the collector of prints on a vast scale. To be sure there had been collectors in previous centuries, the Fuggers, Imhoffs, Welser (Dürer and van Leyden complete), Paul Praum, 1548-1616 (Dürer and Italian masters); and prints were included among the contents of the countless *Wunderkammern*, or Chambers of Curios, along with shells, insects, minerals, stuffed animals, cameos, etcetera. (Evelyn as late as 1651 notes: "I went to see the collection of one Monsieur Poignant which for variety of agates, crystals, onyxes, porcelain, medals, statues, relievos, paintings, taille-douces [prints], and antiquities, might compare with the Italian virtuosos.") And artists such as Dürer and Rubens, as

96

we have seen, and Rembrandt who at one time owned over one hundred paintings and a huge collection of prints by Mantegna and many other artists, were passionate collectors. But the first real print collector was Claude Maugis, Abbé de St. Ambroise, 1600–1658, who spent forty years amassing a collection which eventually passed into the hands of Michel Marolles. Michel Marolles, Abbé de Villeloin, who had been given a fat living by Mazarin, was one of the world's great print collectors. No sooner had he disposed of his first huge collection, than he started all over again. As he wrote:

God has given me grace to devote myself to pictures without superstition, and I have been able to acquire a collection numbering more than 70,000 engravings of all subjects. I began it in 1644, and have continued it with so much zeal, and with such an expense for one not wealthy, that I can claim to possess some of the work of all the known masters. . . . I have found that collecting such things was more suited to my purse than collecting paintings, and more serviceable to the building up of a library. Had we in France a dozen such collectors among the nobility, there would not be enough prints to satisfy them all, and the works of Dürer, Lucas, and Marcantonio for which we now pay four and five hundred *écus* when in perfect condition would be worth three times that amount.

In 1666 his collection had grown to 123,400 prints and drawings by over 6000 artists. The entire collection was bought by Colbert for the King and became the foundation of that huge public collection numbering over 4,000,000 prints now housed in the Bibliothèque Nationale. In England there were collectors like Lord Pembroke and the Earl of Arundel (Hollar's patron), but it was in Paris that Marolles' suggestion was really followed. In 1673 there were eighty-five large collections of prints, often in connection with libraries; towards the end of the century there were one hundred and thirty. It became so much the fashion that La Bruyère took note of it in his "Characters":

You wish to see my prints, says Democenes, and he forthwith brings them out and sets them before you. You see one that is neither dark nor clear nor completely drawn, and better fit to decorate on a holiday the walls of the Petit Pont or the Rue Neuve than be treasured in a famous collection. He admits that it is engraved badly and drawn worse, but hastens to inform you that it is the work of an Italian artist who produced very little, and that the plate had hardly any printing; that, moreover, it is the only one of its kind in France; that he paid much for it, and would not exchange it for something far better. I am, he adds, in such serious trouble that it will prevent any further collecting. I have all of Callot but one print, which is not only not one of his best plates, but actually one of his worst; nevertheless it would complete my Callot. I have been looking for it for twenty years, and, despairing of success, I find life very hard indeed.

5. Eighteenth Century

THE history of eighteenth century prints may be summed up as a year in Paris, a month in London, and a week-end in Italy. France was the artistic center of Europe, and France meant Paris. No city was ever so documented by its artists as Paris. It was, however, essentially an urban culture, highly civilized and highly artificial. Paris was the apex of the pyramid which rested on the broad base of the peasants of France. The flowers that grew in the hothouse at the apex had no strong roots in the free soil of the country. Nevertheless they were in many respects beautiful flowers, among the most extraordinary the world has ever seen. The documentation of Paris may be said to have proceeded on four separate levels. At the top, the most artificial and the most completely documented, was the life of the court. Below was the life of the middle class, sober, industrious, and urbane, untainted by the excesses of the court. The third was the life of the artists themselves, another aspect of the middle class. Below all these, the most meager in detail, yet represented in the *Cries of Paris*, the representations of the lower artisan class and the *imagerie populaire*, was the level of the workers.

At the beginning of the century there lived and dreamed and painted a rare artist, Antoine Watteau. His work may be said to symbolize, in its most ideal and beautiful aspects, the spirit of Louis XV. He was born in Valenciennes of Flemish ancestry in 1684. He died of consumption at the early age of twenty-seven. He was supported by wealthy patrons like M. de Julienne; he had access, through his friend the great collector Crozat, to drawings and paintings by Rubens, Titian, Giorgione, and Campagnola. Out of the leisure which good fortune brought him and out of the contacts with the great art of the world, and impelled by the heart-breaking nostalgia of the consumptive, he proceeded to make con-

99

crete one more dream of an ideal world. It was the world of the *fête galante*, the *Embarkation for the Isle of Cythère* (Love), exquisite glimpses of picnics in beautiful gardens, of couples in amorous conversation, of music and dancing and the theater in the open. He made a few unimportant etchings: he poured himself out in his drawings and paintings. It was his lifelong friend, M. de Julienne, who undertook at his expense to have his work engraved by the best engravers of the time and published in four huge volumes in 1734 at a price of five hundred livres. It is from this magnificent *Recueil* that our three reproductions are drawn (illustrations 243 and 244 and 271). Never has the spirit of play, of cultivated pastime, the *otium cum dignitate* of the ancients, been clothed in more enchanting dress. This escape from reality, this flight to a carefree island of love and beauty, strikes a responsive chord in every one of us at some time in our lives. It is Watteau's great achievement that he made the dream so tangible and so beautiful. All his contemporaries, Gersaint, De Caylus, testify to the unhappiness of his personal life. He was melancholy, irritable, and diffident. It was only when he was actually painting or drawing, said De Caylus, that he was the Watteau of his own pictures. It may be, as Wilenski suggests, that this unhappiness was due not only to the inroads of his malady, but also to his dilemma as a creative artist. He had every reason to be grateful to his rich patrons who had rescued him from a life of hack work (he had started as a painter outside the pale of the all-powerful Academy) and to his dealers Sirois and Gersaint (illustration 271) for their affectionate and continued assistance, but they were all men of the world and did not look at a picture in the way he looked at it, nor see what he saw in it. He lived in the apartments which Crozat provided for him in his palace, but after a year he ran away. The world was not fashioned according to his heart's desire, and he was driven to his dreams. Yet, curiously enough, in this instance, the world, that is to say the court of Louis XV, tried to imitate his dream. Such a utopia as Watteau's Isle of Cythère can exist only in the world of art or imagination. When its happy irresponsible existence was translated into reality, it predicated the support of countless servants or slaves. Its grace and sensibility, its tender note of ideal love became tainted with wanton extravagance and display, sordid intrigue and unbridled licentiousness. And so it was, as history tells us, at the court of Louis XV. Yet comparatively little of the sordid side is carried over into the pictorial record by the artists of the time. The obverse of the shield we discover from other sources and from the fact that suddenly the whole system collapsed. The artists set out to glorify the reign of Louis XV as they had that of the Grand Monarch, and they did a magnificent job. They did it in two ways: **by** embellishing the setting and by recording it.

First of all there were the decorators, Boucher for example. François Boucher (1703–1770) was one of the most accomplished artists in France, director of the schools of the Academy and of the tapestry manufactory of Beauvais and the Gobelins, painter of murals for the king and for Mme de Pompadour. We know his features from the striking portrait by Roslin, an unassuming, somewhat cynical man of the world with able hands and piercing eyes. He is represented by the decorative composition engraved by Demarteau, *Venus Desarmée par les Amours* (illustration 241), and the color print, *Femme à la Rose*, engraved by Bonnet (illustration 265). We all remember Renoir's estimate of Boucher as recorded by Vollard:

As if being a decorator made any difference! Why Boucher is one of the painters who best understood the female body. What fresh youthful buttocks he painted, with the most enchanting dimples. It's odd that people are never willing to give a man credit for what he can do. They say they like Titian better. Good Lord so do I! But that has nothing to do with the fact that Boucher painted lovely women superbly. A painter who has the feel for breasts and buttocks is saved!

The second decorator, Jean Honoré Fragonard (1732-1806), was typical of the more frivolous spirit toward the end of the century. Pupil of Chardin, protégé of Boucher, influenced by Rembrandt and Tiepolo, he painted decorations for Du Barry and other fashionable women, and made countless drawings and paintings. He made among others a series of four etchings of *Bacchanals* (illustration 240) of great spirit and charm in a form probably suggested by the *Caprices* of Tiepolo. Some delightful engravings were made from his paintings, including the *Chiffre d'Amour, La Bonne Mère,* and *The Happy Accidents of the Swing* (illustration 246), frivolous yet charming, and filled with a certain gallant suggestiveness.

The setting was embellished in many ways. The enormous impetus given to architecture and the applied arts had its repercussion in ornament prints. The earlier academic tradition is represented in the *Rape of Europa* after Le Moyne (illustration 245). The gestures have become very elegant and rococo; it is interesting to contrast this with Claude's treatment of the same subject. There were two trends of ornament in the eighteenth century: one, the Rococo, was a development of the Baroque, carrying its mannerism and eccentricity to even greater limits, and the other a reaction against it in favor of the antique (stimulated perhaps by the excavations at Herculaneum and also by the work of Piranesi) which culminated in the severely classic style of the Directoire and Empire. In flower arrangement and design there was a range from the seventeenth century Monnoyer (illustration 287) through the early eighteenth century van Huysum (illustration 298) to the late eighteenth century Ranson. Characteristic Rococo ornament was supplied by Meissonier, Oppenordt, Gillot, Watteau, Oudry, Huet, Huquier, Nilsen, Habermann, and notably in the delightful inventions of Pillemont (illustration 66). Chinoiserie and other exotic notes were fashionable. Among the notable furniture designers in France were Oppenordt, Toro, Pineau, and Cornille; in England Heppelwhite, Sheraton, Chippendale (illustration 284), Ince and Mayhew, and Robert Adam. The classic style in France was developed by Neufforge, Delafosse, Forty, Babel, and Lalonde (illustration 67). One field was specially cultivated, under the patronage of the Regent Philippe d'Orleans and of Madame de Pompadour both of whom dabbled in design, by the luxury-loving age—the illustrated book. Sumptuous and expensive editions were published, illustrated with engravings and vignettes by the best artists of the time: Molière's *Works* illustrated by Boucher, 1734 (illustration 263), the *Fermiers Généraux* edition of La Fontaine (an allusion to the source of its financing) illustrated by Eisen and others, 1762, Corneille's *Works* illustrated by Gravelot, 1764, Marmontel's *Contes Moraux* illustrated by Gravelot, 1765, the *Metamorphoses* of Ovid illustrated by Boucher,

102

Eisen, Gravelot, Moreau, and Choffard, 1767–1771, *Les Baisers* illustrated by Eisen, 1770, the *Choix de Chansons* de M. de la Borde illustrated by Moreau-le-Jeune, 1773 (illustration 288), one of the most beautiful books ever made, and finally Rousseau's *Works*, 1774–1783, also illustrated by Moreau-le-Jeune. And so "Monsieur" and "Madame" were provided with books to look at (though perhaps not to read), furniture, wall decorations, jewelry, costumes, china, gardens, coaches, and rooms to live in, designed and executed by the greatest talent in France.

How they looked and acted amid these luxurious surroundings we discover from *Les Estampes Galantes, Estampes de la Mode,* and *Gravures des Mœurs.* There is a close resemblance between these engravings and Dutch seventeenth century prints. There is the same factual literal representation of a contemporary scene. There is to be sure a greater perfection of execution, a more magnificent sense of style, a more effective feeling for the dramatic aspect, in the French engravings, but the ultimate aim is the same—it is "giving the customers what they want." In spite of certain notable exceptions there is a spiritual poverty about both, a lack of creative conviction or passion on the part of the artists that prevents the work from being classed with the world's greatest art. It was a faithful, impersonal, and business-like reflection of the age, and since the milieu was hardly a spiritual one, the art never rose above it, as the works of the greatest artists and thinkers always do. Incidentally Dutch genre pictures of the seventeenth century were assiduously collected by French amateurs of the eighteenth century. Both groups catered definitely to a certain class, the Dutch seventeenth century prints to a rising middle class; the French *éstampes galantes* to the nobility and the underlying strata which imitated them. Who was it that bought these French prints? Certainly not the impoverished peasants and workers, for they had no money, nor even the lower middle class. Nor was it in general the principal personages of the court; there was no reason why they should buy pictures of the scenes they saw every day. It was rather that class which had a slight or indirect contact with the court and had grown rich through it, that sought these prints in order perhaps that their wives and daughters might see the latest fashions. Or it was

103

the roué who bought the *sujets grivois*, the suggestive subjects, to add piquancy to his relations with his mistress in the sumptuous apartment where he maintained her. Or it was the rich amateur with a taste for art and nothing to do who succumbed to the collecting mania.

French eighteenth century prints have been the subject of much argument pro and con. Even in their day, they and the paintings from which they were often derived, were savagely attacked by Diderot as a symbol of a society of which he disapproved. Diderot incidentally was one of the first of the professional art critics. It was in the eighteenth century (1699 to be exact) that official exhibitions of paintings and drawings by many artists were inaugurated by the Academy (Gabriel de St. Aubin made a delightful etching of the "Salon" of the Academy held at the Louvre in the year 1753). Of course pictures had been exhibited, as we have seen, at the fairs and markets in Germany, Italy, and Holland, and also at the Foire de St. Germain in Paris, but these had no official recognition. Therefore when society was confronted with several hundred pictures at a Salon which it was *de rigeur* to attend, the writers stepped in, as has been said, to tell it what to talk about, and thus art criticism or rather art journalism began. Unquestionably, the tone of society, pampered and protected as it was from reality, was highly artificial and frivolous. In Chamfort's words: " 'A genuine sentiment is so rare,' said M. de V——, 'that when I leave Versailles I sometimes stand still to see a dog gnaw a bone.' " French eighteenth century prints, on the other hand, have had apologists who maintain that their licentious and irresponsible tone has been exaggerated, and point to the number of prints which extol the virtues of happy family life (illustration 252). Even those subjects which are rather free are never gross: they tell their story as a *double entendre*, with subtlety and a proper regard for the conventions. It is quite likely that the moral degradation of the age has been exaggerated, that it was confined to a few sensational and destructive examples at the court, and that the main body of the people went on in their accustomed ways. After all, even in our day financiers have kept mistresses and squandered fortunes without having overthrown the structure of society. A case can be made out on both sides. In either case the prints themselves build up a complete picture

104

of a mode of life that is elegant, refined, and luxurious. It is only when we go beyond the picture to examine its implications that we are compelled to exercise moral judgment. Incidentally it is interesting to discover that nearly all the engravers welcomed the Revolution and some took an active part in it.

After this rather philosophic preamble let us visit Paris and with the artist to give us entrée, let us visit the court and participate in its functions. First, having been introduced to Augustin de St. Aubin and his charming wife paying each other compliments in *Au Moins Soyez Discrets* and *Comptez sur mes Serments* we accompany him to the *Concert* or to the court ball, *Le Bal Paré*, following an invitation engraved by Choffard. With the Swede Lavreince we might visit two other functions *chez* le Duc de Luynes, the *Assemblée au Salon* and *Assemblée au Concert*, or listen to Beaumarchais reading extracts from his *Figaro* in *Le Mercure de France*, or explore with him such crises of sentiment as *Consolation de l'Absence*, *L'Heureux Moment*, *L'Indiscretion*, or *L'Aveu Difficile*, or, entering the more formal salon, hear *Qu'en dit l'Abbé* or see the furtive passing of the *Billet Doux* (illustration 249). Walking through the park with Baudouin, we might glimpse a charming tête-à-tête in *La Soirée des Tuileries* (illustration 247) and witness in the boudoir an intimacy close to the border line in *Le Danger du Tête-à-tête* and especially in *Le Carquois Épuisé* (*The Empty Quiver*) with its double meaning (illustration 248) or participate in the dramatic scenes, *Le Couché de la Mariée* or *L'Enlevement Nocturne*. We might see and purchase the latest portraits of the king and queen, or Pompadour (illustration 264) or Du Barry, or as a novelty that of Mr. Franklin, the new Philosopher from America who made such a hit at court and among the savants (illustration 267). We might with Carmontelle patronize the concert of a new infant prodigy of music, the seven-year-old Mozart (illustration 260). With the Swiss artist Freudeberg we might trace the round of daily life in luxury: *Le Lever*, *Le Bain*, the charmingly domestic *Le Petit Jour*, and *Le Coucher*. For a taste of gallantry there are Baudouin's *Marchez Tout Doux*, and *L'Épouse Indiscrète*, Fragonard's *Le Verrou*, Boilly's *L'Amant Favorisé*, Boucher's *La Cour-*

tisane Amoureuse, Debucourt's *L'Escalade*, or Lavreince's *La Comparaison*.

Jean Michel Moreau-le-Jeune was perhaps, all things considered, the finest and most accomplished designer and engraver of French manners. He was born in 1741 and studied engraving with jolly old Le Bas. In 1760 he married the daughter of Pineau the furniture designer. In 1770 he was appointed *Dessinateur des Menus-Plaisirs du Roi* and in 1781 he was made an associate of the Academy. His engravings, the *Coronation of Louis XVI* in 1776, the *Festin Royal*, the *Bal Masqué*, the *Feu d'Artifice* (the last three are in the Chalcographie du Louvre), and his engravings of *Le Couché de la Mariée* and *Le Modèle Honnête* after Baudouin are well known, but his chief title to fame rests on his book illustrations and the great *Monument du Costume* of 1776 and 1783. Confronted with the problem of designing a series of costume plates, he composed them as scenes from daily life with such perfection of draughtsmanship and incomparable dramatic power that the twenty-four plates may almost be said to sum up a complete age and mode of society. Certainly the society of Louis XVI has never been displayed in a better light. The young king and queen were weak and mildly benevolent characters; they believed in a happy family life and asked nothing better than to play at being shepherds and shepherdesses in an irresponsible pastoral life. They merely reaped the whirlwind that was sown by the grandfather. Thus, true happiness, *Le Vrai Bonheur*, is visualized in the *Monument* as a happy farmer surrounded by his family and his pet animals. No more charming picture of domestic felicity has been made than the *Délices de la Maternité* (illustration 252). Has there ever been a more charming dinner party than *Le Souper Fin* (illustration 254)? The grace and glamor, the polished and distinguished manners of an aristocratic court will live forever in such plates as *Les Adieux*, or *La Sortie de l'Opera* (illustrations 255 and 253). They seem like concrete embodiments of the maxims of one who was perhaps the most eloquent apologist of the courtly manner, Lord Chesterfield:

Courts are the best keys to character; there every passion is busy, every art exerted, every character analyzed; jealousy, ever watchful, not only discovers, but exposes, the mysteries of the trade, so that even bystanders, *y apprennent à déviner*. There, too, the great art of pleasing is practiced, taught, and learned, with all its graces and delicacies. It is the first thing needful there; it is the absolutely necessary harbinger of merit and talents, let them be ever so great. There is no advancing a step without it. Let misanthropes and would-be philosophers declaim as much as they please against the vices, the simulation, and dissimulation of Courts; those invectives are always the result of ignorance, ill-humor, or envy. Let them show me a cottage, where there are not the same vices of which they accuse the Courts; with this difference only, that in a cottage they appear in their native deformity, and that in Courts, manners and good breeding make them less shocking, and blunt their edge. No, be convinced that good breeding, the *tournure, la douceur dans les manières*, which alone are to be acquired at Courts, are not the showish trifles only, which some people call or think them; they are a solid good; they prevent a good deal of mischief; they create, adorn, and strengthen friendships; they keep hatred within bounds; they promote good-humor and good-will in families, where the want of good breeding and gentleness of manners is commonly the original cause of discord.

From the court to the middle class—from Moreau to Chardin. Jean Baptiste Siméon Chardin was born in Paris in 1699 and died there in 1779. He was a simple kindly man who loved the city and its ways—especially the middle-class life that he lived and knew. He poured into his simple genre pieces and still lifes such a wealth of feeling, such love and tenderness, such consummate craftsmanship and perfection of design and placement that they seem to come to life before our eyes. He had much in common with Vermeer of Delft. About fifty engravings were made after his paintings, which had considerable vogue in his day. Among the best known are *Le Bénédicité, Le Dessinateur, L'Écureuse, L'Étude de Dessin, La Mère Laborieuse, La Pourvoieuse, La Bonne Éducation*, and *L'Instant de la Meditation*. All of them have an intangible quality, a certain inwardness that haunts the imagination. We identify ourselves with the characters, and experience in a magic moment the simplicity and charm they so beautifully express. Two of the most charming are reproduced here, *La Gouvernante* and *Le Négligé* (illustrations 251 and 250). When the painting of *Le Négligé* was exhibited in the Salon of 1741, Chamarande reviewed it as follows: "No woman of the third estate of the Realm stands before one of Chardin's canvases without discerning a reflection of her own morals, manners, and daily avocations, of the ways of her children, of her household gods and wardrobe." Furthermore there is a story that "when Le Bas [the engraver of this picture] was asked what instructions the painter had given him for the interpretation of his colors, he, knowing very well that for the complete harmony of a picture there can be no fixed rule, replied: to use sentiment."

Chardin, sure of himself, pursued his own quiet way, and, though an academician through the influence of Largillière, seldom exhibited with them and had little sympathy with their historical grand manner. There was one other, a profoundly original artist and a rare personality, who did not fit into the academic mold—Gabriel de St. Aubin (1724–1780). He had a brother, Augustin de St. Aubin, who was a man of the world and became *Graveur du Roi* and an artist of influence (illustration 267). But Gabriel, after competing unsuccessfully for the Prix de Rome, renounced academic ambitions and was content to remain an obscure professor of drawing at Blondel's School of Architecture.

He drew [recounts his brother] at all times and in all places. If he was taking a walk his crayon would be taking note of the passers-by. The lectures of the Academy were for him but a moving tableau for his sketches. One holiday, having placed himself in the nave of Notre Dame to hear a celebrated preacher, he drew out his sketchbook from habit and started to draw the orator. People nearby watched him as he worked; those in front of him turned around, those behind raised themselves in their chairs. Finally the attention of the listeners was so completely distracted that the preacher, interrupting his discourse, said, "When the eyes have been satisfied, I hope you will lend me your ears." This passion, joined to the desire to see everything and know everything, made him extremely negligent of his person and his health. He died completely worn out at the age of fifty-five. He was singular, bizarre: often before going out, he would rub white chalk from his crayons either on his hair to powder it or on his stockings to whiten them. He left a great number of curious drawings. We have several prints engraved after his designs and some etchings which display his genius.

108

He was in truth a singular and profoundly original artist. In an age and country where line engraving was supreme he gave his preference to etching and made some fifty plates, probably largely for his own pleasure and amusement. At a time when all expression was keyed up to the grand manner he came out with modest little etchings singularly free from pretense, each one a masterpiece of mood and atmosphere. His work strikes a very modern note: he is concerned only with entering into the spirit of a scene and reflecting with rare art his personal impression of it. Since he was an artist of great feeling and sensibility, his "impressions" have great charm for us. Take for example the *Spectacle de Tuileries* (illustration 256); with what subtlety and penetration he has invoked the spirit of the scene, the summer night under the swaying trees, the cool fragrance, the buzz of the conversation, the play of shadows and half-lights. On one proof of this etching St. Aubin wrote the following quatrain:

"Le faste se repose en ces jardins charmants;
Les cercles sont formés autour de chaque belle.
Nonchalamment assis, mille couple d'amants
S'y jurent à leur age un flame éternelle."

How simply and effectively he has re-created an eighteenth-century Coffeehouse in *Les Nouvellistes* (illustration 257). "There are," wrote the traveler Nemeitz in 1727, "an infinite number of coffeehouses in Paris, often ten or twelve on the same street. . . . There are still others where one finds *Les Nouvellistes* (news mongers) who discuss the news and the latest affairs of the state. Since there are a number of idlers in Paris, some of them do nothing else all day but frequent the cafés to hear the latest bit of news or gossip." Daumier later took up the same theme in his *Coffeehouse Politicians*. Two contemporary theatrical representations form an instructive contrast: Moreau-le-Jeune's *The Crowning of the Bust of Voltaire* (illustration 272) and St. Aubin's *Théâtre Italien* (illustration 261). The first is brilliant and polished, a showy panorama of stage and audience with Voltaire in a box bowing to the applause; the other is simple and unpretentious and enters into the very spirit of Harlequin and Columbine. St. Aubin's picture reminds one of Degas' studies of the essential gesture, the "magic moment" in his pictures of ballet dancers. In fact in many of St. Aubin's works we find anticipations of the modern point of view.

Another charming little etching is the *Académie Particulier* (illustration 268) a glimpse of the artist drawing from a model. There were many delightful pictures made of artists' life in the eighteenth century, such as for example, the *Cabinet d'un Peintre* (illustration 269) by the Polish engraver Chodowiecki living in Berlin. The engravers generally lived uneventful lives concerned with apprenticeship, technique, commissions, etcetera, and were more or less conscious of their middle-class station. The younger Cochin in his memoirs, when recounting a dispute with Comte de Caylus, said, "I was met by that contempt which, I know only too well, is felt by men of birth, in spite of their fine seeming politeness, for all who are, like artists, but of the bourgeoisie." The diary of J. G. Wille abounds in illuminating passages relating to contemporary life. He was an uninspired, rather mannered, but highly successful reproductive engraver (illustration 289) but he was a delightful social historian. He tells of his contacts with patrons and dealers, of the immense speculation in art at the time, how long it took to engrave a plate (two years and four months on the *Family Concert*) and the prices he received for his work (six livres or about $1.20 for the same print). Like many of the engravers, such as Cochin, Tardieu, Poilly, Chereau, and others, he was his own dealer, that is to say he also sold prints from his engraving studio. Pierre François Basan, a glimpse of whose shop is given in Choffard's engraving (illustration 270), was more a dealer than engraver. He was the first to establish the practice of printing a large number of "proofs before letters" to supply the vast demand on the part of amateurs for such "rarities." He acquired a number of the coppers by Rembrandt and other Dutch etchers which he published in collected form. He organized and managed auction sales, printing for them illustrated auction catalogues in the modern manner, of such important collections as those of Bouchardon, van Loo, Marigny, and Wille. But the most important sale of all under Basan's management was that of the tremendous private collection of Pierre Jean Mariette in 1775 and 1776. The three generations of the Mariette family, the grandfather Pierre, the father Jean, and Pierre Jean, were among the greatest print-dealers the world has ever known. They had had dealings with Marolles, Charles I, Crozat, and many others, especially the genial Prince Eugene of Savoy whose own enormous collection of prints was eventually housed in the Imperial Library at Vienna under the curatorship of Adam von Bartsch and formed the basis of Bartsch's monumental catalogue of prints still in use today. Another important engraver, publisher, and dealer was Gabriel Huquier, whose shop was the center for the ornament prints of France. Still another dealer, C. F. Joullain, in his *Reflexions sur la Peinture et la Gravure accompagnées d'une courte dissertation sur la commerce de la curiosité et les ventes en général*, offers further sidelights on the traffic in prints, the psychology of collecting, the excitements of auction, and a complete description of how unscrupulous dealers formed a ring to control prices at an auction. In the eighteenth century picture-selling had become the business that it is today.

In the eighteenth century several discoveries in printmaking technique were made which resulted in a widening of the range of its expression. Chief of these was the invention of aquatint by Jean Baptiste Le Prince about 1768 (illustration 242). This process allowed for a wider use of tonal effects in intaglio printing and also made possible one form of printing in colors which was developed and perfected by Janinet, Debucourt, Descourtis, Alix, Jazet, and Sergent-Marceau. The most original of these perhaps was P. L. Debucourt (1755–1842) who engraved much after his own designs. He seems to have had no strong political convictions since he issued plates that found favor with the *Ancien Régime*, the Revolution, Napoleon, and the Restoration. Perhaps he had a contempt for the whole human race, and political convictions did not matter, since much of his work has a strong satiric tendency. He spent his last years raising rabbits, pigeons, and chickens which he allowed to run wild and never would kill. Among his most famous plates are *Les Deux Baisers*, *Le Menuet de la Mariée* and *La Noce au Château*, *La Matinée du Jour de l'An*, and *La Promenade de la Galerie du Palais Royal*. But his greatest print undoubtedly is the *Promenade Publique* of 1792 (illustration 291), a vivid panorama of society in the picturesque and stirring days of the National Convention.

III

It is probable that Debucourt received the impulse to make his picture from Rowlandson's equally famous color print, *Vauxhall* (illustration 290). Still another technique developed in the eighteenth century was the stipple and crayon process. The crayon manner was developed by François and Demarteau (illustration 241) to reproduce the effect of crayon drawings, and by Marin and Bonnet (illustration 265) to reproduce the quality of a pastel drawing. The most famous practitioner of the stipple technique was Francesco Bartolozzi (illustration 299) an Italian who settled in London in 1764. Indeed stipple engraving was popular chiefly in England where it was used to reproduce the sweet and sentimental works of Cipriani, Cosway, Angelica Kauffmann, and others.

Still another technical discovery was the invention of the Physiono-trace about 1768 by the court musician Gilles Louis Chrétien. The machine is really an adaptation of the pantograph idea to the making of outline silhouettes of the head. By this means the foundation of a good workman-like likeness can be made in a sitting of less than five minutes. This tiny drawing could then be worked up on a copper plate with roulette work and etching into a complete portrait from which any number of prints could be taken. The speed of its production and its consequent cheapness ensured to the process an immediate success, especially with the rising middle class. Hitherto portraiture had been necessarily confined to distinguished people or to those few who could afford to commission an artist for a regular portrait. With the new process people of moderate means could afford to have portraits made of themselves (illustration 285). In addition to Chrétien there were other practitioners of the art, Quenedey and the émigré Favret de St. Memin, who came to America and made about eight hundred portraits (illustration 286). St. Memin charged thirty-three dollars for the original drawing, the copper plate, and twelve impressions.

Meanwhile, side by side with all these activities of the *haute monde*, flowed the daily life of the people. Some reflection of this—patronizing to be sure—was given in several series of *Cries of Paris* or pictures of various crafts and professions by Boucher and Bouchardon, and in such genre pictures as *La Place des Halles* and *La Place Maubert* by Jeaurat.

These were prints of the people but not for them. Such prints as they had were the rude woodcuts from chapbooks, in direct tradition from the fifteenth century through generations of obscure craftsmen, such as the *Robinson Crusoe* (illustration 68) or in religious pictures like the *Notre Dame de Bonne Deliverance* of which 500,000 proofs had been printed by 1766. Or they were the peep-show prints exhibited by wandering showmen like the *View of Lammerk* (illustration 274) or crude engravings of famous events like the *Boston Massacre* by Paul Revere (illustration 275) or the woodcut image, *View of the Place de Grève on the Day of the Fall of the Bastille* (illustration 72). Or else they were slightly satiric prints like the *World Upside Down* (illustration 71), which indirectly suggested that perhaps the world could be made a better place to live in, and which had their small share in the factors bringing about that experiment of direct action known as the Revolution. Yet there was relatively little use of pictures as propaganda. This form of persuasion and conversion was to receive a much wider development in the nineteenth century.

In 1789 began the debacle of the *Ancien Régime*. Very many of the artists and engravers such as Moreau, Choffard, Debucourt, Ponce, welcomed the ideas of the Revolution; some of them like Sergent took an active part in it; but trained as they had been in the faithful delineation of an old order, they were unable to transfer their new convictions to their art. In spite of the eloquent appeal to artists of Minister Benezech on the ninth Floreal of the Year IV ("Liberty invites you to retrace its triumphs. . . . You should acquire a national character in order that succeeding generations can not reproach you with not having been French in the most remarkable epoch of our history"), most of the work was cold and uninspired. New forms were required for a new conception of society, and the academic, Roman classicism of David or Regnault was not adequate. Prud'hon, in many ways perhaps the most characteristic painter of the Revolutionary period, is here represented by an allegory on *Liberty* engraved by Copia (illustration 293). There was a great deal of documentation of the Revolution, much of it interesting to the historian rather than to the art-lover. *The Interior of a Revolutionary Committee under the Terror*, engraved by Berthault after the younger

113

Fragonard (illustration 273), does manage to dramatize some of the emotional currents of the Revolution—members of the nobility, often innocently suffering for the sins of their class, on the defensive before a group of "roughnecks" of the Terror. Such minor tragedies are enacted in every revolution. One of the most vivid pictures of those stirring times is Sergent-Marceau's color print, the *People Running through the Streets with Torches* (illustration 292). The tenseness of passions unloosed, the uncertainties of alarms and excursions have been admirably suggested. Antoine François Sergent, called Sergent-Marceau (for he added his wife's name to his own), was a fiery and picturesque character. He married the sister of General Marceau, Maria Marceau, to whom he paid the tribute of the ardent devotion of a lifetime. On her death at the age of eighty he published a pamphlet giving a detailed description of her mental and physical charms. When the Revolution broke, he threw himself into the thick of it, was one of the deputies who voted for the death of the king, celebrated at Chartres Cathedral the Festival of Reason, was instrumental in preventing the destruction or mutilation of many works of art during the Terror. After the reaction of the ninth Thermidor he fled to Switzerland; he returned later and was again exiled after the eighteenth Brumaire, and lived in Italy for the rest of his life. Eight days before his death in 1847, totally blind and ninety-six years of age, he declared to Carnot that "far from repenting his revolutionary activity, he considered it, on the contrary, as his chief title to fame."

We have had little to say about printmaking in England during the centuries. The country had been backward as far as the visual arts were concerned; its genius was expressed in other ways, in literature and science, in empire-building, in commerce and manufacture. Whatever production of art there had been, was through foreign talent such as Holbein, Hollar, Sir Anthony van Dyck, Sir Peter Lely, and Sir Godfrey Kneller. But in the late seventeenth century and in the eighteenth century there was perfected a new printmaking medium eminently suited to the English taste—mezzotint—and native artists quickly sprang up to develop its possibilities. The process was invented by Ludwig von Siegen (1609–1676) and the first dated mezzotint was a portrait of the

Landgravin of Hesse of 1642. The secret of the process was communicated to Prince Rupert, to whom Evelyn in his "Sculptura" gives the credit for its invention by what appears to have been a willful juggling with the facts. The romantic Prince Rupert executed several plates himself, of which *The Great Executioner, The Standard Bearer,* and a *Self-Portrait* are the most famous. Even if he did not invent the art he did much to encourage its development in England, with the result that in due course of time mezzotint was practiced chiefly in England, and labeled as "the English manner" everywhere on the Continent. The mezzotint process was based upon gradations of tone and was particularly suited to reproduce paintings, and since the English were interested chiefly in portrait painting, the great bulk of mezzotints are portraits.

In Holland [wrote Hogarth] selfishness is the ruling passion; in England vanity is united with it. Portrait painting therefore ever has, and ever will succeed better in this country than in any other; the demand will be as constant as new faces arise. . . . Upon the whole, it must be acknowledged that the artists and the age are fitted for each other. If hereafter the times alter, the arts, like water, will find their level.

And Horace Walpole wrote to Sir Horace Mann:

Another rage is for prints of English portraits: I have been collecting them above thirty years, and originally never gave for a mezzotint above one or two shillings. The lowest are now a crown; most, from half a guinea to a guinea. . . . In short, we are at the height of extravagance and improvements, for we do improve rapidly in taste as well as in the former. I cannot say as much for our genius. Poetry is gone to bed, or into our prose; we are like the Romans in that too. If we have the arts of the Antonines— we have the fustian also.

England had become a prosperous nation, that is to say there were many noblemen owning much of the land who had grown rich through the enclosing of communal lands for sheep raising and through the improvements in agriculture during the seventeenth and eighteenth centuries, and there were many merchants who had grown rich in commerce. Manufacture, chiefly of woolen cloth, had made great strides in the seventeenth century and had been aided materially by the influx

115

of great numbers of skilled artisans possessing considerable capital, the Dutch and Flemish weavers who fled from the Spanish invasion, and the Huguenots, the pick of France's industrial population, who were expelled from France by Louis XIV. The beginning of the eighteenth century witnessed the naval and commercial supremacy of the English over the Dutch and Spanish; henceforth Britannia ruled the waves. In the conflict between the French and the English over India, England emerged victorious with the whole of India in her possession, an enormous source of wealth procured at very little cost. Furthermore in 1769 James Watt took out his patent for a steam engine; and further inventions by Hargreaves, Arkwright, and Crompton benefited the spinning and weaving industries and brought about the Industrial Revolution, the full effects of which were not felt until the nineteenth century. All of these factors, however, combined to make England the richest nation in Europe. And how did the English spend their money? The merchants invested theirs for further profits, but many of the noblemen, with the Grand Tour in Italy as a traditional part of their education, posed as collectors, dilettantes of the arts, connoisseurs or virtuosi as they were called. Unfortunately they purchased chiefly Italian pictures since there was little native art which had any prestige. The only native art which they patronized was portrait painting, and the fact that they patronized this one branch was largely due to the achievement and personality of one man, Sir Joshua Reynolds.

Sir Joshua, shrewd man of the world, suave member of Dr. Johnson's circle, dignified first President of the Royal Academy, continued the aristocratic tradition of van Dyck. As a portrait painter he substituted for elegance the glamor of the Grand Manner. He evolved an eclectic style based upon the achievements of the Venetian and Flemish Schools, believing that genius was a power acquired by long labor and study.

Study consists in learning to see nature [he said] and may be called the art of using other men's minds. . . . We should to the last moment of our lives continue a settled intercourse with all true examples of grandeur. Their inventions are not only the food of our infancy, but the substance which supplies the fullest maturity of our vigor.

116

On which Blake commented later:

Reynolds endeavours to prove that there is No such thing as Inspiration and that any Man of plain Understanding may by Thieving from Others become a Mich. Angelo. . . . Reynolds Thinks that Man Learns all he Knows. I say on the Contrary that Man Brings All That he has or can have Into the World with him. Man is Born Like a Garden ready Planted and Sown. The World is too poor to produce one Seed.

Reynolds was not a great artist, but he was a successful one. He had enough tricks of the grand manner to impress his contemporaries, and envelop his fashionable portraits with a flattering dignity. Through connection with the Academy and his *Discourses*, his careful cultivation of friends, and his countless commissions, he exerted an enormous influence on the London art world, and hundreds of mezzotints were made after his paintings by such skillful engravers as McArdell, Houston, Fisher, J. Watson, T. Watson, Green, Dickinson, Jones, Walker, and others. A typical example is the portrait of Mrs. Carnac engraved by J. R. Smith (illustration 295). The portrait of Dr. Johnson engraved by Doughty (illustration 297) displays more sincerity and sense of character. It was of another and earlier portrait of himself that Dr. Johnson said to Boswell: "He may paint himself as deaf as he please but *I will not* go down to Posterity as Blinking Sam." Reynolds set the style of fashionable portrait which was continued with minor variations by Hoppner (illustration 294), Romney (illustration 296), Gainsborough, Raeburn, Wright, Lawrence, and their engravers. There is a certain sameness about all these mezzotint portraits, due partly perhaps to a limitation of the medium which emphasizes softness and smoothness at the expense of honest or subtle delineation of form, but also due to the fundamentally artificial approach of the painter to his problem. It is a highly aristocratic and superficial art, grandiloquent, flattering, and sentimentalizing, and without that exquisite taste and sense of style which gives distinction to the equally aristocratic art of France.

It is with some sense of relief—a touch of reality or a breath of fresh air—that one turns to the work of Gainsborough and Hogarth. With regard to Gainsborough, it is not so much the portraits (though most

117

of these are executed with more originality and feeling than is visible in the other portraits of his time) as it is the landscapes which he executed for his own pleasure. "I'm sick of Portraits," he wrote to a friend, "and wish very much to take my viol-da-gamba and walk off to some sweet village where I can paint landskips and enjoy the fag-end of life in quietness and ease." He made a small number of soft ground etchings which were published in 1797 by Boydell after his death. They have caught the charm and freshness of the English countryside (illustration 276), and thus stand as precursors of the development of the English landscape school which took place in the nineteenth century. Incidentally these rare soft ground etchings are among the earliest examples of the process.

The artist who placed himself most directly in opposition to Sir Joshua Reynolds and what he stood for was William Hogarth. He espoused a popular tradition as against the aristocratic and academic tradition of Reynolds. His genius found its completest expression in the creation of universal types under the stress of dramatic situations rather than in fashionable portraits or in historical compositions in the grand manner. Hogarth was born in 1697, and like Reynolds was the son of a schoolmaster. He was apprenticed to a silversmith and later studied at the academy of Sir James Thornhill. In 1729 he ran away with Thornhill's daughter. In 1733 he moved to a house in Leicester Fields in which he lived until his death in 1764. Meanwhile he had painted in 1731, and a year later engraved, the series of six pictures entitled *Harlot's Progress*. They had such a widespread success that he became reconciled to his father-in-law Thornhill, who said "the man who can furnish representations like these can also maintain a wife without a portion." It is recorded that there were over one thousand two hundred subscriptions entered for the engravings at a guinea per set. In describing the inception of this work Hogarth wrote that portrait painting to a conscientious and self-respecting artist was "not sufficiently profitable to pay the expenses my family required."

I therefore turned my thoughts to a still more novel mode, namely painting and engraving modern moral subjects, a field not broken up in any country or any age. . . . I have therefore endeavoured to treat my subject

118

as a dramatic writer; my picture is my stage, and men and women my players, who by means of certain actions and gestures, are to exhibit *a dumb show.* . . . This I found was most likely to answer my purpose, provided I could strike the passions, and by small sums from many, by the sale of prints which I could engrave from my own pictures, thus secure my property to myself.

The pictures were much copied and pirated; so much so that Hogarth with other artists, Vertue, Vandergucht, petitioned Parliament to pass a law vesting in the artist the exclusive right to his own designs and restraining reproduction without consent. This Copyright Act was passed in 1735, and Hogarth's next series of engravings, *Rake's Progress*, appeared under that protection, the first prints to bear the inscription *Published according to Act of Parliament.* There had been previous attempts by artists, such as Rubens and others, to prevent plagiarism of their works, and some of them were successful in obtaining exclusive privileges from the king or ruler, but in every case they were "privileges" obtained by influence or favor, as the correspondence of Rubens clearly shows. For the first time the general principle of copyright was established: any artist could avail himself of its protection. The third famous picture sequence was *Marriage à la Mode* satirizing high society in the same manner that he had dramatized episodes in the life of a harlot and a rake. The six prints were published in 1745 but were not engraved by Hogarth himself. Plate II, the *Breakfast Scene*, or the *Morning After*, engraved by Baron is reproduced herewith (illustration 258). The setting is supposed to have been copied from the drawing-room at No. 5 Arlington St., once occupied by Horace Walpole. The theme of the series is the tragic unfolding of a marriage of convenience between an earl and his rich but plebeian wife.

Hogarth was in the habit of specially engraving some little subject and presenting it to the subscribers of his various large prints or series of prints, as a subscription receipt. One of these, the receipt for *Rake's Progress*, entitled *Laughing Audience*, is reproduced (illustration 262). It is a most delightful print, perfect in composition, and expressive of character by the simplest and directest means. Hogarth engraved many famous single plates such as *The March to Finchley, Southwark Fair,*

Strolling Actresses Dressing in a Barn, Midnight Modern Conversation, Beer Street and Gin Lane, and *Garrick as Richard III. The Enraged Musician* (illustration 259) is characteristic of his rich and humorous observation of life in the London of his time. The picture, as Fielding said, is "enough to make a man deaf to look at it." Hogarth also made political caricatures, being one of the first to cultivate that form of print-making, specially favored in England and later developed by Rowlandson, Gillray, Dighton, and others. Allied to these, though not a caricature, was his *Portrait of Lord Lovat* (illustration 266), just before his execution for high treason. It was quickly etched to satisfy a popular demand so great that he sold prints, priced at one shilling, at the rate of two hundred and forty per day for many weeks. For vigor of characterization it ranks among the greatest portrait prints of the world.

Hogarth was not a realistic artist; he worked rather in the style of the dramatist or comic writer like Fielding. He combined realistic elements for a theme that was either humorous or moral or descriptive. He was not the first artist to depict low life or the contemporary scene, nor the first to conceive of a picture sequence as connected episodes with a central theme, as we know from the many series of the Passion which preceded him. But he combined the two ideas with such vigor and dramatic power that he may be said to have perfected a new form. His painting has been called literary or didactic. This is true only of his less successful work; at his best it expresses its theme in purely pictorial terms rich in observation of life and character. His book *The Analysis of Beauty* shows him to have been a theoretician and technician of considerable ability and common sense. To say that his work has mankind for its central theme is merely to point out that it has social content. This is thoroughly within the legitimate province of art, although many critics disagree, just as in literature the purists are more likely to relish "Kubla Khan" than *Tom Jones*. For a print or picture to have a meaning should be an advantage not a disqualification. Hogarth was in many respects typically English: he had the Englishman's contempt for foreigners as his caricatures of the French testify. His training was more or less indigenous; he never traveled abroad. He allied himself with the democratic tradition of Bruegel and the seventeenth century Dutch. He

120

aimed for expressive character, never for ideal beauty or elegant style, though, as Dobson says, when beauty came his way he drew it. It was a curious quirk of his character that although he despised the historical painters, he tried to beat them at their own game—with lamentable results. His genius was of a different order. One of the first great partisans of the bourgeois or middle class, he found his patrons among the many instead of the few.

Life in eighteenth century Venice—if we believe the memoirs of Casanova, Carlo Gozzi, and Goldoni—was one long *fête galante* or carnival interrupted by short periods of Lent equally picturesque and beautiful. At any rate it was somewhat in this spirit that Giambattista Tiepolo (1696–1770) worked at his decorations for villas and palaces and occasionally for churches. He was a facile painter and draughtsman, and inventions came bubbling from his fertile brain. In the midst of a busy career he found time to etch about thirty-eight plates. They are truly what he called the two leading series of his etchings: *Capricci* and *Scherzi*, or whimsical inventions (illustration 282). The subject matter is most varied and fanciful, scenes of magicians, occultism, satyrs, Roman soldiers, Pulchinello, and the like, all executed with a light and airy grace, with much spirit and little meaning. The Tiepolos must have been a happy jolly family: Giambattista married Cecilia Guardi, the sister of the painter Francesco Guardi. It is said that she was such a gamester that once during the absence of her husband she gambled away all his sketches and even their country house with all his frescoes in it. They had nine children, two of whom, Domenico and Lorenzo, assisted their father with his decorations, and etched a number of plates after his paintings. Domenico was an able artist in his own right, and composed a series of twenty-five etchings entitled *Idee Pittoresche sopra La Fugga in Egitto*, 1753 (illustration 283), an elegant and fluent lenten meditation suffused with soft Italian atmosphere and charm.

If the Tiepolos may be said to have pictured the actors in the Venetian carnival, then Canaletto may be said to have provided the setting or backdrop. His thirty-odd etchings, also made in the intervals of a busy painting career, depict scenes in and around Venice, and are filled with brilliant sunshine and quivering atmosphere. Such plates as the *Torre di Malghera* and the *Porch with the Lantern* are justly famous, but some of the smaller plates, the *Terrace* (illustration 281), the *Prison* (illustration 280), the *Market on the Giudecca*, are equally attractive. Canaletto had numerous contacts with English connoisseurs and collectors, and the collected edition of his *Vedute* or etchings was published with a dedication to Joseph Smith, the British Consul at Venice.

The third great name in eighteenth century Italian etching was Giovanni Battista Piranesi. He too was a Venetian, born in 1720, the son of a stone mason. He was educated to be an architect but the great passion of his life was Roman antiquities. And passion was a mighty force in a man of his fiery temperament if one can judge from the anecdotes told of him. How for instance when sketching in the old Roman Forum he saw a young girl who he was convinced was descended from the noble Romans and how after a cyclonic courtship lasting five days was married to the daughter of the gardener of Prince Corsini. How he threatened to kill the doctor called in to minister to a member of his family if the patient did not recover within a few days. How when he was absorbed in the making of an etching, his wife and five children suffered agonies of hunger, not daring to disturb him or eat without him. It was in Rome, the city of his dreams, that he spent most of his life, pursuing his archaeological researches and bringing to completion his stupendous *œuvre* of over one thousand three hundred huge etchings. He became an authority on Roman archaeology throughout Europe, and exercised an influence on the development of the classic style in the France of Louis XVI and in England through his friendship with Robert Adam. His mastery of draughtsmanship and perspective, his knowledge of Roman antiquities, the sense of drama suggested by the picturesque figures with which he peopled his romantic ruins, and above all his epic imagination all combine to make his etchings the most effective dramatization of Rome's past grandeur ever known (illustration 277). Piranesi also made many etchings of the Rome of his day; a typical and skillful example, showing the home of the French Academy in Rome from 1725 to 1800 on the Via del Corso, is reproduced (illustration 278). Early in his career he etched a series of fourteen (later sixteen) large etchings called *Carceri d'Invenzione* or *Prison Scenes* (illustration 279). They

122

seem to have been caprices in which he allowed his imagination to run riot in a fantastic interplay of light and shade among architectural forms. De Quincey in his *Confessions of an Opium Eater* mentions these prints in a celebrated passage, which probably reads into it meanings which were not in Piranesi's mind. In spite of its distortions it does manage to convey something of the spirit of these etched phantasmagoria:

Many years ago, when I was looking over Piranesi's *Antiquities of Rome*, Mr. Coleridge, who was standing by, described to me a set of plates by that artist, called his *Dreams*, and which record the scenery of his visions during the delirium of a fever. Some of them . . . represented vast Gothic halls, on the floor of which stood all sorts of engines and machinery, wheels, cables, pulleys, levers, catapults, etcetera, expressive of enormous power put forth and resistance overcome. Creeping along the sides of the walls, you perceived a staircase; and upon it, grasping his way upwards, was Piranesi himself; follow the stairs a little further, and you perceive it comes to a sudden, abrupt termination, without any balustrade, and allowing no step onwards to him who had reached the extremity except into the depths below. . . . But raise your eyes, and behold a second flight of stairs still higher, on which again Piranesi is perceived, by this time standing on the very brink of the abyss. . . . With the same power of endless growth and self-production did my architecture proceed in my dreams.

6. Nineteenth Century

THE nineteenth century was a drama of personalities, and Goya, working in two centuries, wrote its prologue. The outstanding qualities of the nineteenth century were its diversity and its emphasis on personality. There were, to be sure, movements and schools of artists, plenty of them in bewildering succession, but they were usually grouped around a few outstanding personalities. Hitherto an art style or epoch lasted for a century or longer, now it lasted for a generation. Once the epoch molded the artist, now the artist created the style. Classicism, Romanticism, Realism, Barbizon, Impressionism, post-Impressionism all had their say within a hundred years. The nineteenth was the century of rugged individualism.

Francisco de Goya y Lucientes was a picturesque and outstanding personality who in expressing himself also expressed truths about mankind. He was a combination of court-painter and satirist, of philosopher and *aficionado* of the bull-ring, that could occur only in Spain. Spain has always been a strange and mysterious land where all things are possible. As Joseph, who tried to rule the country for six years, ruefully said to his brother Napoleon: *"L'Espagne n'est pas un pays comme les autres."* A backward and reactionary country, priest-ridden and king-ridden, its peoples displayed in many respects an astonishing wisdom of life, a real feeling for life as a fine art. Its beggars had the manners of grandees. Nowhere in Europe were bourgeois ideas and ideals so completely discounted and ignored as in Spain.

Goya was born in Fuendetodos in Aragon in 1746. There are many legends of his early life, a record as violent and vivid as Cellini's, filled with love affairs, murderous quarrels, exploits in the bull-ring, travels in Italy. In 1776 he was settled in Madrid, married to Josepha Bayeu who was to bear him twenty children, leading an active, hard-working

124

life, designing cartoons for tapestries saturated with the gay spirit of Madrid life, painting murals and portraits of the nobility and the royal family. In 1780 he was elected to the Academy of San Fernando; in 1789 he was made *Pintor de Camara;* in 1799 he was *Primer Pintor de Camara,* chief painter to the king. He enjoyed the friendship and patronage of the Duke and Duchess of Ossuna; he had an intense love affair with the alluring but fickle Duchess of Alba. In all these years he drew and painted incessantly, tried his hand at etching, copies of Velazquez. But his direct and passionate temperament also had opportunity to reflect on the pageant of human folly as he saw it: greed, fickleness, pride, lust, cruelty, stupidity. In 1791 Le Prince's secret of aquatint etching had been published to the world in the *Encyclopédie Méthodique.* Goya must have come across it, and in the aquatint process he found a medium eminently fitted to reproduce his pen and wash drawings. In the last years of the century there began to crystallize in his mind the idea of a series of satiric compositions executed in etching and aquatint. The miracle of it was that he should want to publish to the world, in Spain of all places, such a series of prints. Perhaps he had to do it to keep his self-respect amid the corrupt and artificial surroundings of the court, perhaps he was a bit *afrancesado,* tinged with French revolutionary ideas. In any case the series was announced to the public in 1797 in a prospectus containing the following explanation written, if not by Goya, by Cean Bermudez under the inspiration of his ideas:

Believing that the criticism of human errors and vices, although first and foremost the business of rhetoric and poetry, may also come within the province of painting, the author has chosen as subjects for his work some of those extravagances and stupidities, common to all classes of society, some of those prejudices and falsehoods, hallowed by custom, by ignorance or by interest, such themes indeed as seemed to him to offer matter for ridicule and scope for the free play of the artist's imagination. As the subjects are idealized it may not be too daring to assume that their faults will be leniently judged by people of intelligence. . . . I crave the public's indulgence in consideration of the fact that the author has made use of no strange models, nor even of studies from nature. The imitation of nature is as difficult as it is admirable if one can really attain it and carry it

125

through. But he also may deserve praise, who has completely withdrawn himself from nature and has succeeded in placing before our eyes, forms and movements which have hitherto existed only in our imagination. . . . Painting, like Poetry, selects from the universe what she can best use for her own ends. She unites, she concentrates in one fantastic figure circumstances and characters which nature has distributed among various individuals. Thanks to this wise and ingenious combination the artist merits the title of an inventor and ceases to be a mere subordinate copyist.

Two years later the set of eighty plates of the *Caprichos* was put on sale at 320 reals (about $25.00)—one of the world's masterpieces of graphic art, a savage yet detached commentary on human kind. For once the façade was ripped off and the essential type laid bare. Yet not only types were attacked, but society, which allowed certain things to happen—*Because She Was Sensitive* (illustration 311), or the fickleness of fortune in *To Rise and Fall* (illustration 312). In spite of Goya's disclaimer that the satire was general and not particular there were rumors—as was natural in a society where gossip and the malicious story were raised to a fine art—that certain reigning court favorites and even the king and queen were attacked. Furthermore there were certain inquiries and investigations by the Inquisition, for some of the shots at superstition and fanaticism had hit a bull's eye. Goya deemed it prudent to dedicate the series to the king, Charles IV, who graciously accepted it and duly rewarded the artist. Nowhere but in Spanish countries could such a thing have happened, in Spain where the technique of the deadly thrust in the bull-ring is appreciated with discriminating connoisseurship, where scepticism and faith, idealism and materialism, Don Quixote and Sancho Panza go hand in hand, and where flourishes the ironic laugh, the *vacilada* of the Mexicans, that laugh that is relished by its victims if only the sally be delivered with sufficient art. The frontispiece of the set was a portrait of Goya himself (illustration 364). We see him as he appeared at the height of his powers, the piercing, all-seeing eyes, the protruding underlip, the determined chin—the master of illusion and disillusion. Deafness was already upon him, that deafness which was eventually to cut him off from all society except a few intimates. Meanwhile things were happening in Spain. In 1808 Napoleon invaded Spain

126

to establish his brother Joseph upon the throne. The Spaniards should have welcomed him, for any rule would have been preferable to the old regime of Spain, but most of them did not, and there ensued a guerrilla warfare of unparalleled savagery on both sides. For six long years it lasted, aided by Napoleon's implacable enemy, England, until finally reaction, bigotry, cruelty, and the Inquisition returned triumphantly in the person of Ferdinand VII in 1814. Goya watched it all and set it down in a series of etchings which were not published until long after his death as the *Disasters of War*. Not all the plates refer to the Napoleonic War; several are covert satires against the French and against Ferdinand; still another group refer to the great famine of 1812, indirect consequence of the war, when over twenty thousand people died in Madrid alone. A reflection of this is given in that magnificent composition *Thanks to Millet Seed* (illustration 316). "Men women, and children," says Romanos in his *Reminiscences*, "lay dying in the streets, they begged for a scrap of green stuff, for a potato, for a drop of soup, however thin and bad. It was a scene of despair and pain." But most of the etchings relate to the invasion (illustrations 317 and 319), a terrific and awe-inspiring indictment, not of the enemy, but of war itself, its senselessness and incredible brutality. Only a Voltaire in *Candide* could do justice to the scope of Goya's savagely ironic portrayal:

He crept over a heap of dead and dying and at last reached a neighboring village which he found in ashes. It was a village of the Avares and the Bulgarians had burnt it down according to the rules of the international game. Here aged men, sinking beneath the blows that were showered upon them, saw their wives throttled to death, pressing their children to their bleeding breasts to the last. There girls lay dying, their bellies ripped open when they had served to satisfy the lust of conquering heroes; others, half burned, begged for death. On the ground one saw splashes of scattered brains and limbs lopped from bodies.

Goya worked on, more and more withdrawn into himself in the Quinta del Sordo, the deaf man's villa. On one of his *Caprichos* there was an inscription, "The Sleep of Reason produces Monsters." Dreams

127

and nightmares seemed to haunt him, visions far more fantastic and monstrous than those he pictured in the *Caprichos*. Out of pleasure or necessity he recorded them on the walls of the Quinta and in the series of twenty-two etchings and aquatints known as the *Disparates*, or *Extravagances*. Like Titian and Rembrandt, Goya suffered no diminution of imaginative power in his old age. The *Disasters* were realistic, the *Caprichos* were a mixture of realism and fantasy, but the *Disparates* were pure fantasy, a direct outpouring of his unconscious. What powerful and haunting visions they are, a group of people huddling on a rotten branch, a stallion biting a woman, flying men (illustration 313), a man haunted by demons! One of them, entitled *Disparate de Bestia* (illustration 315), shows priests and lawgivers anxiously holding a law code before an elephant who may or may not symbolize the People unconscious of their strength. It is a superbly vital composition.

In 1825 he was in Bordeaux for his health—old, in a strange land, deaf, with eyesight failing, "but very pleased with life and anxious to meet people." "He obstinately continued to work," wrote his friend Moratin, "painting everything that comes into his head and unwilling ever to correct what he paints." In his seventy-ninth year he made a number of lithographs, then a comparatively new medium, including the four great bull fights (illustration 314). He had already etched forty good-sized plates (thirty-two of which were published in 1815) as a sort of illustrated history of the *corrida de toros* and its heroes. But his invention continued undiminished. These four great stones are a veritable orgy of bull fighting, the compositions built up with broad strokes and large masses, brimming with energy. They are amazingly spirited achievements from a man almost eighty and count among the great masterpieces of lithography. Goya had extraordinary energy and an indomitable will; in a letter he excused his bad penmanship, "I have neither sight, nor pulse, nor pen nor inkpot, I lack everything, only my will survives." But even the will to live was quenched by a stroke in 1828 brought on, it is said, by joy over the arrival of his son Xavier.

On one of the preliminary drawings for the *Caprichos*, the one which originally was to serve as the frontispiece, Goya wrote "*Idioma Universal*." Universal language, the ultimate aim of the print, that was what

128

was in the back of his mind, and he came as close to it as any print-maker ever did. His only peers are Rembrandt and Daumier who approached humanity from the side of love and understanding. Goya perhaps probed deeper into the unconscious, into those devious but powerful forces which motivate our every action. He has brought into the light of day and made concrete in the shape of recognizable types certain essential drives that lie buried in most of us, impulses of vanity, pride, greed, gluttony, lust, cruelty, and the like. There is nothing like war or the vision of sudden death for uncovering the essence of man. This is strong medicine and bitter: many people will be repelled by Goya's work. But for those who can accept one aspect of reality without sugar-coating, it can become a most illuminating catharsis.

Another personality who was active in two centuries was Thomas Rowlandson. He was born in London in 1756, the son of a fairly prosperous merchant. He studied at the Academy School for a short time. In his sixteenth year, about 1771, he was sent to Paris to live with his aunt, née Mlle Chattelier, whose favorite he became. He learned to speak French like a native, plunged with eagerness into the life of the gay capital, and entered the École de l'Académie Royale to continue his art studies. He became acquainted with Debucourt, and with Janinet, a fellow pupil at the École. In 1775 when he was nineteen, he returned to London and continued his studies at the Royal Academy. Angelo in his *Reminiscences* recounts:

Bannister and Rowlandson were prankish youths. The latter once gave great offense by carrying a pea-shooter into the life academy, and, whilst old Moser was adjusting the female model and had just directed her contour, Rowlandson let fly a pea, which, making her start, threw her entirely out of position, and interrupted the gravity of the study for the whole evening.

In spite of such pranks Rowlandson was well liked; and a great future was predicted for him by the academicians, two Presidents, Reynolds and West, having expressed the greatest admiration of his talents. In 1775 he exhibited for the first time at the Royal Academy, and continued to do so for about a dozen years. He gradually, however, lost interest in the so-called serious or historical art in favor of a more free and easy

129

and rollicking social commentary, partly through the influence of such friends as Bunbury, Wigstead, and Gillray, and partly through the bent of his own temperament. He launched into a career of extravagance and dissipation aggravated by the receipt of a legacy of over seven thousand pounds from his French aunt. Yet his wild life did not interfere with his production: it rather spurred him on to tap the apparently inexhaustible springs of his fancy. His work combined French elegance with English animal spirits. He had a ready gift for characterization combined with a rich knowledge of life gained from actual experience. His opulent and exuberant forms exactly mirrored his uncommon zest for life. His *Vauxhall Gardens* (illustration 290) has been mentioned as having influenced Debucourt. Vauxhall was a famous London amusement resort of the eighteenth century, and Rowlandson is supposed to have introduced caricatures of many well known people in his picture. The two fashionably dressed women under the singer on the balcony are supposed to be the Duchess of Devonshire and her sister Lady Duncannon. Farther to the right the man whispering into the ear of a lady linked to a deformed husband is the Prince of Wales, afterwards George IV. In a supper box Dr. Johnson is oblivious to everything but the pleasures of the table, with the ever-watchful Boswell diagonally on his left. On the right of Johnson, the blue-stocking Mrs. Thrale may be seen talking to Oliver Goldsmith. Rowlandson made many illustrations, chiefly for Ackermann's publications, the *Dance of Death*, the *Dance of Life*, the various *Tours of Dr. Syntax*, and the *Microcosm of London* (illustration 302) in collaboration with Pugin who supplied the architectural features. This last is a survey of the activities of a great city in 104 plates, furnishing a wealth of information regarding the manners of the time. He made a number of genre scenes, the *Cries of London*, such as the charming *Ballad Singers* (illustration 304). For such publishers as Ackermann, Fores, and Tegg, he produced several political caricatures (illustration 303) and countless social caricatures, etched on copper and crudely colored by hand. *More Miseries or the Bottom of Mr. Figg's old Whiskey [a type of carriage] Broke Through* (illustration 305) is typical of these and of the robust humor of the

130

time. The caricatures of Gillray, Bunbury, Dighton, and Cruikshank are in the same genre.

Rowlandson also did a few sporting prints, a genre that was popular in the early nineteenth century in England. The hard-drinking, hard-riding English country squires and the young bucks of the city were collecting art, and the demand was ably supplied. The appreciation of these connoisseurs, however, was strictly limited: they demanded that a picture be factual, accurate, and pleasant, and, in subject matter, entirely within the range of their experience, either genre pictures of the English countryside (Morland and Ward), or sporting pictures, hunting, shooting, racing, or coaching prints. A large group of able, decorative but esthetically limited prints were produced by Alken, Pollard, Wolstenholme, Howitt, and others. Two prints, *Hare Hunting* by Hodges (illustration 307) and *False Alarm on the Road to Gretna Green* by Newhouse (illustration 306), may serve as representative of the class. There were other groups of prints appealing to a specialized public, such as flower prints, here typified by Redouté's charming color print of *Roses* (illustration 308) or natural history prints, represented by a plate from the monumental *Birds of America* (illustration 309), the life work of J. J. Audubon. Mention should also be made of the lithograph genre subjects, popular in America, and published by Currier and Ives, and others. Many of these have little artistic merit but the best of them have both decorative charm and historical interest. The clipper ships especially bring back the thrill and glory of a vanished era (illustration 310). Thousands and hundreds of thousands of specialized prints have been made, relating to science, natural history, travel, genre, illustration, which in their humble way have contributed to the amusement and instruction of mankind.

A new and cheap printmaking medium was perfected at the beginning of the century which was greatly to extend the range of popular prints—lithography. The inventor was Aloys Senefelder. He was not an artist, but was ambitious to write for the stage. Being poor, he saw no way of getting the world to look at his work unless he became his own publisher. In the course of his attempts to find a cheap method of printing plays with engraved plates, he happened upon the germ of lithography. In his own words:

I had just ground a stone plate smooth in order to treat it with etching fluid and to pursue on it my practice in reverse writing when my mother asked me to write a laundry list for her. The laundress was waiting but we could find no paper. My own supply had been used up by pulling proofs. Even the writing ink was dried up. Without bothering to look for writing materials, I wrote the list hastily on the clean stone with my prepared ink of wax, soap and lampblack, intending to copy it as soon as paper was supplied.

Curiosity as to the possibilities of this chance application of ink and stone led him to further experiments till he had evolved the complete process. Later unscrupulous promoters were to defraud the unworldly inventor of some of his just benefits and dues, but in the end he received a pension from the King of Bavaria, and painstaking biographers and autobiographers have set the whole record straight for the benefit of grateful posterity. In Germany and Austria the new medium did not stimulate any far-reaching response. At the beginning of the century these countries were in a state of depression artistically, economically, and politically. Schinkel made a few prints and the Quaglios some romantic scenes including an interesting portrait of Senefelder printed with two stones like a chiaroscuro (illustration 320). The portrait, dated 1818, was undoubtedly done from life and thus punctures the legend that Hanfstängl's lithograph of 1834 was the only life portrait. The legend is that Senefelder had a deadly fear of having his picture taken; Hanfstängl persuaded him to sit for a portrait, and three days later he sickened and died. Strixner, Piloty, and Hanfstängl used lithography to reproduce paintings. Portrait lithographs were made by Reuter, Krüger, Schadow, and the Viennese Kriehuber, who drew the charmingly romantic *Une Matinée chez Liszt* (illustration 324) with portraits of Liszt, Berlioz, the pianist Carl Czerny (remembered for his Études), the violinist Ernst, and Kriehuber himself. It is one of the most famous of musical portraits.

It was in France, however, that lithography first came into its own.

132

Not only was art in demand there, but there were also distinguished artists who were willing to try their hand with the new medium, Prud'hon, Guerin, Géricault (illustration 325), Baron Gros, Boilly (illustration 321). Distinguished amateurs took it up (as they had the physionotrace). They included the Duc de Montpensier, brother of the future king Louis Philippe, and Vivant-Denon, one of Napoleon's savants who gathered together in the Louvre famous paintings from all over Europe as spoils of war, and of whom it was said that his chief occupations were "*la gravure et les femmes.*" But lithography flourished in Paris chiefly because it satisfied a popular need. Amid all the ups and downs of the Revolution, the Directorate, the Empire, and the Restoration, the middle class had been slowly and steadily gaining in power and influence. A quick and inexpensive reproducing medium was needed in order to reach the bourgeoisie for purposes of propaganda. Woodcut and etching, as Edouard Fuchs has pointed out, were too complicated and costly; lithography was as if made for the purpose. Political caricature flourished as never before at the beginning of the reign of *le Roi Bourgeois.* Furthermore, the middle classes had still other uses for lithography beside political propaganda; they wanted pictures, decorations for their walls and illustrations for their books. Thackeray in his *Paris Sketch Book* has drawn a pretty picture of this aspect of French bourgeois culture:

The same love of ornament which is shown in their public places of resort, appears in their houses likewise; and everyone of our readers who has lived in Paris, in any lodging, magnificent or humble with any family, however poor, may bear witness how profusely the walls of his smart *salon* in the English quarter, or of his little room *au sixième* in the Pays Latin, have been decorated with prints of all kinds. In the first, probably, with bad engravings on copper from the bad and tawdry pictures of the artists of the time of the Empire; in the latter, with gay caricatures of Grandville or Monnier: military pieces, such as are dashed off by Raffet, Charlet, Vernet; or clever pictures from the crayon of the Deverias, the admirable Roqueplan, or Decamps. . . . We get in these engravings the *loisirs* of men of genius, not the finikin performances of labored mediocrity, as with us: all these artists are good painters, as well as good designers; a design from them is worth a whole gross of *Books of Beauty*. . . . Can there be a more pleasing walk in the whole world than a stroll through the Gallery of the Louvre on a fête-day; not to look so much at the pictures as at the lookers-on? Thousands of the poorer classes are there: mechanics in their Sunday clothes, smiling grisettes, smart dapper soldiers of the line, with bronzed wondering faces, marching together in little companies of six or seven, and stopping every now and then at Napoleon or Leonidas as they appear in proper vulgar heroics in the pictures of David or Gros. The taste of these people will hardly be approved by the connoisseur, but they have *a* taste for art. Can the same be said of our lower classes, who, if they are inclined to be sociable and amused in their holidays, have no place of resort but the tap-room or tea-garden, and no food for conversation except such as can be built upon the politics or the police reports of the last Sunday paper? So much has Church and State puritanism done for us—so well has it succeeded in materializing and binding down to earth the imagination of men, for which God has made another world (which certain statesmen take but too little into account)—that fair and beautiful world of art, in which there *can* be nothing selfish or sordid, of which Dulness has forgotten the existence, and which Bigotry has endeavored to shut out from sight.

Thackeray, in speaking of onlookers, might also have been describing the group in front of *Delpech's Lithograph Shop* (illustration 327), so apt is his account. It is interesting to note the boy carrying a lithograph stone on his head. Carle Vernet who drew the lithograph was of a long line of artists reaching back to the *Ancien Régime*. He also was one of the artists, along with Raffet, Charlet, Marlet, and Bellangé, active in building up what was called the Napoleonic Legend. Almost a generation had passed since the great wars, and the old soldiers now indulged in fond and pleasant recollection. Nor was the comfortable bourgeois averse to tasting a little vicarious glory. And so the idea went over big, as they say. Hundreds of lithographs were brought out, anecdotes of the war, details of uniforms, of battles, anecdotes of the Emperor, presenting him in a grand or kindly light, all executed with zest and a big dash of sentimentality. One of the most imaginative is Raffet's *Revue Nocturne* (illustration 318) where a phantom Emperor nightly reviews his phantom troops. The reality of the Napoleonic Legend we get in Goya's *Disasters*.

134

Another large-scale enterprise carried through with the aid of lithography was the *Voyages Pittoresques et Romantiques dans l'Ancienne France,* in twenty-four huge folio volumes brought out by Baron Taylor, Inspector General of the Fine Arts and of the Museums of France. Taylor was quite alive to the possibilities of lithography: "Bourgeois showed me his first lithographs. I saw in this new art a means of realizing an idea which was to occupy the greater part of my life: I believed I could foresee that lithography was to be for the arts of drawing almost what typography had been for literature." The 2700-odd lithographs included in this stupendous work cover every part and province of France, recording picturesque scenes and romantic ruins, and were made by the best artists of France and England, Ciceri, Isabey, Charlet, Vernet, C. Nanteuil, Ingres, Bonington, Prout, Boys, Harding, Haghe, and others. Two examples of this work, which did so much for landscape lithography, are reproduced (illustrations 328 and 329), Bonington's *Tour du Gros-Horloge* at Evreux, and Eugène Isabey's *Église de St. Nectaire in Auvergne,* of which Pennell wrote: "The gems of the collection are the drawings of Eugène Isabey. The way he could seize upon the most pictorial point of view and use chalk, stump and scraper, or anything to work up his design until one hardly knows how his effect has been obtained, how he managed to fill it with color and light and air and beauty, is truly marvelous."

The technique of color lithography had been developing along with lithography in black and white, and reached perhaps its highest technical proficiency in the Paris portfolio of Thomas Shotter Boys (illustration 330). Color lithography later was to fall into the hands of commercial printers and artists without any taste, and to acquire the opprobrious label of chromo. Color printing as a sensitive art was again revived at the end of the century by such artists as Toulouse-Lautrec, Bonnard (illustration 331), Vuillard, and Signac. Lithography found another great field in the genre pictures, the social commentary, the gay caricatures which Thackeray speaks about, by Monnier, Lami, Decamps, Deveria, Beaumont, Travies, and Gavarni.

Sulpice-Guillaume Chevalier, called Gavarni, was born in Paris in 1804 and died there in 1866. In him the wit and elegance and feminine grace of Parisian life found a worthy interpreter. One of his most famous prints is his portrait of the two De Goncourt brothers (illustration 376). His name is often coupled with that of Daumier. In a sense they complement each other: although Gavarni has none of the virility or depth or grandeur of Daumier, he has a delicacy and a flair for a pretty woman and a modish dress that is lacking in the work of the great caricaturist.

It is said that when Balzac saw some of Daumier's work he exclaimed: "This fellow has a lot of Michelangelo inside of him." It is quite true that there is much of Michelangelo's heroic and plastic monumentality in his work, as there is of Rembrandt's deep feeling for humanity. Daumier presented the complete drama of humanity in the dress of the middle class. Never has the life of the solid bourgeois and his equally solid wife been presented in greater detail or with greater understanding and humor. All its hopes and fears, its virtues and prejudices, its little crises of happiness or unhappiness found expression in Daumier's crayon. As Baudelaire pointed out, Daumier was the pictorial complement to Balzac's *Comédie Humaine*. There were limitations to his range: neither the extremes of proletarian poverty, starvation, and degradation nor the elegance of the demi-monde (so delightfully portrayed by Gavarni) and luxuries of the ruling class were pictured by Daumier. Daumier was the middle class writ large, the bourgeois in his noblest aspect, the tireless fighter for political freedom against censorship and monarchical reaction, against war and extreme exploitation, ecclesiastical obscurantism, against police brutality and the venality of the law. In so far as the middle class represented the ideals of humanity —and it has come as close to it as any single class ever has—Daumier was a universal artist. "*Je suis de mon temps*," he said—I am of my own time. No heroics, no ideal figures, no search for the beautiful or the sublime, merely scenes and incidents of daily life, topical, factual, often of ephemeral interest. But through his genius he has made these scenes live for all time. We turn to them again and again, long after the stimulus that gave them birth has been forgotten, as inspiring and illuminating pages in the history of mankind—fresh and pertinent today as they were the day they were published.

Honoré Daumier was born in Marseilles in 1808, the son of an impecunious glazier with poetic aspirations. In 1814 the family moved to Paris and young Daumier grew up in the great city whose life he so heroically depicted. He wanted to draw; the family finally consented, but not until he had served his term as a bookseller's clerk and as a process-server in a lawyer's office (where perhaps he got his first insight into the legal mind). He entered the studio of Lenoir and drew ears and noses from casts. But this was not to his liking either, and he went out into the streets of Paris to watch and observe and store his memory with impressions of life. He had a visual memory astonishing even for an artist. An anecdote is told of him later, that illustrates this forcibly. He was out one Sunday with the Daubignys at Valmondois. He asked if there were any ducks to be seen, since he had to draw some in one of his lithographs. They led him to the canal where there was a whole flock of the birds, and after he had observed them for a few minutes, they asked him if he did not want a pencil and paper to make some sketches. Smilingly he said, "No thanks, you know I cannot draw from nature." A few days later the lithograph appeared with the ducks drawn to the life. What he meant when he modestly said that he could not draw from nature, was that he did not have to.

One does not know what turn the career of young Daumier might have taken if the times had not been crying out for an outstanding political caricaturist. France was getting heartily sick of the stupid and reactionary king Charles X. Political pamphleteering and caricature were in a ferment. In 1831 Daumier met Charles Philipon, founder and editor of *La Caricature* and *Le Charivari*, militant fighter for liberal democracy, ardent republican (which in 1835 excited the same opprobrium that the epithet communist does today); and so began the collaboration of these two kindred spirits which lasted a lifetime. Daumier found his metier. He was perhaps the greatest political caricaturist the world has ever seen; he had the faculty of dramatizing an abstract or political idea and clothing it in such convincing and universal terms that it still has meaning for us. Has there ever been a more vivid and complete embodiment of a prostitute press than in the picture of *Mlle Constitutionnel*, the "official" newspaper (illustration 339)? Look at those two great master-

137

pieces, *Le Ventre Législatif* (illustration 332) and *Rue Transnonain* (illustration 333). They were separate prints issued by *La Caricature* at one franc apiece in order to defray the expense of fines that had been imposed upon the periodical. The *Ventre Législatif*—as superb in design as a grand fresco—was the caricatured portrait of a corrupt Chamber of Deputies. Daumier had made many careful studies of the members by visiting the Chamber day by day and returning to his studio to model busts of nearly everyone in clay (these busts exist today), and finally he composed the lithograph from these modeled sketches. It was by this means perhaps that he attained that plastic feeling, that tactile sense which is so marked a characteristic of his work. *Rue Transnonain* represented an incident of police brutality in which a whole family, man, woman, and cihld, were murdered by the civic guard. Burning with indignation Daumier drew the scene, so charged with emotion yet so grandly simple and monumental in feeling that it is one of the most moving pictures of all time. It is said that people lined up daily in long queues to see the picture when it was exhibited in Aubert's window in the Galerie Vero-Dodat. From this time on, Daumier's fame was secure. He had already served a six months' term in the prison of Ste. Pélagie in 1832 for a caricature against Louis Philippe. This king with liberal pretenses had been swept into power by popular discontent in 1830, but he soon proved to be as reactionary as Charles X, and in 1835 he clamped down a censorship of the press so severe that any political caricature was quite out of question. Daumier therefore turned to social caricature and began the huge opus of over three thousand lithographs which appeared in *Charivari* from 1833, off and on, to 1872. He received at first forty and later fifty francs per stone, and his work for *Charivari* constituted his chief source of income during his life. He often brought out series of from ten to fifty lithographs on the same subject, as for example *Blue Stockings*, *Les Artistes*, *Le Bon Bourgeois*, *Les Beaux Jours de la Vie*, *Histoire Ancienne*, *Croquis Parisiens*, *Landlords and Tenants*, *Hunting*, *Country Life*, *Railroads* (just being built), *Les Papas*, *Théâtre*, *Mœurs Conjugales*, *Bathers* (copied by Delacroix as studies of the nude), *Professeurs et Moutards*, *Croquis Musicaux* and many others. There was one class which he was merciless in satirizing,

138

Les Gens de Justice (illustration 338). Another famous series was that of Robert Macaire, a type whose adventures gave a complete picture of the rascality of the time. He also designed a large number of woodcut illustrations for books, notably the *Nemesis Médicale, Les Français Peints par Eux-mêmes* (illustration 79), *La Grande Ville*, and the various *Physiologies*, and for magazines such as *Le Monde Illustré* in the years 1862–1868 (illustration 335). But in spite of his manifest achievements Daumier never felt quite at home in this medium. He told Théodore de Banville that "he was sick and tired of designs on wood and did not wish to do any more; the lithographic crayon alone followed his thought, whereas the lead pencil was refractory and would not obey him; in short he had a violent dislike to this kind of design where nine times out of ten one is betrayed and dishonored by the engraver."

Daumier lived quietly and modestly on the Ile St. Louis. He liked to go to the theater and to chat with a few intimate friends; far into the night or on a Sunday excursion, he would be with such confrères as Delacroix, Corot, Millet, Rousseau, Dupré, Daubigny, and Geoffroy-Dechaume. He painted also in his leisure moments and in those years (1860–1863) when there was no demand for his caricatures. In his painting and drawing, *Don Quixote, Les Blanchisseuses, Christ Presented to the People,* he voiced those deep and moving intuitions which somehow never found expression in his lithographs. In his later years the style of his lithographs changed. Color, rich blacks, and minuteness of form, no longer were important; the figures became bathed in atmosphere and light; only the barest essentials were given. His line became fluid, form-enclosing, and supremely vital. He always had the gift of creating types. His distortions, his deviations from the norm, always were convincing: every figure he ever drew had in it the breath of life. But now his expression became truly monumental. Take for example the *European Equilibrium* (illustration 336) or the *Witnesses* (illustration 337), an unpublished lithograph said to be the last one he made: grandeur of conception and inspired breadth of execution lift them out of the limbo of ephemeral caricatures into the small class of the elect of all time. The *Witnesses* with its group of skeletons of men, women, and children picketing, as it were, the Council of War, is one of the grandest war pictures ever made. Great and satisfying as were these paintings and lithographs of Daumier, they brought him little material recompense. Old and blind, he eked out a modest existence with a tiny pension from the government in a cottage at Valmondois generously given to him by his old friend Corot. He died in 1879. Van Gogh in a letter has perhaps summed him up as well as anyone:

But I remember being so very much impressed at the time by something so strong and manly in Daumier's conception that I thought: it must be a good thing to think and to feel in that way, and to overlook or to pass by many things, in order to concentrate oneself on things that furnish food for thought, and that touch us as human beings much more than meadows or clouds.

A number of the great painters of the time also tried their hand at printmaking. Ingres made a notable portrait etching of Pressigny and several lithographs including an *Odalisque* (illustration 374) similar to one of his paintings. It is a miracle of tight drawing and carefully built up effects. Ingres, the brilliant pupil of David, broke from the classical tradition of his master, and was considered a "Gothic" by him and others. However, as the Romantic School gained in favor and influence, Ingres became the chief bulwark of classicism against the Romantic vagary. His work was based on line and drawing highly finished, and, within its narrow limits, attained a rare perfection, but in Delacroix's words, it was "the complete expression of an incomplete intelligence." His great rival was Delacroix, the champion of the Romantic School. Eugène Delacroix was born in 1798, the natural son—as has been rather generally admitted—of Talleyrand. Delacroix was one of the most richly endowed personalities in the history of art. He was passionately devoted to music; he had a gift for writing, published many articles and from his twenty-fourth year kept a diary which is a most revealing document on the temperament and character of an artist. "He was a man of general education," wrote Baudelaire in a sensitive appreciation of his genius, "unlike the other modern painters who are for the most part either illustrious or obscure daubers, sad specialists old or young, or pure artisans, some making academic figures, others fruits, and still

140

others animals. Delacroix loved everything, and surrendered his mind to every kind of impression." His writings on art praising order, reason, and clarity, Baudelaire continues, reveal that duality in most great artists, "which compels them, as critics, to praise and analyze with all voluptuousness the qualities of which as creators they are most in need, and which are the antithesis of what they possess in abundance."

If Delacroix had praised and extolled what we specially admire in him, the violence, the precipitateness of his gestures, the turbulence of his composition, the magic of his color, we would indeed be astonished. Why search for something one already has abundantly? . . . In the last years of his life all that might be called pleasure had disappeared from his life, a single, avid, exacting, terrible passion having taken its place—work—which was no longer merely a passion, but would have been better described as a fury.

In his one hundred and twenty-six etchings and lithographs Delacroix spoke the language of the Romantic artist. The Romantic School of artists, in reaction against the growing crystallization of bourgeois culture, sought either to combat it or shock it (as did Berlioz or Victor Hugo) or to run away from it to exotic lands or to a Gothic Middle Ages of their own imagination. Delacroix, although not indulging in the excesses and exaggerations of some of the Romantic fraternity, nevertheless was one of their acknowledged leaders. We find therefore in his work many of the leit-motifs of Romanticism, the portrayal of the elemental qualities of wild animals, the exotic note of African sketches, and illustrations for *Les Chroniques de France*, for *Hamlet*, and for *Faust*. The lithograph, *La Sœur de Dugesclin*, from *Les Chroniques de France* (illustration 323) is a most inspired reconstruction of medieval romance. It has color, movement, drama, it is beautifully drawn; in a word a *chef d'œuvre*. Eckermann in his *Conversations with Goethe* in 1826 records the poet's reactions when the first proofs of the *Faust* lithographs (illustration 322) were sent to him from Paris:

The longer this excellent design was looked at, the greater seemed the intelligence of the artist; who made no figure like another, but in each expressed some different part of the action. "M. Delacroix," said Goethe, "is a man of great talent who has found in Faust his proper nourishment.

141

The French censure his wildness, but it suits him well here. He will, I hope, go through all Faust, and I anticipate a special pleasure from the witches' kitchen and the scenes on the Brocken. We can see that he has a good knowledge of life, for which a city like Paris has given him the best opportunity." I observed that these designs greatly conduce to the comprehension of the poem. "Undoubtedly," said Goethe, "for the more perfect imagination of such an artist constrains us to think the situations as beautiful as he has conceived them himself. And if I must confess that M. Delacroix has in some scenes surpassed my own notions, how much more will the reader find all in full life and surpassing his imagination."

Delacroix's aquatint of *The Blacksmith* (illustration 348) shows that he could treat an everyday scene with dignity and grandeur.

In the career of that short-lived genius Théodore Chassériau (1819–1856) the conflicting principles of Ingres and Delacroix were resolved and blended. He combined the purity of Ingres with the richness of Delacroix. His print *œuvre* consists of a series of etchings for *Othello* and a few other etchings and lithographs, of which the *Venus Anadyomène* is an outstanding example (illustration 371). It is interesting to discover that in the nineteenth century artists made more and more use of the nude as a compositional element. They might call their composition by some fancy name such as *Odalisque, Olympia, Venus, Bather, The Horoscope*, but the chief interest after all was in the nude human figure. A half-dozen prints (illustrations 368, 369, 370, 371, 374, and 375) give an idea of the great variety of approach to a single theme. The point of view expressed by these artists begins to approximate the conception of art for art's sake: subject matter is less important than the personality of the artist and a new and original manner of expressing it. Whistler was to establish the doctrine in its most complete form. The theory works successfully in those cases where the artist's personality is richly endowed, where the artist's mentality and feelings become the lens which concentrates some leading idea of humanity or nature as a whole, a definite *Weltanschauung*. In the hands of a petty or incomplete personality, the result becomes banality.

The great painter Gustave Courbet (1819–1877) made only one lithograph, *The Apostle Jean Journet Setting out for the Conquest of*

142

Universal Harmony (illustration 377). Courbet, an expansive, robust, somewhat demagogic personality, championed the doctrine of realism (which viewed in the perspective of time turns out to be far from photographic realism). Not abstract or ideal or exotic subjects, he maintained, but real life was important. However, when he thought that he was copying nature, he really was being only an honest, vigorous, and skillful painter. He was filled with the radical and humanitarian notions current in his time, was persecuted for his active participation in the short-lived Paris Commune of 1871, and died in exile in Switzerland.

One offshoot of the realistic movement was the program of the Return to Nature which animated a group of artists who went to live around the Forest of Fontainebleau. The leading members of this School of Barbizon, as they were sometimes called, were Jacque, Millet, Daubigny, Théodore Rousseau, and Dupré. The names of Corot, Diaz, Barye, and Daumier, are often associated with them. They produced landscapes and rustic scenes in much the same spirit as the Dutch landscape etchers and painters of the seventeenth century. Charles Jacque, an industrious landscape and genre painter, made almost a thousand etchings which, though not deep or profound, nevertheless exhibit a great variety of technical approach in etching, drypoint, and roulette work. His etching, *Pastoral* (illustration 362), portrays the peasants' noonday rest with great economy of means. Jean François Millet (1814–1875) in his dozen important etchings shows a greater depth and nobility of feeling. Norman, peasant-born, Millet, after years of struggle in Paris, returned to the country to consecrate himself to the epic of the soil.

Peasant subjects [he wrote] suit my nature best, for I must confess, at the risk of your taking me for a socialist, that the human side is what touches me most in art, and that could I only do what I liked, or at least attempt to do it, I would paint nothing that was not the result of an impression directly received from Nature, whether in landscape or in figures. . . . I have been reproached for not observing detail; I see it, but I prefer to construct the *synthesis* which as an artistic effort is higher and more robust. You reproach me with insensibility to charm; why, I open your eyes to that which you do not perceive, but which is none the less real: the dramatic.

143

Many of his famous prints were variations of subjects used in his paintings: the etchings of *The Gleaners*, *The Diggers* (illustration 360), *The Churner*, *The Man with the Wheelbarrow*, *The Shepherdess Knitting*, *Woman Feeding a Child*, *The Woolcarder*, and the lithograph of *The Sower*. Millet's work in a sense was a reflection of certain social theories of the time, as promulgated for example by P. J. Proudhon:

To paint men in the sincerity of their nature and their habits, at their work, accomplishing their civic and domestic duties, with their actual countenances, above all without posturing; to surprise them in the undress of their consciousness, as an aim of general education: such seems to me to be the real starting point of modern art.

The purely landscape aspect of the Barbizon School was expressed in the few etchings of Rousseau and the thirty-four etchings and lithographs of Jean Baptiste Camille Corot (1796–1875). Once during a discussion of Delacroix, Corot said, "He is an eagle and I am only a skylark." In a sense this gives the keynote of his character and achievement, at least as far as his prints are concerned. In his prints he is never the great figure painter, but rather the lyric poet celebrating the delicate and subtle moods of nature (illustration 361). In his etchings he built up his effects with a free, almost careless interweaving of lines which suggested rather than defined the forms. He always painted from imagination rather than *en plein air*. When Corot was asked by a colleague for the secret of his painting he replied, "All you have to do is to look at the large masses with half closed eyes." Yes and when you want to see the details? "Then I close my eyes completely." He always had trouble with the biting of his plates, and this service was usually performed for him by his friends Bracquemond, Michelin, or Delaunay. Similar in spirit to the Barbizon landscapes, though not by an artist associated with them, are the thirty-odd etchings of the Dutchman Johann Barthold Jongkind (1819–1891). Like Corot's, his effects are built up by wild and wayward lines, though with greater economy than Corot and with a more vital and nervous stroke. The *Porte d'Honfleur* (illustration 355) is a marvel of direct and forceful approach to a landscape scene.

144

The discussion of landscape painting and etching inevitably leads us to England, for English poets and artists, especially in the last two hundred years, have shown a notable and sensitive appreciation of landscape. At the beginning of the century the activity in oil and watercolor painting was paralleled by the production of many prints, etchings by Crome, Daniell, and Read, soft ground etchings by Cotman, Girtin, and J. R. Cozens, aquatints by Alexander Cozens, Prout, and David Cox (the *Treatise on Landscape Painting* of 1814). But the two most important artists in landscape were Turner and Constable. Turner's *Liber Studiorum* was projected in direct emulation of Claude's sketches in his *Liber Veritatis* which had been translated into etching and mezzotint by Earlom in 1777. The set was planned to consist of one hundred combined etchings and mezzotints but the project was abandoned by Turner owing to lack of popular support after seventy-one had been formally published between the years 1807 to 1819. In most cases the preliminary etched outline was made by Turner himself and proofs exist of the plates in this state. In ten subjects, including the one here reproduced (illustration 300), Turner then added the tone and washes by means of mezzotint. For the balance of the plates he employed such mezzotinters as Charles Turner (no relation), Say, Dunkarton, Clint, Lupton, and others. The *Liber Studiorum* expressed not Turner the great colorist and pathfinder admired by the modern artists of today, but Turner the traditionalist who summed up the landscape schools of the past (especially of Claude) and, in his delineations of wild scenery, the Romantic School current in his day. In his "Prospectus" to the series in 1807 he announced that he "intended in this publication to attempt a classification of the various styles of landscape, viz. the historic, mountainous, pastoral, marine, and architectural." It is as examples of composed or heroic landscapes rather than for their direct observation of nature that Turner's plates are valued today. For direct transcripts from nature, for the moving and subtle delineation of atmospheric effects, for wind and clouds and rain, for sunset and dawn, for the freshness of dew and the brightness of sun, we turn to the collaboration of the painter John Constable and the mezzotinter David Lucas. The first set, *Various Subjects of Landscape*, from which *Summer Evening* is

145

taken (illustration 301), was published in its completed form in 1833. In a tribute to Lucas, Constable wrote, "His great urbanity and integrity are equaled only by his skill as an engraver; and the scenes transmitted by his hand are such as I have ever preferred. For the most part, they are those with which I have the strongest associations—those of my earliest years, when in the cheerful morn of life, I looked to nature with unceasing joy." Constable as a painter was to have considerable influence on Delacroix and others of the French School, for the freshness of his color and the fidelity of his observation of nature. These qualities have been admirably translated into mezzotint by Lucas. In his hands mezzotint became for the first and last time a rich and flexible medium for the interpretation of nature in all its moods.

The revival of interest in the woodcut began in France and England in the 1830's. The way had been prepared by Thomas Bewick of Newcastle (1753–1828). This provincial engraver began in the tradition of the crude and popular woodcut, but in the course of his long life perfected a new style of xylography, the white line engraving. He was not the first to have made such engravings but he was the first to have worked up the technique into a practical method. By working on end grain wood with engraving tools instead of a knife, he was able to build up compositions in which white lines of hitherto unachieved fineness became the dominant motive. This procedure was more in the true spirit of the medium since it is easier to work from black to white on wood and engrave high-lights and break up black masses with fine white lines than it is to scoop out wood on both sides of a black line. His two most famous works were the *History of British Birds*, 1797–1804, and the *History of British Quadrupeds*, 1790, written and illustrated by himself. His plates of natural history are interesting for their able rendering of textures, plumage, and the like. But we turn especially to the tailpieces and vignettes which he inserted at various places in his books. They are filled with charming, racy, and humorous observation of English country life (illustrations 77 and 78). It is England seen by a man of the people, which Bewick always was. In the hands of his followers in England and France white line wood engraving became an efficient reproductive medium especially in connection with book illus-

146

tration. Xylography had always had this great advantage over lithography and the intaglio process—the cuts could be printed simultaneously with the letter press. The regular woodcut, however, had the disadvantage of being crude and lacking in subtlety. With the new method this disability was obviated, since wood engraving could reproduce tonal effects with great flexibility. The impulse of a new technique combined both with the demand of the rising middle-class culture for cheap illustrated books and the existence of a flourishing school of artists produced the so-called renaissance of French book illustration. In 1835 appeared *Gil Blas* with Gigoux's romantic illustrations; in 1838 Curmer's edition of *Paul and Virginia* (illustration 81) with engravings after Huet, Isabey, Meissonier, Français, and Johannot. There is not space enough to consider all the charming and interesting works that came out in the first half of the century with illustrations by Vernet, Raffet, Meissonier, Grandville, Daumier, Gavarni, the Johannots, and others. The name of Doré is associated with imposing illustrations of the Bible, Dante, Coleridge, Rabelais, and Balzac's *Contes Drolatiques*. Doré (1833–1883) was an exuberant, fantastic, and at times melodramatic and superficial illustrator. His fertility of invention was remarkable. Less known are his extraordinary illustrations to Blanchard Jerrold's *London* (illustration 83), a spirited, comprehensive, and somewhat lurid commentary on the heights and depths of a great city. One of the most striking of his designs of their series, the *Prisoners Taking Their Exercise in a Courtyard*, was the inspiration for one of van Gogh's famous paintings.

In Germany woodcut illustration also was popular. Inspired by Vernet's *Napoleon*, Kugler and Menzel brought out in 1840 their monumental *History of Frederick the Great* (illustration 70). Adolph Menzel (1815–1905) was in many ways an amazing artist, amazing in his mastery of minute and factual detail, which he marshaled, by patient research, into some of the most extraordinary historical reconstructions the world has ever seen. He had what might be called a factual imagination: facts inspired him to his highest flights. His reconstruction of the life and times of Frederick the Great in the aforementioned history as well as in the illustrations to Frederick the Great's literary works, and the costumes of his army, was truly unique. Other outstanding works

147

out of an unusually productive *œuvre* are his illustrations to Kleist's *Der Zerbrochene Krug* and the series of lithographs entitled *Versuche auf Stein mit Pinsel und Schabeisen.* The popular uprisings throughout Europe in 1848 found a satiric reflection in Alfred Rethel's *Auch ein Totentanz, Another Dance of Death* (illustration 102). These six woodcuts, though conceived in a hostile spirit, have in the course of time lost something of their partisan animus and remain as a moving and dramatic portrayal of stirring and turbulent times. Ludwig Richter (1803–1884) stands revealed through his work as a charming, benevolent, and sentimental personality, a child who never grew up. It is interesting to note that in his drawings there are no grown-ups: his men and women are never of adult stature, they are merely bigger children. He is at his best when illustrating folk song or fairy tale. A sweet and sentimental charm shines through all his work, a nostalgia for the good old times when life was *gemütlich* and pleasures simple. The complement to Richter's pious and sentimental picture of German life is provided by the woodcuts and text of Wilhelm Busch (1832–1908). Here we find gentle satire and good-humored insight into the foibles of Herr Biedermeyer and his family (illustration 80). The pictorial adventures of his characters, Max and Moritz, were prototypes of our comic strips. Although the new technique of wood engraving was perfected in England, it did not at first stimulate the artists in the production of illustrated books; it was used rather in the interests of factual journalism such as the *London Illustrated News.* In the sixties much notable work was done for wood engraving by Rossetti, Sandys, Keene, and Whistler. Later William Morris, Walter Crane, Shannon, and Ricketts revived the use of the woodcut for book illustration. *When Adam Delved*, designed by Burne-Jones, with the decorative border by William Morris, was the frontispiece to the Kelmscott edition of Morris's stirring socialist romance, *A Dream of John Ball* (illustration 84).

The name of William Blake carries with it the magic of an ineffable secret: he was a man apart, a mystic whose values were created not of this world but of an inner and transcendent light. He would have been the same had he been born at any time and place. It was one of the ironic touches of history that he was born in 1757 and lived for seventy

148

years in the city where Reynolds and Stothard were great and popular. He was an engraver by profession and spent a large part of his life doing hack-work for publishers to earn his daily bread. At the age of fourteen he was apprenticed to a second rate engraver named Basire, whose rather mechanical system of engraving he absorbed. It is unfortunate that he had no better model, for it was not until the end of his life that he was able to shake off some of these mechanical mannerisms and evolve a more beautiful and flexible medium for the expression of his ideas. After his apprenticeship he studied for a time at the Royal Academy School. He already had very definite ideas about art and recounts an anecdote about Moser the academician (of whom we have already heard in connection with Rowlandson):

I was once looking over the prints from Rafael and Michel Angelo in the library of the Royal Academy; Moser came to me and said, "You should not study these old, hard, stiff and dry unfinished works of art. Stay a little and I will show you what you should study." He then went and took me down Le Brun's and Rubens' galleries. How did I secretly rage. I also spoke my mind. . . . I said to Moser, "These things that you call finished are not even begun. How can they then be finished? The man who does not know the beginning never can know the end of art. . . . I am happy to say that Rafael never was from my earliest childhood hidden from me. I saw, and I knew immediately the difference between Rafael and Rubens."

These two artists symbolized for Blake the difference between good and bad art. Drawing, the firm and precise outline, was to him more important than color, tone, and chiaroscuro; in this he was truly Gothic. Art was never the imitation of natural objects, always the expression of an abstract idea. For this reason the sensuousness of Rubens repelled him.

Blake had two great vehicles of expression, poetry and art, and they went hand in hand. He had a momentary flash of acclaim with his *Poetical Sketches* in a circle of fashionable ladies and bluestockings. But the productions of his genius were not understood and he was driven to find a cheap way of setting down in permanent form the thoughts and images that teemed in his consciousness. To this end he perfected

149

the method of "relief etching." John Thomas Smith describes it as Blake told it to him:

Blake, after deeply perplexing himself as to the mode of accomplishing the publication of his illustrated songs, without their being subject to the expense of letter-press, his brother Robert stood before him in one of his visionary imaginations, and so decidedly directed him in the way in which he ought to proceed that he immediately followed his advice, by writing his poetry, and drawing his marginal subjects of embellishments in outline upon the copper plate with an impervious liquid, and then eating the plain parts or lights away with aqua-fortis considerably below them, so that the outlines were left as a stereotype. The plates in this state were then printed in any tint that he wished, to enable him or Mrs. Blake to color the marginal figures in imitation of drawings.

In this manner he produced whole books with text, illustrations, and marginal decorations. The first work to be published was the *Songs of Innocence* in 1789. In 1794 he finished the complement to this, the *Songs of Experience*, in which appears that superb poem on the nature of evil, "Tyger Tyger" (illustration 345). He made numerous other books, *The Book of Thel*, 1789, *The Marriage of Heaven and Hell*, 1793, and the various *Prophetic Books* ending up with the *Milton* of 1808 and the *Jerusalem*, finished in 1821. As illustrated books they are perfection, for the artist-author has completely realized his intention. If much of his writing and visual symbols are seemingly obscure, it is because we have not taken the trouble to learn his language or are not sensitive to mystical experience. Blake had a definite world-conception that was as complete as any single man has ever worked out. It was, however, so far beyond the ken of his contemporaries that he was for the most part misunderstood and neglected. Even when Blake exhibited and later engraved his large picture of the *Canterbury Pilgrims* (1810) —surely understandable enough in its delineation of types—he met with failure. He was given a commission to illustrate the first Eclogue of Virgil for an edition of translations published by Dr. Thornton in 1821. He made seventeen small wood engravings which narrowly escaped recutting since they were not in the style of the mechanical wood engrav-

150

ings of the time. Underneath the first cut the following apology was printed:

The Illustrations of this English Pastoral are by the famous Blake, the illustrator of Young's Night Thoughts and Blair's Grave; who designed and engraved them himself. This is mentioned, as they display less of art than genius, and are much admired by some eminent painters.

Today the book is remembered only because of these wood engravings, for they are among the most lovely designs ever made (illustrations 73 and 74).

Blake's last years would have been passed in abject poverty, had it not been for the friendship and generous aid of John Linnell. It was he who commissioned Blake to engrave the *Illustrations of the Book of Job*, published in twenty-one plates in 1826. This is unquestionably Blake's masterpiece and one of the choicest treasures in the world of art. It is an epic of the imagination, outstanding in pictorial design and felicity of execution, and endowed with a profundity of hidden meaning which only years of study will reveal. Blake has made the problem of Good and Evil the central theme of his drama, for such it may properly be called; and he has resolved this everlasting problem by departing somewhat from the original Bible story and conceiving the conflict in terms of man himself, by making it, in the words of Joseph Wicksteed, "a primarily subjective experience; the account of a man's inward struggle and triumph; the conflict between his indwelling Good and Evil powers." It is Blake's great achievement, alas not recognized during his lifetime, that he not only conceived this stupendous cosmic drama of the human soul, but he also carried it out in a moving and beautiful and precise formulation. One of the loveliest engravings of the series is number fourteen, *When the Morning Stars Sang Together*, and it is reproduced herewith (illustration 344). Two years later Blake died while he was working on a series of engravings for Dante's *Inferno*. Samuel Palmer thus gives his recollection of the man:

He was energy itself, and shed around him a kindling influence, an atmosphere of life, full of the ideal. . . . He was a man without a mask, his aim single, his path straightforward, his wants few, so he was free, noble, and happy. His voice and manner were quiet, yet all awake with intellect. Above the tricks of littleness or the least taint of affectation, with a natural dignity which few would have dared to affront, he was gentle and affectionate, loving to be with little children and to talk about them. . . . Those may laugh at this who did not know such a one as Blake, but of him it is the simple truth.

A small band of young artists gathered with John Linnell in admiration of the venerable Blake. Chief among them were Edward Calvert, George Richmond, and Samuel Palmer. Blake the mystic they did not understand, but they loved and revered the pastoral Blake of the *Songs of Innocence*, and Virgil's Eclogue. Under the direct inspiration of Blake (for he never made a print after 1830) Calvert made a dozen engravings on copper and wood and two lithographs. *The Bride, The Cyder Feast, The Brook*, and *The Return Home* (illustration 75) are filled with sweet arcadian charm. The *Chamber Idyll* (illustration 76) in particular for its delicacy and ecstatic mood and masterly execution is one of the most perfect little prints ever made. Calvert lived until 1883, very much introverted, destroying almost more than he produced. Samuel Palmer (1805-1881) continued the pastoral tradition in his elaborate, minutely worked out etchings (illustration 351). "Those who have seen him," wrote his son, "sitting, sable in hand, hour after hour behind tissue paper, pencilling, in varnish, silver cloudets round a moon; or have seen him revelling in the ferocity of seething mordant with which he sometimes loved to excavate an emphatic passage, will not wonder that he achieved only thirteen etchings." He was a typical Victorian artist; and the *Memoir of Palmer* written by his son gave the Victorians an insight into what they thought was artistic temperament.

In every century, as we have seen, there are one or two artists who stand apart from the main current of their time by the intensity of their inner life or their difficulties in adjusting themselves to their surroundings. In the fifteenth century there was the Master of the Amsterdam Cabinet; in the sixteenth Duvet and Baldung Grien; in the seventeenth Elsheimer, Seghers, and Rembrandt; in the eighteenth Gabriel de St. Aubin and possibly Goya; in the nineteenth Blake and possibly Calvert.

152

To this company of what might be called the Brotherhood of the Inner Life four more names must be added, Meryon, Bresdin, Redon, and Ensor. Charles Meryon (1821–1868) had a tragic life: there was in him a strain of morbid melancholia, he suffered poverty, and he died insane. But no one has ever drawn a portrait of a city with such vivid intensity, or endowed every brick and stone with such personality. And this in spite of the fact that he had no great technical facility in etching. Such etchings as the *Petit Pont*, the *Galerie de Notre Dame*, the *Rue des Mauvais Garçons*, the *St. Etienne du Mont*, the *Abside de Notre Dame*, all etched in the years 1850 to 1854, are immortal. Especially moving is the *Morgue* of 1854 (illustration 340) as successful in its evocation of a mood as it is in its superb rendering of buildings. Jules Andrieu reports Meryon's comment on his etching, *Le Stryge* (illustration 341), which gives a clue as to why his prints have such a moving effect: it is because he was a visionary who lived not in the present but in the past or in a world of his own. Picking up an impression of *Le Stryge*, Meryon said:

You can't tell why my comrades, who know their work better than I do, fail with the Tower of St. Jacques. It is because the modern square is the principal thing for them, and the Middle Age tower an accident. Even if they saw, as I see, an enemy behind each battlement and arms through each loophole; if they expected, as I do, to have the boiling oil and the molten lead poured down on them, they would do far finer things than I can do. For often I have to patch my plate so much that I ought indeed to be a tinker. My comrades are sensible fellows. They are never haunted by this fellow [Le Stryge]. The monster is mine, and that of the men who built this Tower of St. Jacques. He means stupidity, cruelty, lust, hypocrisy; they have all met in that beast.

A legend has been built up by certain critics around the name of Rodolphe Bresdin (1825–1885). They nicknamed him Chien-Caillou and endowed him with an ultra-bohemian character and a garret to live in after the manner of Murger. Redon, whose teacher he was, gives a more sensitive and reasonable estimate of his character. Like Redon himself, he was a gentle visionary, and Redon recounts how "his words directed the painter's eye toward the two worlds of life, toward two realities which it was impossible to separate without a diminution of our art." *La Comédie de la Mort* (illustration 346) is characteristic of his miniature-like workmanship and his fantastic and subtle humor. Redon's own expression is more austere and noble. He sought to give form—always in plastic terms—to the contents of dream and to flights of imagination, inspired by Poe, Goya, the Bible, and Flaubert's *Temptation of St. Anthony*. Among his hundred lithographs are many of startling originality, notably the *Pegase Captif, Yeux Clos, L'Aile* (illustration 347), *Buddha, L'Arbre, Le Jour*, and *La Mort*. Technically they exhibit a range from delicate greys to rich vibrant blacks. Walter Pach has pointed out the extent to which Redon was a precursor of certain modern movements. Blake, of course, had said many of the same things as Redon, but Blake was not known in France. James Ensor, the last of the great visionaries, was born in 1860 and is still alive today. His highly personal and somewhat macabre art is represented in a characteristic etching, the *Cathedral* (illustration 343).

In 1862 Baudelaire wrote an article with the title *"L'Eau-forte est à la Mode"*—Etching is in Fashion—in which he speaks of the work of Meryon, Legros, Manet, Ribot, Whistler, and Jongkind and of the activities of the print-publisher Cadart. Quite a number of professional etchers were attracting notice: the amiable and accomplished Bracquemond (1833–1914), who etched some interesting birds and two striking portraits of Edmond de Goncourt and Meryon (illustration 367), and who gave technical instruction to Corot, Millet, Rousseau, Manet, and Degas. There was Lalanne, who produced a new textbook in etching and many uninspired plates, and Felix Buhot (1847–1898), who etched a number of picturesque and whimsical scenes in Paris and London in the seventies and eighties (illustration 350). This print of the *Débarquement en Angleterre* is technically of interest because it is a counterproof. Such a proof is made by placing a clean sheet of paper on top of a freshly printed proof and running the two through the press. Most of the design will come off in offset, and since the image is always reversed in printing, the design appears as it does on the original copper. Alphonse Legros (1837–1899) started by making crude but powerfully felt etchings of monastic life; later he went to England and turned out soft, innocuous landscapes. The etching, *Death of the Vagabond* (illus-

tra————, —— ——lk—— midway between these two activities. The leading
Bri——h ——cher of the time was an amateur, the well-known surgeon Sir
Fra—cis ——y—— H—den (1818–1910). He was an able and somewhat
dic—to—al Victorian gentleman who had very definite ideas and knew
how to express them both with his pen and his etching needle. He liked
etch——s and collected them. He did not like engravings and repro-
duc—ve work in general, and he wrote against them, exalting etching
at th—r expense, and making a fetish of spontaneous originality. Perhaps
a rea—tion against mediocre reproductive engraving was needed, but he
went too far and condemned it all from Marcantonio to Moreau-le-
Jeune. He himself also etched and used to carry around with him in his
carriage a copper plate ready to draw upon. He made over two hundred
etchings and there was nothing amateurish about them except that they
were done in his leisure time. Like many English country gentlemen
he had a real feeling for landscape, and since he was never at a loss to
express his feelings positively, the best of his etchings are vigorous and
even tender transcripts from nature. Rembrandt was his master, and he
made good use of his instruction. Such plates as *Egham, Water Meadow,
Egham Lock* (illustration 142), the five Welsh plates, *Sunset in Ireland,
Kensington Gardens, Windmill Hill No. 1, Nine Barrow Down,* and
Challow Farm, are a contribution to landscape etching.

Haden's brother-in-law was the American James A. McNeill
Whistler, and as they both had rather peppery personalities they did
not get along very well together. Whistler was born at Lowell, Massa-
chusetts, in 1834. He attended West Point for a while, but not finding
military discipline to his liking, went to Paris to study art. He made
friends with Legros, Bracquemond, Degas, and Fantin-Latour. In 1858
he published a set of etchings. *The French Set,* containing such notable
plates as *La Kitchen, La Vieille* and *Loques, The Mustard Woman,*
and *Street in Saverne.* In some of them the influence of Jacque's and
Meryon's etchings is visible. In the same year he went to London which
became more or less his headquarters until his death in 1903. He was
as able with his tongue and pen as he was with his brush and etching
needle, and remained a thorn in the flesh of British philistinism all his
life. In his famous lawsuit with Ruskin, resulting in an award of one

155

farthing damages, he scored a moral triumph over the very British dicta-tor of prevailing taste. Shortly after his arrival in London he made a series of sixteen carefully worked out etchings known as the *Thames Set* (published in 1871), of which the outstanding examples are the *Black Lion Wharf, Rotherhithe*, the *Limeburner* (illustration 349), the *Hungerford Bridge*, the *Thames Police*, and *Limehouse*. In these early etchings, inspired by the bustle of London's shipping and industry, he made a complete statement of what he saw. In his painting he was influ-enced to a certain extent by Velasquez and Rossetti, by the Impres-sionists, and by Japanese prints. He painted a number of well-known portraits including *Carlyle*, his *Mother, Duret*, and the *Leylands*. A reflection of this phase of his activity is seen in the dry point of his niece Annie Haden (illustration 359). He was very fond of this plate, and wrote on the proof in the Avery collection, "One of my very best." Mansfield quotes him as saying that if he were required to rest his reputa-tion on any one print, as a matter of technical achievement, he would be willing to rest it on that. Other notable portrait prints are *Bibi Lalouette, Becquet, Riault the Engraver, Drouet*, and *Fanny Leyland*. In the course of the years his artistic expression changed. His signature developed from the name Whistler into a stylized Butterfly. He became interested not in portraying a scene in its detailed form but in suggesting a mood, in rendering and setting down a definite "impression" from which all but the contributing details were tastefully excluded. In this he was allied to the French Impressionists, but where their leading motive was a greater sense of reality or scientific management of light, his keynote was largely decorative, a poetic impression of exquisiteness and irre-sponsible beauty. He truly became the Butterfly that composed lyrics in a lighter vein. His etchings have all the spontaneous charm of an improvisation, but many of his lesser plates suffer from this very quality, for the sketch can easily become trivial. "Taste," wrote Arthur Symons, "in Whistler was carried to the point of genius and became crea-tive." The full expression of this attitude appeared in the twelve etchings known as the *First Venice Set* published in 1880, and which contained the *Palaces*, the *Nocturne* (illustration 353), the *Traghetto*, the *Door-way*, and the *Riva*. He repeated this success with another *Venice Set*,

156

the *Twenty-six Etchings of 1886, San Biagio, Turkeys, Nocturne: Palaces, Upright Venice, The Garden, The Balcony, Nocturne: Furnace,* and *Lagoon: Noon*. In these etchings the effect is greatly enhanced by Whistler's masterly printing. Indeed so dependent was he on printing that an etching like *Nocturne* is practically a monotype. In addition to his four hundred and sixty etchings he made about one hundred and sixty lithographs which have much the same qualities, fugitive visions, delicate and poetic effects of atmosphere, such as the *Thames, St. Giles in the Fields, Little Evelyn, Steps: Luxembourg Gardens, The Horoscope, Dancing Girl,* and *Old Battersea Bridge*. The effect produced by a lithotint such as *Nocturne: The Thames at Battersea* (illustration 352), he has also produced in words:

And when the evening mist clothes the riverside with poetry, as with a veil, and the poor buildings lose themselves in the dim sky, and the tall chimneys become campanili, and the warehouses are palaces in the night, and the whole city hangs in the heavens, and fairy land is before us—then the wayfarer hastens home; the working man and the cultured one, the wise man and the one of pleasure, cease to understand, as they have ceased to see, and Nature, who, for once, has sung in tune, sings her exquisite song to the artist alone.

Whistler, in his writing and in his work carried to its extreme the doctrine of art for art's sake, where the artist's personality and taste become the sole source of value. In his reaction against the stodginess of the Victorian story-telling picture he went to another extreme. In spite of his ruthless wit and striving for effect, he had his integrity as an artist, and he was a patient and tireless and fastidious craftsman.

A picture is finished [said he] when all trace of the means used to bring about the end has disappeared. To say of a picture, as is often said in its praise, that it shows great and earnest labor, is to say that it is incomplete and unfit for view. Industry in Art is a necessity—not a virtue—and any evidence of the same, in the production, is a blemish, not a quality; a proof, not of achievement, but of absolutely insufficient work, for work alone will efface the footsteps of work. The work of the master reeks not of the sweat of the brow—suggests no effort—and is finished from the beginning.

157

Whistler has his place in history as an aristocratic and exquisite poet, a high priest of Personal Art, that "goddess of dainty thought—reticent of habit, abjuring all obtrusiveness, purposing in no way to better others —seeking and finding the beautiful in all conditions and in all times."

In France a group of Whistler's contemporaries were making art history. They were all great painters, and because they were distinguished artists their prints have an importance and significance greater than that of the often larger production of the professional printmakers. First there was Manet (1832–1883). In his famous *Manifesto to the Public* in 1867 he wrote: "M. Manet has always recognized genius wherever he found it and he has never aimed to overthrow an ancient tradition of art or to establish a new one. He has merely sought to be himself and no other." This sums up his achievement in a few words. In neither his life nor his works was Manet deliberately subversive of tradition; viewed in the perspective of time, much of his art, that was so excoriated by contemporary criticism, is seen to be merely a purification of the academic tendencies of his day. The one thing he insisted on was that art be true to life and to the personality of the creator, and he sought for a technique which would most adequately give expression to this for himself. Manet had independent means and was essentially a gentleman of the world. He went to his studio and painted pictures, "as regularly," said Zola, "as other people go to their offices and counting-houses." He made seventy-five etchings and twenty-one lithographs. His etchings are typically painter's etchings: he was more interested in color and tactile values than in line work as an end in itself. He had what Baudelaire called *"un gout decidé pour la realité."* With Manet this enhanced vision of form was instinctive and immediate: he did not have to perform a laborious synthesis in order to give it expression, and it is this that gives his prints their vigor, spontaneity and verve (illustration 357). His etching, *Olympia* (illustration 375), a free translation of his famous painting, was etched as a frontispiece to a pamphlet which Zola wrote in defense of Manet's art.

Degas, like Manet, had independent means, but he was more aloof and sardonic in temperament. He had an absorbing passion to draw and paint, a passion to capture the elusive, to set down for all time the fleet-

158

ortalize the significant gesture or movement. "You sell my work," he grumbled. "I always hope eventually to do better." Degas had a trenchant wit and many stories are told about him. Vollard relates:

someone call Monsieur Degas! It was Vibert, the he Cardinals. You must come to see our exhibition Then he gave a sidelong glance at the old mackintosh Degas was wearing, and added: "You may find our frames and rugs a little too fancy for you, but art is always a luxury, isn't it?" "Yours, perhaps," retorted Degas, "but mine is an absolute necessity."

He painted and made pastels; he modeled in wax; he made drawings, countless studies which he hoarded in his studio; he experimented with etching and aquatint and lithograph. He made about sixty prints altogether, some of them frankly experimental but others among the most perfect and completely realized prints ever made. Take for example the lithograph, *Mlle Bécat aux Ambassadeurs* (illustration 378); how complete and moving is the evocation of the scene in the *café chantant*, the sight, the smell, the sound of it; or the *Sortie de Bain* (illustration 368), what wealth of meaning there is in that intimate picture of a fat woman. The etching and aquatint, *Au Louvre* (illustration 358), contains a portrait of his friend and fellow-artist Mary Cassatt. "Cassatt has infinite talent," Degas remarked musingly. "I remember the time we started a little magazine called *Le Jour et la Nuit* together. I was very much interested in print processes then, and had made countless experiments. . . . You can get extraordinary results with copper." Mary Cassatt, though American born, lived most of her life in France and painted chiefly mothers and children. She made a number of charming etchings and drypoints and some aquatints in color inspired by Japanese prints (illustration 356).

Pissarro had the largest print *œuvre* of any of the Impressionists, having made 122 etchings and 67 lithographs. His best work, as exemplified by the charming *Goose Girl* (illustration 363), has the smell of earth and moist fresh dew upon it. Renoir, the healthiest and most sensuous and natural of the group, put the stamp of his expansive personality upon everything he touched, be it oil painting, pastel, sculpture, or his few etchings and lithographs (illustration 370). He created instinctively and elementally. He loved color and sunlight and children and mother-hood and the ruddy skin and rounded forms of buxom women; and this love of his radiated from his every work. No greater contrast can be imagined than between Renoir and van Gogh, both sun-worshipers. But where Renoir just basked in the sun, van Gogh reached for it passionately to illumine the dark night of his soul. Van Gogh made only one etching, the striking portrait of Dr. Gachet (illustration 366). Van Gogh wrote to his brother:

I have seen Dr. Gachet, who gives me the impression of being rather eccentric, but his experience as a doctor must keep him balanced enough to combat the nervous trouble from which he certainly seems to me to suffer at least as seriously as I do. . . . When he spoke of Belgium and the days of the old painters, his grief-hardened face grew smiling again, and I really think that I shall keep on being friends with him and that I shall do his portrait.

Dr. Gachet was the same doctor who knew Meryon at the asylum of Charenton.

The name of Gauguin has been surrounded with a halo of romantic legend. His life, to be sure, was picturesque enough, wild adventures between Europe and South America, a successful business career, the renunciation of business and family for the pursuit of art, and finally the renunciation of a whole civilization in favor of a savage Eden which Strindberg dramatically rejected: "You have created a new heaven and a new earth, but I do not enjoy myself in the midst of your creation. It is too sun-drenched for me, who enjoy the play of light and shade." In his life there was much travail of flesh and spirit.

I have known [he wrote] extreme misery, that is to say I have been hungry and I have been cold and all that follows therefrom. That is nothing or almost nothing; one gets used to it. But what is terrible in one's misery is the frustration of one's work, and of the development of one's intellectual faculties. It is true that suffering sharpens the faculties. But it must not be too much, otherwise it kills you.

160

There is no trace of poverty, suffering, and sickness in his works from the South Seas: the forms are big and serene, the mood exalted. Out of odd flat bits of wood he made wood engravings such as never had been made before, blocks that were cut and scratched and sandpapered in unconventional ways, forms that were distorted in the interest of design or emotive effect, subjects that were taken from Tahitian life and legend.

It is because these prints go back to the most primitive time of engraving [he wrote to de Monfried] that they are interesting. Wood engraving for illustration has become like photogravure, detestable. A drawing by Degas beside a copy of the drawing done by hatchers! I am sure that in time my wood engravings being done now will have a certain value.

(At the time there were no buyers at eight francs apiece.) The best of these, such as *The Night*, *Maruru*, *Fair Land*, *Te Faruru*, and *Te Atua*, have a strange and moving beauty. *Mahna no Varua Ino* (illustration 373) is filled with the magic and mystery of the jungle at night. Stripped of legend and fable the story of Gauguin is simply the story of a man with a terrific urge to create, the triumph of a demonic will.

Spend yourself, spend yourself again! . . . I believe that life has no meaning unless one lives it with a will, at least to the limit of one's will. Virtue, good, evil are nothing but words, unless one takes them apart in order to build something with them; they do not win their true meaning until one knows how to apply them.

Cézanne was the painter's painter, that is to say his great contribution was technical and only indirectly in terms of the human spirit. He was absorbed during his whole life in what Read calls "the knitting together of form and color into a co-ordinated harmony," or as Cézanne himself put it "to make a Poussin out of nature," to combine the architectonic concept of the classical painters with the color perception of the Impressionists.

Everything we see [said Cézanne] is dispersed and disappears. Nature is always the same, but nothing remains of it, nothing of what we see. Our art should give to nature the thrill of continuance with the appearance of all its changes. It should enable us to feel nature as eternal.

All this is related to the problem of Cézanne as a painter, but some reflection is given in his prints—he made but six—such as the color lithograph, *The Bathers* (illustration 372). Here the artist has created a microcosm, as Wilenski calls it, of planes and forms and color in which each part is pleasurably and vitally connected with every other part. To do this successfully, to make the parts all fit together harmoniously, a certain amount of distortion is necessary. The distortion which most people notice is the deviation from their preconceived notion of the appearance of the human figure, although there are equally wide deviations from the appearance of other natural objects. If these people would stop fixing their eyes on the figures in their effort to correct the supposed defects of anatomy, and, instead, look directly into the picture beyond the figures and enjoy the pleasurable perspective of space, then the figures would take their proper place and seem strangely solid and real. This is the beginning of an adventure in perception and appreciation which will bring great delight and continued satisfaction to the seeing eye. The people who are bothered by distortion are like the people who refuse to enjoy Chaucer because the words are so queer.

And now we come to the Gay Nineties. There were the posters, a new and fascinating art by Lautrec, Steinlen (illustration 381), Cheret, Willette, and Léandre. There were the woodcuts and wood engravings which the etcher and engraver Auguste Lepère (illustration 408) and his associates were trying to revive as a popular art in the publication, *L'Image*. Bonnard and Vuillard were setting down their breezy impressions of Paris in color lithographs (illustration 331) so different from the precise statements of Boys or Girtin. Fantin-Latour was still making his soft lithographs inspired by the music of Berlioz and Wagner (illustration 383) and the young Swede Zorn was already etching his brilliantly superficial plates (illustration 382). Forain was drawing and etching (illustration 406) and Vallotton cutting bold woodcuts (illustration 104). Across the channel Beardsley and Max Beerbohm were making drawings, and Conder and Rothenstein and Shannon making their lithographs (illustration 403). But the artist who perhaps best summed up the period, its odd mixture of glamor and tinsel, its decadence and *fin de siècle* pose was Henri de Toulouse-Lautrec. He was born in 1864, a descendant of the famous Counts of Toulouse. He died of drink and dissipation at the age of thirty-seven. He was crippled and conspicuously ugly: fate cast him for the role of observer. He watched life, but was never of it, the sporting life at the race course (illustration 380), the gay life of the theater, music hall, and cabaret (illustrations 365 and 379). He lived for a while in a *maison close* and became the friend and confidant of the inmates. It was out of this intimate knowledge that he drew the set of ten lithographs, *Elles*, and the vividly realized *Étude de Femme* (illustration 369). He started making lithographs in 1892 and in the next nine years drew more than three hundred and fifty. He had a trenchant and vital line and a sardonic sense of character. "*Vraiment, vous êtes le génie de la déformation,*" exclaimed Yvette Guilbert when she saw one of his caricatures of her, but she grew to like it just the same. Yvette Guilbert, the greatest of music hall singers, summed up the period, too, in her way. "Yvette begins to sing," wrote Arthur Symons, "and immediately the gay world that you see across the smoke of your cigarette, seems to unmask itself, becomes too suddenly serious, tragic, a piece of real existence."

So we come to the end of the nineteenth century, extraordinary in its variety and complexity, and brimming over with startling contrasts. No century has had richer material. There was a great impetus to printmaking not only through the enlargement of the buying public but also through the invention of new techniques, lithography and aquatint and the new wood engraving. But the technique which was to have the widest influence on nineteenth-century art was photography. It is less than a hundred years since the perfection of its technique by Wedgwood, Davy, Niépce, Daguerre, Talbot, and others, but it has already completely revolutionized printmaking. Through the development of photo-engraving, the line cut and the halftone, it stripped regular printmaking completely of its reproductive function. It could make a facsimile of an artist's drawing more quickly and more cheaply than the other processes, and it had the further advantage that it could be printed simultaneously with letter press. It was the Gillotype or early version of the line cut, that supplanted lithography as the medium for political caricature in the fifties. Photography, as an art for itself,

163

has passed through stages of experimentation, of commercialization, and of creative mastery. It is foolish to maintain that photography can never become an art because of the mechanical elements inherent in the process. If one does so, one must logically banish all the print processes for lithography, engraving, and the rest of them, also make use of mechanical aids, and are capable of indefinite reproduction. Many of the old woodcuts and engravings which we so admire as works of art, were commercial productions in their day. A photograph is as much of a "print" as an etching or a lithograph. The essential element in every case is the conscious use of common materials by the human mind and imagination. There are photographs by recognized masters that have a singing quality of perfection as obviously and definitely as any etching or woodcut. Out of the wealth of material at hand three examples have been chosen to typify the achievement of photography. No attempt has been made to follow its production through all its ramifications in the twentieth century—that would require a book in itself. All three examples reproduced have a definite art quality, expressive of the personality of the creator. The first is the *Portrait of Mrs. Anna Jameson* (illustration 384) by David Octavius Hill (1802–1870). Hill was a Scotch painter who turned to photography in collaboration with the chemist Adamson, to help him in his painting. Now he is remembered for his photographs and not for his paintings. Eugène Atjet (1856–1927) devoted most of his life to making a straightforward portrait of every aspect of Paris life with stand camera and dry plate. In his photograph of a shop window on the Avenue des Gobelins (illustration 385), the skillful use of the accidentals of window reflections contributes greatly to the vividness of the scene. Another genius of photography in technical skill, psychological insight, and creative vision is Alfred Stieglitz (1864–   ). His control of every detail of selection, angle of vision, exposure, and printing builds up in *The Hand of Man* (illustration 386) definite esthetic and psychological values that haunt the imagination. A born experimenter and keenly alive to the significant currents of his time, he was among the first to photograph night and rainy scenes, airplanes, skyscrapers, and industrial scenes. His portraits and those

164

interpretations of nature's moods called *Equivalents* are true master-pieces.

Photography functions at its best as a faithful transcript of external reality. It has served science more than it has served art. Only in the hands of a few masters have its art possibilities been developed. I have mentioned the enormous influence that photography has had upon print-making in freeing it of many of its reproductive or practical functions. Does this mean that prints now have no *raison d'être* whatsoever? Not at all. As I have said in *Fine Prints Old and New:*

There still remain some things that photography cannot do, and that the printmaker can do very well. Photography is of the moment, a snap-shot, an instantaneous cross-section of reality more or less faithfully re-corded. In a portrait, photography can reproduce a thousand different moods and expressions in the subject, each one of them more or less true, but no one of them the whole subject. Synthesis—that is where the artist comes in. He can fuse many separate aspects into one significant whole. Of course it does not follow that the artist's is necessarily a truer portrait, since it will be a portrait of one personality filtered through another personality. But at least, if the artist is proficient and psychologically aware, it will con-tain a greater number of aspects, and thus more nearly approximate the whole. It is possible, no doubt, given photographic genius and an infinite amount of patience, to seize upon the significant or characteristic expression at those rare moments when the sitter himself approaches it. But such things do not happen often. Again, photography has by its nature certain funda-mental limitations. It is focused toward the outward aspect of things; it records behavior rather than motives. It does not readily lend itself to the creation of types or to symbolic expression generally. Since, however, photography has taken over certain of their functions, the graphic arts are free to carry on in another plane. In the objectifying and stimulation of collective emotions, in satire and caricature, in symbolism and synthesis of all kinds, in all purposive directions difficult to express in photography, the artist and printmaker have ample opportunity to give forth the best that is in them.

7. Twentieth Century

IF the keynote of the nineteenth century was personality, the keynote of the twentieth century is flux. The tempo of civilization had been steadily increasing: lightning changes, violence, tumultuous upheavals, epach-making discoveries are the order of the day. An old order is crumbling. The individual is being submerged in the coalescing of vast collective forces. World movements are on their way. The greatest and most devastating war the world has ever known was fought in this century. Countries, nations, and peoples are shuffled about on the world map as never before. Treaties are made to be broken, wars are waged without being declared. Generals die in bed; defenseless civilians, women, and children are murdered in cold blood. International morality is declared bankrupt; diplomacy becomes a sordid and shoddy piece of chicanery. The Frankensteins of destruction are creeping up on mankind. Heroism, self-sacrifice, and idealism function side by side with cruelty, profiteering, and exploitation. Speed and more speed, power and more power! Man talks to man in the antipodes. We travel across a continent in a day, and around the world in a week. Man has become master of stupendous forces which he knows not how to use. Nature is in harness for monopolists and not for humanity at large. Values are shifting from day to day, concepts of justice, of courts, of property rights and human rights, movements of labor; nothing is stable and secure. A man was rich yesterday and is poor today; a country is at peace today and may be embroiled in war tomorrow. Everybody is bewildered, the leaders as well as the led. "We don't know where we are going but we are on our way." Orozco made a powerful lithograph, *Leaders*—a restless sea of sombreros above which, through the exigencies of time and chance, have been tossed up two or three other sombreros, no bigger or better than the rest: these are the leaders. Values are

166

changing in literature, music, and art. The artists are searching for a unifying or stable principle. Styles are born and flourish in bewildering succession. In addition to the older styles still current, there have appeared in the course of the century such movements as Fauvism, Cubism, Expressionism, Futurism, Orphism, Suprematism, Constructivism, Dadaism, Purism, Neo-classicism, Neoplasticism, *Die Neue Sachlichkeit*, and Surrealism. Once, as we have seen, an epoch or a century dominated the artist's expression; later he molded his own manner of speech. Now the artist, Picasso for example, runs through a half a dozen styles during his lifetime. Not only in their expression but also in their lives are the artists drawn into the stress and turmoil of today. They are forced to reckon with a community apparently indifferent to their contribution and welfare, to reinterpret through bitter experience the old patterns of collector, patron, and dealer, and to come to terms with society economically as well as esthetically. Gone are the ivory towers of yesterday.

Such is the background that the twentieth-century artists have tried to interpret or come to terms with in their own tentative and experimental way. And they have done it in various ways. A few, such as Davies (illustration 389), have tried to escape into a world of poetic imagination; a few, such as Eric Gill (illustration 85), have found stability in the dogmas of the Church. Many have tried to ignore it and go on with their accustomed ways by holding fast to traditional modes of expression and subject-matter, either the medieval tradition as in Austin or Griggs (illustration 390) or the tradition of 1880 as in the main body of conservative English and American etchers. Still others, strong individualists, have concentrated upon their own personal expression and style in the hope that they can create works so original and striking that society will come to their doorstep. But still others try to interpret the background honestly to the best of their ability. The problem of the artist and his time can be summed up in a sort of parable of river currents. Artists either swing with the current of their times and derive power from it, or else they swim against it if they are powerful and individualized enough. Those who add their own motive or creative power to that of the current, travel far and have much to see. Those who fight against the current either make a big splash or sink beneath the stream to find a fairy grotto there, or else it is said of them after their death that they saw much and traveled in strange directions and discovered new streams. There are some who do not swim against the current yet do not exert much motive power of their own. These are the traditionalists. They just drift down stream, they see things, too, but not much more than others have already seen, and sometimes they land in stagnant waters.

The conservative etching is, as I have said, largely of the tradition of 1880 and is based upon the work of Rembrandt, Whistler, Meryon, Haden, Cameron, and their derivatives. It is more concerned with literal representation than with emotive design. Yet even its literal representation has been corrupted by the impressionist approach; it is neither accurate representation or powerful impression; it falls somewhere between into a vague and sentimental picturesqueness. It is interesting to contrast the average architectural etching of today with similar old prints by Malton, Pugin, Boys, Girtin, and Meryon: one could almost reconstruct the buildings from the prints by the older artists, whereas it would be much more difficult to do so from the average print of today. There is a difference, too, between the characters created by Rembrandt and the sentimental and picturesque types in contemporary etching; or the crisp and vital approach to nature exhibited by past printmakers (up to and including the Impressionists) and the innocuous and repetitive versions of most of the present etchers. The conservatives are not doing their duty by posterity, since posterity will not be able to look at their work and get much idea of how we looked and felt and acted. Of course there are exceptions to this rule, but an enormous amount of second- and third-rate work has and is being done in the conservative tradition, and it has overshadowed whatever meritorious work has been done in this genre (illustrations 92, 93, 388, 408, 410, 411, 413, and 423). Mediocre work, to be sure, is also being done in the modern tradition, but for the moment there is more vitality in the movement. The conservatives have nothing new to say and have discovered no new way of saying it. An artist, even if he does not invent a new form, can at least say something new about his own time, which is constantly chang-

168

ing. When an artist works in a pattern or formula that is well known, he must speak with unusual creative intensity in order to overcome in the beholder the indifference of familiarity. The moderns, then, have the advantage of a vital momentum: they have something new to say and they say it in a forceful manner. It is forceful because they make use of design and distortion to emphasize the impression they wish to create. A comparison of two prints by Benson and Benton will illustrate what I mean. The *Mallards at Evening* (illustration 388) is a literal representation of birds in flight very much as the lens of a camera might register it. But it is static: there is no suggestion of motion. In Benton's *Locomotive* (illustration 401) every element of the composition is designed to communicate the sensation of motion and speed. A similar comparison could be made between Zorn's *Waltz* (illustration 382) and Covarrubias's *Lindy Hop* (illustration 422), or between Forain's *Témoins à l'Audience* (illustration 406) and Gropper's *The Judge* (illustration 431), in which the artist's purpose and intention have determined the form and given it a dynamic quality absent in the first work.

On the basis of their work, modern artists may be divided into two broad classifications: the artists for whom subject-matter is important, and the artists for whom personal expression is important. Under these two headings nearly all the modern artists can find their place. Among the artists for whom the subject-matter is important are naturally included all those who attempt to interpret the background of today. There is, for example, Pennell's lithograph of the building of the Panama Canal (illustration 391). Joseph Pennell, disciple and biographer of Whistler, was one of the first to glorify modern industry and the Wonder of Work. He took Whistler's impressionistic technique and made of it a facile descriptive formula. Murihead Bone's *Ship-building* (illustration 392) and Kravchenko's *Dnieprostroi* (illustration 100) are examples of straightforward and somewhat more solid reporting. Artists have reacted to the industrial scene in several other ways: as the basis of ingenious and beautiful design in Cook's *Bridge* (illustration 397) or Huntley's *Coke* (illustration 399); as a synthesis of an industry as a whole in Lozowick's *Tanks* (illustration 398); and as a symbolic representation of man's relation to the machine in Sternberg's *Construction*

169

or *Dance of the Machines* (illustrations 400 and 436). The significant aspects of traffic and speed have been dramatized in such typical examples as Benton's *Locomotive* (illustration 401), Spruance's *Road to the Shore* (illustration 395), Gertrude Hermes' *Through the Windscreen* (illustration 393), Nevinson's *Airplane* (illustration 441), and Marin's *Downtown New York* (illustration 394). Other aspects of the material of today are treated by artists in what might be called reportage flavored by temperament and a dash of powerful design. There is, for example, the world of sport, exemplified by Murphy, Segonzac (illustration 412), Spruance, or by Bellows in *A Stag at Sharkey's* (illustration 404), involving not only description but movement and psychological values as well. The world of the theater and dancing may be utilized for an impressionistic sketch in Sickert's *Gaité Montparnasse* (illustration 387), for flavor and atmosphere in Pascin's *Cabaret* (illustration 405), or for the stylized significant gesture in Covarrubias's *Lindy Hop* (illustration 422). Landscapes are made, not by formula but under the impulse of a personally felt vision, the attempt to see things as they are or to communicate to the beholder a definite mood or impression, as in the work of Dehn, Wickey, Mahonri Young (illustration 409) and Hopper (illustration 407). There is the discovery that figures in everyday life can be monumental as well as rowdy or picturesque in the etchings of Cadmus, Hayes Miller, Isabel Bishop, and Marsh. John J. A. Murphy has combined the use of modern subject-matter with important research in technique and optics, in the breaking-up of forms for emotive effect and in the application of optical focus for the suggesting of planes in recession (illustration 96).

In much of modern work there is at least the nuance of a psychological approach. In the old sporting prints nothing but the scene was portrayed; nowadays an attempt is made also to enter into the feelings of the participants and spectators. The moderns suggest psychological subtleties never employed before: a plate such as Brockhurst's *Adolescence* (illustration 418) could not have been made before modern times. Likewise Dwight's *Queer Fish* (illustration 420), Cook's *Mexican Interior* (illustration 416), and Soyer's *Mission* (illustration 419) suggest character against a background of genre in a way undreamed of by the

170

Dutch genre etchers. Wanda Gág's *Lamplight* (illustration 415) dramatizes psychological values in spite of the absence of figures, and conversely Kent's *Pinnacle* (illustration 402) dramatizes the feeling of a mountain-top through a human figure. Some artists have carried the psychological approach still farther in their effort to set down the essence of things. Franz Marc's *Annunciation* (illustration 88) is an illuminating example of this. Contrast its treatment with that of an older master such as Baroccio (illustration 165). In the modern print all the emphasis is concentrated upon the inner feelings of Mary, feelings so exalted and profound that for the moment they have become cosmic and are shared by all the world of nature and animals. Everything in the picture, the design, the darting rays, the staccato accents, all contribute to this feeling of ecstasy; everything unessential, mere representation, has been left out. The artist has truly dramatized ecstasy. Similarly Gerhard Marcks has dramatized the feeling of triumph in *Cats* (illustration 95). Leon Underwood, Raoul Dufy, and Wanda Gág (illustration 91) have made similar contributions. Max Weber has brought out the essence of the mother-and-child feeling in his woodcut (illustration 86) and Edvard Munch, a pioneer in this approach, has suggested the psychological reverberations of death in his woodcut (illustration 97). Munch had considerable influence upon the German Expressionists, but they took his method and applied it to the expression of their own inner psyche, whereas his own work, though highly charged with psychological values, is still, I believe, an attempt to get at the essence of an external object or situation. In *Downtown New York* (illustration 394) Marin has registered an impression of the speed and noise of city traffic. It is impressionistic in approach but it differs from the Impressionists in that the field of its drama is largely an inner consciousness. It is not decorative or charming: it is an attempt to record a psychological truth. An interest in and concern with psychological values, then, is one of the touchstones of modern art.

Another touchstone is the growth of social consciousness. This feeling had been developing in many artists all through the nineteenth century (Daumier, Millet, Courbet, Pissarro, Steinlen, and William Morris), but it received a powerful impetus through the devastating

171

World War and subsequent depression. Social consciousness, in brief, is a stressing of the essential solidarity of all human beings and a feeling that the world might be made a better place to live in. It was a new quest for an earthly paradise. This feeling had existed for centuries in a vague sort of way. In the second half of the nineteenth century several sociologists and economists, notably Marx and Engels among others, not only analyzed the injustices of the present scheme of society but also suggested a technique for their abolition. This is no place to judge of the rightness of their analysis and plan; it is merely necessary to record that more and more people are believing it to be right and are acting accordingly. The impact of so powerful an idea has had an effect upon artists as it has upon men and women in every walk of life. It has become a living issue capable of swaying people into action very much as religion used to do. The reaction of artists varies according to their temperament and conditioning. With most of them social consciousness goes no farther than a generalized feeling for humanity as a whole, a sympathy for the downtrodden and oppressed, and a painful realization of the horrors of war. Most of them would deny the appellation of communist or even socialist, and rightly so: they are fellow-travelers who go only part of the way. Social consciousness is in the air and they have absorbed it from the exigencies of the times and not from the doctrines of the political economists. There are a few artists, however, who have acquired such a burning conviction about the teachings of Marx that they have been impelled to master all the intricacies of its dogmas and carry its issues into their lives and works.

For an artist holding a communist ideal and working in what is admittedly a transition period, there are, it seems to me, two main avenues of expression. The first is critical, directing satire and tragic irony against the present social order, in particular against such bulwarks of the system as organized religion and politics and such fearful manifestations as war and fascism. The second is constructive, a glorification of the heroes of the class struggle and a vision, in general terms, of a better world. This last must necessarily be expressed in general terms since with so far-reaching and complicated a structure as modern society, the artists, no more than the political economists themselves,

172

have any clear idea of the ultimate working out of a new order. The artists express themselves both in personal and in general terms. In Dehn's *All for a Piece of Meat* (illustration 429) and Peggy Bacon's *Patroness* (illustration 424) the satire is personal; in Beckmann's *The Curtain Falls* (illustration 427), Kent's *Twilight of Man* (illustration 89), and Orozco's *Mouths* (illustration 430) we have an ironic reflection of society as a whole. In Soyer's *Bowery Nocturne* or *The Mission* (illustration 419), in Mabel Dwight's *Derelicts*, in Orozco's *Requiem* (illustration 439), in Picasso's *Le Repas Frugal* (illustration 428), and in numerous prints by Käthe Kollwitz we sense a deeply felt sympathy for humanity; whereas in Rouault's moving *Misère* (illustration 425) we see all man's misery concentrated in a single human figure; and in Käthe Kollwitz's equally moving *Death and the Mother* (illustration 426) we see the agonizing conflict between life and death in a mother's consciousness. More definitely class-conscious are Gropper's *The Judge* (illustration 431), Masereel's and Kollwitz's *The Strike* (illustrations 99 and 432), Sternberg's *Dance of the Machines* (illustration 436), and Grosz's *The Robbers* (illustration 434). In some of Orozco's murals and in Lamar Baker's *Religion* (illustration 433) we find a satiric attack on religion. In relation to war Vallotton (illustration 104), Kollwitz (illustration 438), and Dix (illustrations 440 and 442) have stressed the human side, and Grosz (illustration 437) and Lynd Ward (illustration 101) the more class-conscious aspect. To the glorification of heroes Rivera (*Zapata*), Siqueiros (*Zapata*), Kollwitz (*Liebknecht*), Gellert, and numerous Russians including Sakhnorskaya (illustration 98) have contributed. Just as Christianity, with the aid of its artists, created a mythology, so a symbolism is being built up around the left movement, with heroes, martyrs, and villains (illustration 434), and inspiring and edifying parables.

While artists were making a brave attempt to record the background of a changing world, others were making research in self-expression. The artists for whom personal expression is the primary impulse can be divided into several groups. First there are the artists who are strongly individualized and are concerned chiefly with esthetic self-expression. Most of them have built up a great reputation with their paintings, and carry over into their prints the qualities that brought them renown in their easel pictures. Conspicuous among these is Henri Matisse, who wrote: "What I dream of is an art of balance, of purity and serenity devoid of troubling or depressing subject-matter, an art which might be for every mental worker, be he business man or writer, like an appeasing influence, like a mental soother, something like a good armchair in which to rest from physical fatigue." His lithograph, *Liseuse* (illustration 445), is a swift but vivid realization of a reading figure, and, like others of the group, is characterized by a subtle and unified sense of color, distortion for the sake of esthetic design, and a practiced facility of execution. All these artists have attained a personal style which is their hallmark; collectors acquire their work not for the subject-matter but as specimens of the artist's treatment of any subject whatsoever. Other typical examples are reproduced from the prints of Derain (illustration 443), Charlot (illustration 421), Kuniyoshi (illustration 444), and Ganso (illustration 417).

Other artists carried the flight from subject-matter still farther and became interested in a completely non-representational abstract art. Taking a cue from certain paintings of Cézanne and from Negro sculpture they began a drastic simplification of natural forms into rough cubes and cylinders, masses and planes which they organized into an esthetically satisfying whole. Although certain artists such as Léger built up a theory that such an esthetic was the most complete expression of our mechanized civilization, it has been demonstrated by Schapiro that the whole movement appealed only to a very limited and luxurious class, carefully shielded from the realities of life. This tendency toward abstraction expressed itself in two ways. The first in three-dimensional design, a play of planes and their intersections, *cubism*, in the paintings of Picasso, Braque, Léger, Gleizes, Metzinger, Rivera, and Marcel Duchamp, and in the etchings of Picasso, Jacques Villon, and Braque (illustration 447). The other in flat two-dimensional color patterns often with *collage* of newspaper print and other variations of surface texture. A reflection of this is seen in the black and white patterns of Niles Spencer (illustration 446) and Feininger (illustration 94) and in color patterns through the revival of an ancient reproducing medium—the

174

pochoir or color stencil. The technique was first used in the fifteenth century for coloring playing cards and other woodcuts, and also by the Japanese for decorative design. The stencil is one means of adding the full range of color to prints. In a thin sheet of copper or celluloid or stiff paper, an opening is cut which exactly corresponds in outline and area to the spots to be colored. This sheet is then laid on the print to be colored, and watercolor or gouache is applied with a brush through all the open spaces. When the stencil sheet is lifted off, the print appears from underneath with the color neatly applied wherever required. It is a quick and efficient method of coloring prints by hand with one or two colors. In modern times, however, such artists as Picasso (illustration 450), Braque, Severini, and Gleizes have used this technique to build up a complete colored picture with or without the use of any other medium. By making stencil cut-outs of each form and color (all the spots of red, all the spots of blue, etcetera) and applying them successively on the same sheet of paper with their appropriate color, a complete composition can be built up, which is at once an original and yet capable of indefinite duplication. A considerable amount of skill in abstraction and stylization is required to compose a picture in this way, and the compositions are often so elaborate as to necessitate the use of as many as fifteen stencils to supply all the tints and colors. In general, however, the color range is limited to five or six colors, since one of the chief charms of the medium is its flat and stylized color pattern. Whatever else it may have, abstract art has a decided decorative value.

A movement in reaction to the surface preoccupations of Impressionism arose also in Germany where it was labeled Expressionism. Kandinsky may be said to sound its keynote when he writes: "When religion, science, and morality (the last through the strong hand of Nietzsche) are shaken, and when the outer supports threaten to fall, man turns his gaze away from the external and towards himself." The Expressionist was largely preoccupied with his inner psyche: he externalized his inner conflicts, the tragedies and turbulences of his feelings by projecting them outwards, by endowing nature with a pathetic fallacy. These artists, to be sure, also made landscapes that were recognizable as landscapes and portraits that were interpretations of people, but in all cases

175

the impulse was subjective, the expression of the artist's feeling. Kokoschka, for example, used the Christian legend (illustration 448), as he used the inspiration of a Bach Cantata, as the framework around which to express his own emotions. Other artists, the Surrealists, carried the preoccupation with the inner psyche still further in the discovery of the unconscious and its deliberate use as a creative impulse. It is doubtful whether Surrealism would ever have been possible had it not been for the discoveries of Freud and the psychoanalysts. The discovery of man's unconscious, of his powerful irrational impulses, of the devious motivation of sex instincts, of anti-social tendencies which flare up sometimes in spite of all social conditioning, has had a tremendous effect upon the culture of our time. A vast new continent has been discovered which may have reverberations as far reaching as the discoveries of the Renaissance. It was on some such basis, combined with the ironic irrationalism of Dada born of the disillusion of the war, that the Surrealists built their program. It is difficult to explain clearly and logically what they are driving at, since they make a virtue of irrationality. There is no doubt that a complete philosophy of Surrealism would be exceedingly difficult to put into practice in life as in art, combining and stressing as it does such elements as the Freudian unconscious, the anti-social, the pathological and insane, psychic automatism, the emotional shock for the sake of shock, the grotesque outpourings of unfettered imagination, and the attack on reason in general. Man, we know, is an irrational as well as a rational being. He spends about one-third of his life in the state of sleep and dream where much of the surrealist point of view is approximated. There are certain intuitions about life that can be expressed in no other manner but the surrealist. There are surrealist elements in the works of Shakespeare, Swift, Coleridge, Blake, and Lewis Carroll, just as there are in the pictures of Dürer, Bosch, Bruegel, Goya, Callot, Bresdin, and Redon. The works of Picasso (in his later period), Chirico, Klee, Chagall, Miro, Dali, and Castellon (illustrations 456, 453, 455, 452, 457, 454, and 449) astonish, overwhelm, yet fascinate the beholder. The uninitiated spectator can best approach them as if they were the concrete projection of a dream. Picasso's *Minotauromachia* (illustration 456) is a pictorial embodiment of a fantasy of the unconscious; Miro's and Chagall's prints (illustrations 451 and 452) contain elements of fantastic dream-like humor. Dali's etching (illustration 454) is an example of emotional shock for the sake of shock: he has transformed a watch with which in everybody's mind is associated properties of hardness and inflexibility, into an object with the soft and yielding properties of a pillow. The Surrealists are pioneers in the discovery of a new mode of expression. If some of them are pathological and extreme, exhibitionists literally and figuratively; nevertheless they are laying the groundwork of a new symbolic language of benefit to the world at large.

And so, out of the welter of war and destruction, out of flux and ferment, and the transvaluation of all values, the art of the twentieth century is being born. Whither it will lead we know not, nor wherein its true greatness lies. We are too close to it, too much a part of it, to view it with a detached and appraising eye. Our critical standards are too quickly shifting, the artists themselves too uncertain of their goal for us to sit in judgment upon their works. Many many artists, in their life and in their work, are asking the question which is the title of a lithograph of Rockwell Kent's, *And Now Where?* It must be left to time to add its weight and substance to the major works of art of the twentieth century. But meanwhile we can be moved and inspired by the prospect of these stirring times as they are mirrored in the prints of today. We can see in them the faithful reflection of our own hopes and fears and indignations, of our own confusion and doubt, of our dreams and sympathies, our sense of play and fun, our quest for peace and happiness and beauty. And as regards the artist we see that he is leaving, either from choice or necessity, his tower of isolation and is casting his lot with humanity as a whole.

Of the majority of contemporary prints we can safely say that they could have been made only in the twentieth century, that they truly function as *contemporary* prints. It would be impossible in so short a space to make a complete survey of all the prints of the century, to do justice to the sincere and meritorious work in the conservative tradition as well as to trace all the ramifications of modern movements. This summary is all too brief and arbitrary in its selection and condensation. We have attempted, without any presumption of critical appraisal, to deal with tendencies rather than personalities, with general movements rather than with individual lives, and illustrate them with examples that aim to be typical rather than complete in scope. Whatever posterity may decide as to the merit of these works, one thing is clear: there has been an enormous expansion of the modes of expression; the languages of Cubism, Futurism, Expressive Design, Surrealism, and others, give the future artists a greater range of expression than they ever had before. There are, then, certain touchstones, certain qualities that distinguish these modern prints from those of other centuries. In the first place there are all the prints which use distinctively modern subject-matter in a dynamic way. There are those prints which exhibit a greater psychological sensitiveness. There are also modern prints which are deliberately untouched and forceful, just as in modern music the composer consciously uses dissonance to gain emotive effect. There are the prints displaying a social consciousness. Fascism and Nazism have had little if any constructive effect on art: their only expression is repression. There is, on the other hand, a growing body of art, as there is of literature and drama, which has social implications or voices new social ideals. Judging from the work already produced we should say that such ideas seem to be dynamic and life-enhancing—a real source of inspiration to the artist. Possibly the Brotherhood of Man may become as powerful and sustaining an emotional drive as Nirvana or the Redemption. And finally there are the prints based partly on the researches of Freud, the discovery of the new continent of the unconscious. The figures of Marx and Freud thus loom up among the major influences of twentieth-century art. Indeed Freudianism is the only serious challenge that Marxism has received. Who knows where it will lead? Perhaps the question will be resolved in some future higher synthesis. If so, we may be sure that there will be printmakers at hand to record it.

8. A Note on Oriental Art

AFTER the turbulence of the twentieth century, we return, for a moment, to the past and to the detachment and remoteness of an alien civilization. We journey to a far distant continent whose philosophy and thought-forms, whose total outlook on life are at almost complete variance with those of modern occidental culture. The East possesses many secrets not easily revealed—that East where all things have been done, all emotions felt, all thoughts expressed from time immemorial. The East of asceticism and sensuality, of mysticism and rationalist ethics, of fecund life and the equally overwhelming sense of the futility of life, of experiments and theories of government from absolute monarchy through theocracy, aristocracy, militarism, and socialism to anarchy. The East of the great inventions, gunpowder, the compass, printing, and paper money. "To look for the first time at the art of Asia," said Coomaraswamy, "is to stand at the threshold of a new world. To make ourselves at home here requires sensibility, intelligence, and patience." The East that expresses itself in prints is China and Japan; the graphic arts for one or another reason did not flourish in India, Persia, and the Mohammedan countries. Here we are face to face with another esthetic, that definitely subordinates realistic representation to contemplative insight, metaphysical vitality, a quest for essentials or the innate spirit of things. There is an analogy, as Coomaraswamy has pointed out, between oriental art and Gothic or Scholastic art: they both contain linear, calligraphic, and symbolic elements, and are expressive of inner truth rather than external reality. Laurence Binyon has ably expressed some of the leading characteristics of Chinese and Japanese art:

It is always the essential character and genius of the element that is sought for and insisted on: the weight and mass of water falling, the sinuous, swift curves of a stream evading obstacles in its way, the burst of foam against a rock, the toppling crest of a slowly arching billow [illustration 486]; and all in a rhythm of pure lines. But the same principles, the same treatment, are applied to other subjects. If it be a hermit sage in his mountain retreat, the artist's efforts will be concentrated on the expression, not only in the sage's features, but in his whole form, of the rapt intensity of contemplation; toward this effect every line of drapery and of surrounding rock or tree will conspire, by force of repetition or of contrast. If it be a warrior in action, the artist will ensure that we feel the tension of nerve, the heat of blood in the muscles, the watchfulness of the eye, the fury of determination. That birds shall be seen to be, above all things, winged creatures rejoicing in their flight; that flowers shall be, above all things, sensitive blossoms unfolding on pliant, up-growing stems; that the tiger shall be an embodiment of force, boundless in capacity for spring and fury—this is the ceaseless aim of these artists, from which no splendor of color, no richness of texture, no accident of shape diverts them. The more to concentrate on this seizure of the inherent life in what they draw, they will obliterate or ignore at will half or all of the surrounding objects with which the Western painter feels bound to fill his background. By isolation and the mere use of empty space, they will give to a clump of narcissus by a rock, or a solitary quail, or a mallow plant quivering in the wind, a sense of grandeur and a hint of the infinity of life.

The Chinese and Japanese were the first to use the woodcut to print images. One of the earliest dated woodcuts appeared in the *Diamond Sutra*, a Buddhist scripture, with the date 868. There must have been other and cruder woodcuts before this, cuts similar to the tenth-century Buddhist image (illustration 106) printed by stamping. Another block print inspired by Buddhism, with woodcut and text combined, was *Manjusri*, the personification of transcendent Wisdom (illustration 108), a votive offering similar to the European indulgences, found in the Cave of Ten Thousand Buddhas in Chinese Turkestan, and probably made about the year 950. Both of these prints were cut and printed from wood blocks. But there was another reproducing medium in use even earlier—the stone-rubbing. After the invention of paper the Chinese discovered that it was possible to take impressions of inscriptions and designs incised in flat slabs of rock. A dampened sheet of thin paper was

180

laid on the stone and forced into all the incisions, whereupon black ink was applied with a flat pad to the surface of the paper (that side of the sheet which we would call the back) and the design appeared in white against a background of black. In this way was avoided that reversal of image which always takes place when ink is applied *between* the block or plate and the paper. A number of literary and philosophical classics had been cut in stone by Imperial authority, and scholars were enabled by means of stone-rubbings to obtain copies. Later this method was used for the reproduction and dissemination of designs and works of art as well as of literature, wherever flat incised carvings in stone existed. Rubbings are extant of carvings as early as the Han Dynasty (200 B.C. to 200 A.D.), though the rubbings themselves were undoubtedly made at a later date and in some cases are still being made today. We reproduce a rubbing of a *Procession* (illustration 105) taken from a carved pedestal of a Buddhist image of the Northern Wei Dynasty (about A.D. 524), and two others by known artists, which were so famous in their day that they were copied in stone and rubbings taken. The first is a portrait of Confucius from a design in Pei-lin, province of Sian-fu, attributed to Wu Tao-tzŭ (about 700–760), the most famous of all Chinese painters (illustration 112). The T'ang Dynasty during which he worked was one of the most creative in Chinese history. Among his famous contemporaries were the landscape painter, Wang Wei, the poets Li Po and Tu Fu, and the Emperor Ming Huan, poet and musician, whose mad infatuation for the concubine Yang Kueifei, "the most beautiful woman in the world," led to his tragic downfall. Many stories are related about Wu Tao-tzŭ. About 750 the Emperor conceived a longing to see the scenery on the Chia-ling river and sent Wu to paint it. He came back with nothing in the way of sketches; and when the Emperor asked for an explanation, he replied, "I have it all in my heart." Then he went into one of the halls of the palace, and "in a single day he threw off a hundred miles of landscape." Giles recounts another story:

Wu Tao-tzŭ once went to see some priests, and met with a somewhat rude reception. He therefore drew a donkey on a wall in the temple, and at night the furniture and other paraphernalia of the priests were all kicked to pieces. The priests were sure that this was Wu's handiwork, and begged him to erase the drawing, after which there was no trouble.

Even the account of his death is legendary. He painted another great landscape fresco on the palace walls, so marvelous that it aroused the wonder and admiration of everyone from the Emperor on down. In the picture, at the foot of a mountain was a grotto into which Wu entered during the unveiling. Wu Tao-tzǔ was never seen again. The portrait of Confucius is a characteristic example of the Chinese use of a flowing linear rhythm and the emphasis upon an inner likeness. The Chinese ideal of portraiture is expressed by a writer of the twelfth century, Hu Ch'üan:

There is no branch of painting so difficult as portrait painting. It is not that the reproduction of the features is difficult; the difficulty lies in painting the springs of action hidden in the heart. The face of a great man may resemble that of a mean man, but their hearts will not be alike. Therefore, to paint a likeness which does not exhibit these heart-impulses, leaving it an open question whether the sitter is a great man or a mean man, is to be unskilled in the art of portraiture.

The stone-rubbing, the *God of Fortune* (illustration 113), is attributed to the renowned Su Tung-P'o (1036-1101), a universal genius of the Sung Dynasty, poet, essayist, art critic, calligrapher, and painter. The print, distinguished for its exquisite placement of seals, design, and script, illustrates the close relation between calligraphy and drawing in Chinese art. In his practice with written character, every Chinese scholar acquires a sensitive appreciation of the formal and artistic aspects of writing, of individuality of brush stroke, rhythm, symmetry, asymmetry, balance, and vitality of line. Where every written character is in itself a work of art, calligraphy ranks as a fine art. In China there are people who collect examples of writing as we collect works of art. In this picture the artist first drew an ideograph or written character, and then upon that drew a head, thus creating the character of the God of Fortune, both as symbol and as representation.

182

"Why does a virtuous man take delight in landscapes?" asked Kuo Hsi (eleventh century).

It is for these reasons: that in a rustic retreat he may nourish his nature; that amid the carefree play of streams and rocks, he may take delight; that he may constantly meet in the country fishermen, woodcutters, and hermits, and see the soaring of cranes and hear the cry of monkeys. The din of the dusty world and the locked-in-ness of human habitations are what human nature habitually abhors; while, on the contrary, haze, mist, and the haunting spirits of the mountains are what human nature seeks, and yet can rarely find.

It is no wonder that with such an attitude the Chinese developed many schools of landscape painting, and that many landscape paintings were translated into woodcut. A charming example is the *Landscape* by Mi Fei (1051–1107), (illustration 116). In their landscape as in their figure painting the Chinese followed the precepts of the artist Hsieh Ho (sixth century) as to what constitutes the essentials of art. Since the Six Canons of Hsieh Ho throw a great deal of light on Chinese esthetics it might be desirable to quote them in their entirety, in Binyon's translations:

1. Rhythmic vitality or the Life-movement of the Spirit through the Rhythm of things. [Binyon also suggests the Western terms: the Universal in the Particular.]
2. The art of rendering the bones or anatomical structure by means of the brush.
3. The drawing of forms which answer to natural forms.
4. Appropriate distribution of the colors.
5. Composition and subordination, or grouping according to hierarchy of things.
6. The transmission of classic models.

There are certain conventions used by Chinese landscape artists that often prove a stumbling block for Western appreciation. One of these is what is assumed to be absence of or ignorance of perspective but which in reality is the use of a system of perspective different from the Western geometric convention. In Chinese pictures distant objects do not recede along converging parallel lines, but are merely placed a little higher up in the picture. The convention of superposed registers, as Vernon Blake points out, dates back to Egyptian and Assyrian times, and is, in the hands of its practitioners, quite as flexible and expressive an instrument as the equally artificial geometric convention which we have come to regard as infallible. To a certain extent the customary shapes of Chinese pictures were a determining factor, either very tall and narrow or the very wide and not so tall, in neither of which would Western perspective have been very effective. An approximate way of explaining Chinese perspective is to assume that one is on a vantage point and looking down at the picture; in other words that the horizon line is high. Sometimes when the distortions inherent in the system might become unpleasant, the artists will resort to the device of breaking up the whole composition by means of cloud bands and sheets of water into several smaller units each with its own perspective system. This is one of the reasons for the frequent use of bands of cloud and mist, and they, together with the perspective which, for example, makes mountains even more awe inspiring than they are, add greatly to the mystery and dreamy unreality of Chinese landscape art.

The Chinese also made color woodcuts toward the end of the seventeenth century. They were usually, though not always, used as illustrations in books, technical books of instruction such as the painting manuals of *The Ten-Bamboos-Hall* or the *Mustard-Seed-Garden* of about 1701 (illustration 488). This woodcut, as is true of all Chinese prints, was entirely reproductive in character; it aimed to reproduce a watercolor or painting or drawing for scholarly or didactic purposes. Rarely, if ever, were the designs specially made to use in woodcuts. In this, Chinese color prints are distinguished from the later Japanese prints which were definitely designed to be cut in wood. There is no reason to suppose that Japanese color prints, though made later, were derived from Chinese color prints. In Japan the art arose independently and was animated by a different purpose. To be sure Japanese art in its general outlines was strongly influenced by Chinese models, and there likewise exist many prints which reproduce drawings and paintings by famous Japanese artists who were not print designers, such as Korin

184

or Kano Tanyu (illustrations 117 and 111). There was also an indigenous and rather crude tradition of book illustration (illustration 110). But the Ukiyo-ye school of prints in a sense arose as a reaction to the influence of the decadent Chinese classical school dominant in Japan, which had exhausted itself in repetitive and stereotyped themes.

The prints of the Ukiyo-ye school, or Pictures of Transient (or Floating) World of Everyday Life, are among the most beautiful and original manifestations of popular art in the history of prints. It was an impulse toward vitality in the midst of decadence, towards realism as against idealism, but a realism of subject never of treatment, which remained symbolic and suggestive as in all oriental art. The background of the Tokugawa period, during which this outburst of creative energy took place has been graphically described by Fenollosa:

It was like the rise of the industrial classes in the free cities of Europe in those middle centuries when the old feudal system was breaking. There, too, could be seen armored lords of castles flourishing side by side with burghers and guilders. It is the same duality which forms the keynote of Tokugawa culture taken as a whole. . . . The keynote of Tokugawa life and art is their broad division into two main streams—the aristocratic and the plebeian. These two flowed on side by side with comparatively little intermingling. On the one side select companies of gentlemen and ladies, congregated in gorgeous castles and yashikis, daimyos and samurai, exercising, studying their own and China's past, weaving martial codes of honor, surrounding themselves with wonderful utensils of lacquer, porcelain, embroidery, and cunningly wrought bronze; and on the other side great cities like Osaka, Nagoya, Kyoto, and Yedo, swarming with manufacturers, artisans, and merchants, sharing little in the castle privileges, but devising for themselves methods of self-expression in local government, schools, science, literature, and art.

Once again it was an instance of the rise of the urban or middle class, for the lot of the peasant was still almost unbearable. Farmers were treated by tax-gatherers and officials, wrote an old Japanese historian quoted by Sansom, "as a cruel driver treats an ox or a horse, when he puts a heavy burden on the beast, and lashes it unmercifully, getting all the angrier when it stumbles, and whipping more violently than ever,

185

with loud curses." Many of the peasants drifted to the cities where taxation was less onerous.

There was no trace of lofty idealism or religious ecstasy in the Ukiyo-ye prints: the "transient world" was described with power and grace and poetic charm. It was a transient world of actors and the theater, of courtesans and the glamor of the Yoshiwara, and of sweet and lovely genre scenes, glimpses of domestic life. The rise of the popular theater, as opposed to the *"Noh"* drama of the aristocracy, coincided with the development of the Japanese print. Actors, in spite of their being at the bottom of the social scale, were immensely popular and pictures of them in characteristic roles were eagerly sought for. There were, one might say, two types or schools of acting, those like the famous Ichikawa Danjuro I, who employed *aragoto*, "rough business," sound and fury and vehement gestures, and those, like Sakata Tajuro, who employed *nuregoto* or "moist business." Certain plays, like *Chiushingura* or the *Forty-Seven Ronin*, were very popular and furnished themes to many artists (illustration 475). The inhabitants of the Yoshiwara or licensed quarter, were in no sense to be considered merely as prostitutes; they were more like the *hetairae* of the Greeks, professional entertainers, boon companions, women of wit and culture, accomplished poets and musicians. The tea-houses were centers of elegance and gaiety and cultured amusement. An eighteenth century Japanese writer thus describes the quarters of the Yoshiwara: "their splendor was by day like Paradise and by night like the Palace of the Dragon King." The most famous of the courtesans lived in indescribable luxury. They set the fashion in costume and elegant manners; their appearances on the streets were triumphal processions. The situation was not without its sordid aspects, but the whole was invested with a glamor and elegance that has never been surpassed.

The Ukiyo-ye prints were a popular art similar to the theatrical posters and "funnies" of today. They were sold for a few sen and little value was attached to them; they were pasted on walls and on the screens that protected the kitchen fire; they were bought, as are picture post cards today, by visitors as souvenirs to take back to the provinces; they were used as costume plates or as advertisements for

186

houses in the Yoshiwara. They were produced at a time when Japan was completely isolated from the outside world, and thus are peculiarly an expression of Japanese genius. It is extraordinary that a popular art should exhibit such refinement and subtlety of treatment. Arthur Ficke has beautifully described the outstanding qualities of their approach:

This almost symbolic quality is the chief element of the pleasure to be derived from Japanese art. Japanese designs are metaphors; they depict not any object, but remote and greater powers to which the object is related. Often the artist produces his effect by the exaggeration of certain aspects, or by expressing particular qualities in the terms of some kindred thing. If his subject happens to be an actor in some great and tragic role, he will not hesitate to prolong the lines of the drapery unconscionably, to give the effect of solemn dignity, slow movement, and monumental isolation. Westerners may smile at the distortion of such a figure; but they must acknowledge that an atmosphere of lofty and special destiny surrounds the form, precisely because the artist has dared to use these devices. The Japanese artist will draw a woman as if she were a lily, a man as if he were a tempest, a tree as if it were a writhing snake, a mountain as if it were a towering giant. This is the very essence of poetical imagination; and the result of it is to endow a picture with obscure suggestions and overtones of infinite power. Symbols of existence beyond themselves, these designs are charged with an almost mystical command upon the emotions of the spectator. Western art has employed such a method comparatively little in painting. In poetry it appears frequently. The poet, when he wishes to convey the impression of a beautiful woman, does not set out her features and her stature and all the details of her aspect. He tries to awaken some realization of her by a bold and fantastic leap of the imagination straight to the heart of the matter—he makes her a perfume, a light, a music, a memory of goddesses. The prosaic mind will never greatly care for work produced in accordance with this principle; the conventions will seem distortions, the imaginative generalizations will seem inaccuracies, and the transcending of reality to shape a more universal and significant statement will appear nothing more than ineptitude in grappling with fact. But to the poetical mind, all these things will come with a unique and irresistible fascination.

The germ of the Ukiyo-ye idea first appeared in the paintings of an aristocratic artist, Iwasa Matahei (1578–1650), but the real founder of the school was Hishikawa Moronobu (1625–1694). It was he who in the years 1670–1680 first had the idea of using the woodcut medium for making Floating-World pictures and thus channeling Ukiyo-ye into a popular art. With Moronobu (illustration 115) are usually classed Sukenobu (illustration 114), Norishige, Kiyonobu (illustration 458), and his son Kiyomasu (illustration 457) and Okumura Masanobu (illustration 462). They are the primitives, with reference to technique and not to treatment, since Japanese prints were from the beginning highly sophisticated. They were printed in black and white, and sometimes colored by hand with a red pigment called by the Japanese *tan* (first used by Kiyonobu), sometimes with *tan* and a yellow pigment, sometimes with a saffron-red called *beni* used in combination with a greenish yellow or low-toned blues and purples (also first used by Kiyonobu). Sometimes a little lacquer, *urushi*, was mixed with the pigment to give it brilliance (invented by Masanobu). All the primitives are characterized by boldness of execution and a vigorous sweep of linear curves. The prints were mostly of single figures, and little attempt was made at composition except in the book illustrations of Moronobu and Sukenobu. About 1714, Masanobu who was also a bookseller and print publisher, perfected the genuine color print, in which the color was applied with two separate blocks instead of by hand. At first the *beni* color scheme, rose and green, was used, but later other color schemes and three blocks were employed by such masters as Kiyomitsu, Shigenaga, and Toyonobu (illustrations 471, 459, 461). The designs tended to become more elegant and less vigorously heraldic. Masanobu is also credited with having invented a special form, or rather shape, of Japanese print, the pillar print or *hashira-ye*. The shape is very long and narrow, and such prints were made to be hung on the columns that were used for support in Japanese houses. Many artists including Harunobu, Koriusai (illustration 474), Shunsho (illustration 473), Yeishi, Kiyonaga (illustration 472) and others, made pillar prints to supply popular demand, fascinated perhaps also by the challenge of the unusual proportions to their powers of invention and composition. At the beginning of the Meiwa period or about 1765 a further improvement in the printing process was made which rendered possible poly-

188

chrome effects with as many as eleven blocks. Haronobu was the first of the great designers to take advantage of this, and it gave scope to his exquisite and lovely sense of color, in some of the most beautiful prints ever made (illustrations 464 and 465). Henceforth there were no more important technical innovations except possibly the mica backgrounds of Sharaku and Utamaro, and the history of prints is the chronicle of the various artists' approach to the perennial problem of self-expression.

Harunobu (1725?–1770) was the dominant figure in the Meiwa period (1764–1772); he broke with the tradition of making theatrical prints and devoted himself to genre scenes of idyllic charm. There is a magic in his girlish figures, exquisite in their sensitive gestures. It is astonishing how much feeling and sensibility can be expressed by the pose, the gesture, the outline of the figure, for in these woodcuts, as in all Japanese prints, the faces are like masks, expressionless according to Western ideas. In the Anyei period (1772–1781) the honors were divided between Koriusai, of Samurai birth, famous for his bird and pillar prints (illustration 474), Shigemasa, renowned as a calligrapher, Shunsho (1726–93) famous for his actor prints (illustrations 460, 473) and his Samurai pupil, Buncho, whose life exhibited elements of a strange psychological conflict (illustration 463). The Temmei period (1781–1789) was dominated by Torii Kiyonaga (illustrations 467, 468, 472). He was born in Yedo in 1752, the son of a bookseller. He was a pupil of Kiyomitsu, at whose death in 1785 he became head of the Torii clan as Torii IV (Kiyonobu was the founder of the Torii clan or school, Kiyomasu, its second, and Kiyomitsu its third head). He summed up in his work the full flowering of the Japanese print school. In 1792 he gave up print designing and opened a tobacco shop, and in 1815 he died. He developed the diptych and triptych forms of composition, each part a separate unit, yet so designed as to become part of a larger whole. Where Harunobu gave to the Japanese print lyricism and grace, Kiyonaga gave serenity and grandeur. This is Binyon's estimate:

Kiyonaga rarely invents motives beyond the simplest to relate his figures to one another; and his most characteristic women are proudly impassive. He is content with the solid pose of his majestic forms, as if to bend or sway them toward or away from each other would mar their dignity. But

189

out of these so simple harmonies what a magnificent whole he creates, consummate in its equilibrium and authority! If his resources as a designer are strangely limited and easily exhausted, within those limits he is perfect, and he is a splendid draughtsman. His superb feminine forms, calmly sweet in a stable world and breathing the unconscious air of perfect health, are drawn with no parade of power, but impress as by the sensation of actual presence, so wonderfully does the contour evoke the shape of the rounded limbs it encloses. This discovery of a type at once winning and stately, a type founded on reality but imaginatively enhanced so as to be in truth an ideal creation, is one of Kiyonaga's great achievements. . . . The most famous and familiar of the series of twelve diptychs, *Minami Juniko*, one of the classic masterpieces of Ukiyo-ye, is the holiday group on a balcony overlooking Shinagawa Bay [illustration 468]. It is a composition simple in its symmetry. At the left is one standing woman immensely tall; at the right two girls standing close together. In the center are four seated or kneeling figures, a youth and three girls, arranged in groups of two. It is an hour of peace and idleness; one of the seated girls touches her *samisen*, and the imagined notes of music seem to hold the group in happy stillness; only the gesture of the girl, crouching beside the youth and holding up a lacquer wine-cup as she turns her face to the woman behind her, lends a touch of animation. But of what value to the composition is that central space of air and prospect of seashore! What largeness and infinitude seem drawn in among those idle figures! Here is Kiyonaga's new gift to Ukiyo-ye; completeness, *envelope*. The landscape is no mere adjunct, it is an integral part of the conception. There is no effort at realism, no color in the sky; the evocation is made by the simplest means; but one smells the seaweed on the sands and the salt moist air of evening at low tide, one seems to hear faint voices from the distant groups of people near the little cluster of stranded fishing-boats.

The Kwansei period (1789–1801) in spite of the decadence which was gradually creeping in, was a period of great creative activity in prints. Utamaro and Sharaku were the two great figures, and they were ably seconded by Choki (illustration 482), Toyokuni (illustration 483), Shunyei (illustration 480), Shunman (illustration 481), and Yeishi. The latter, Samurai born, and trained in the classical Kano school, carried over a certain nobility of treatment into his popular productions (illustration 469), and is famous for his illustrations to the well-known romance the *Tale of Genji* (illustration 466). The *Surimono* by Shunman (illustration 481) is an example of a print much in vogue from the time of Moronobu, a greeting card for special occasions such as the New Year, and usually commissioned by private individuals. Shunman himself, as described by Fenollosa, "is, like Shigenaga and Buncho, one of those strange personalities who infuse their art with a nameless individual charm. Everything he does has a strange touch. The Kiyonaga face becomes distorted with a sort of divine frenzy; trees grope about with their branch tips like sentient beings; flowers seem to exhale unknown perfumes."

In Sharaku we meet one of the most extraordinary figures in Japanese art. We know little about him other than that he was a *Noh* dancer in the service of the Daimyo of Awa. In the years of 1794 and 1795 he designed some forty-odd prints of actors, inaugurating a new type of bust portrait (illustration 475), and also introducing a technical innovation, the mica background, or *Kirara-ye*. His prints found no favor in his time, their supposed realism being considered repulsive, and after 1795 he gave up print designing and was heard of no more. We do not know how or why he suddenly burst in, full fledged as it were, upon the print world with his terrific characterizations. But it is easy to see why they were not popular: they struck a discordant note in the Ukiyo-ye esthetic by the intensity of their subjective vision. Sharaku was not impersonal and objective as were most oriental artists; he endowed his faces with an expressiveness that was highly personal and subjective. Binyon, again, has ably characterized his work:

The violent and sensational character of the Japanese popular drama partly accounts for the wrung features and desperate attitudes which we find in some of these prints—though not where it is not demanded for the character portrayed. But for Sharaku it was an opportunity of portraying the whole range of human emotions as written on face and form, and these he intensified to an extreme degree, without losing their essential truth. But we must not dwell on these prints exclusively as portraiture. We cannot sufficiently admire the unerring seizure of the one significant line that gives feature or expression (and note that, however extravagant the expression or posture, the delineation is reticent, the brush-line sober though intense) as if the whole force of the artist's mind were in the hand that traced it; just so Sharaku when he danced in the *Noh* plays would have concentrated the whole energy of his being in a gesture.

Fenollosa gives a vivid account of the background of the period in which Utamaro worked, and which furnishes a certain clue to his expression:

The cleavage between the aristocratic and the plebeian strata of Japanese life, which had become placidly conscious of itself in the days of Genroku, now threatened a moral, a social, if not a political disruption. The new factors of popular education—art, prints, illustrated books, the theater, novels, contact with the Dutch at Nagasaki—all had stimulated a spirit of inquiry and of unrest which had penetrated back in investigation to the facts of the Shogun's usurpation; which wrote new, popular histories of the national life; which gave plays and novels a semi-political aim. This deeper wave of self-consciousness on the part of the people was met by the authorities with sterner repressions. The better elements that might have drifted into improving the popular standards in pleasure and in art were driven out by a stricter censorship. There was thus a sort of natural, or unnatural, selection which tended to isolate and give prominence to the coarser side of the popular feeling. If the issue were squarely made between Confucius and rank demoralization, there was little resource for the commoner but to choose the latter. Thus there arose a sort of alliance between the theater and the houses of pleasure on the one hand, and the disaffected among the literary and political agitators upon the other. Men, great men who sowed the seed of the revolution which ripened in 1868, had to flee for asylum, not to Buddhist temples, but to the labyrinths of Yoshiwara, where, in the care of a romantic love lavished upon them by its then highly cultivated *hetairae*, they could print and disperse, from their hidden presses, seditious tracts which set the heart of a nation on fire. It was not the ideals of a ripe self-consciousness, such as Kiyonaga had attempted; it was a struggle of living desires against worn-out conventions and hopeless tyrannies. Hence, the two phases of a new Ukiyo-ye art—its pressure outward to fuller scientific realisms, and its frank recreations in the vulgarities of its surroundings. This passing phase of affairs Utamaro well knew. Himself frequently an inmate of Yoshiwara, he knew the authors, the agitators, the female in-

192

triguers, the pet actors and wrestlers, writers of cheap novels, cutters of vulgar prints—all this feverish life he breathed; of it, so far as Ukiyo-ye allowed him, he became an exponent.

Utamaro was discovered by the West in the 1890's, and was endowed with *fin de siècle* decadent tendencies by the critics. Utamaro is not, in my opinion, a decadent at all, but an artist of great sensibility and sensitiveness to the currents of his time, a restless and daring experimenter in the same sense that Picasso is today. From his early triptych the *Awabi Fishers* (illustration 470), and the *Young Woman Dressmaking* (illustration 477) to the late *Yamauba and Kintoki* series (illustration 476), Utamaro was a superb designer and draughtsman who gave to the perennial themes of woman, motherhood and the like, a new significance and meaning. In 1804 he published, in spite of the censorship, a satiric print which gave offense to the Shogun. He suffered imprisonment, and died shortly after his release.

After the beginning of the nineteenth century, that is to say during the Kyowa, Bunkwa, and Bunsei periods, the decadence of the Japanese print was almost complete. Such artists as Kunisada, Kuniyoshi, the later Toyokuni, and Yeizan lost their mastery in exaggerated and meaningless gesture, in elaboration of unessential detail, and in inferior coloring. Only two figures stand out above the general mediocrity, Hokusai and Hiroshige. Properly speaking they do not belong to the Ukiyo-ye School; they might have started a new and vital landscape school, had the times been propitious. They portrayed the land, as the Ukiyo-ye artists had portrayed the life of the Japanese people, its streets and highways, its harbors and landmarks, the ever changing aspects of the great mountain Fuji. Hokusai and Hiroshige were the artists whom the Western world found easiest to understand and appreciate. At their best they are among the great landscape designers of the world. Hokusai, "the Man Mad about Painting," as he sometimes signed himself, was born in Yedo in 1760. He was a pupil of Shunsho but in his final development was largely self-taught. He was always poor, always changing his name and his lodging, and he was always drawing. No artist has ever shown a more unflagging and undiscriminating delight in the delineation of hu-

193

manity and all natural objects. The fourteen volumes of his drawings, *Mangwa* (illustration 485) were a veritable encyclopedia of graphic representation of birds, insects, animals, fish, rocks, trees, flowers, mountains, every possible trade and craft and expression and gesture of man. In his celebrated epilogue to the first volume of the *Hundred Views of Fuji* he spoke of his own artistic development, saying that as early as his sixth year he felt the impulse to draw the form of things; when he was fifty he had already published innumerable sketches. At seventy-three he began to comprehend approximately the true form and nature of birds, fish, and plants; consequently he hoped to make great progress after the age of eighty, and when he should have reached the age of one hundred and ten, every dot and every line would be alive. He was a fecund, tirelessly inventive artist who would have had to digest the entire visible world before he could arrange it in the hierarchy of its importance. His work is a triumph of externalization. In 1829 he completed the set of *Thirty-six Views of Fuji* (illustration 486), one of his masterpieces. Other famous series are the *Waterfalls*, and *Living Images from the Poets of China and Japan*. He died at the age of ninety. Hiroshige was born in 1797 and died of cholera in 1858. He studied with Toyohiro. He worked for a while with figure subjects, but at last found his true medium of expression in landscape. Few artists have portrayed such a range of atmospheric effects, day and night, wind and sun, snow and rain (illustration 479).

His accuracy to local detail [wrote Fenollosa] is so great that travelers in Japan today can easily recognize his scenes. No part of this picturesque country escapes his observation, but he is especially happy in treating the many aspects of his native Yedo. His figures, like those of his great contemporary, Turner, are sometimes hardly more than lay figures, spots in the landscape, yet vigorous in their suggested action. That some of his most delicate landscape effects can be achieved with flat blocks is a marvel.

His most famous series were *Eight Views of Lake Biwa*, the *Fifty-three Stations of the Tokaido* or road from Kioto to Yedo, the *Thirty-six Views of Fuji* (illustration 484), and the many *Views of Yedo*.

With the death of Hiroshige, and indeed for some time before that,

194

the Japanese print ceased to have any real esthetic significance, and oriental art ceased to exist as far as the print is concerned. Within the last few years a young Chinese artist, Teng-Kuei, has used a Western medium, the lithograph and lithotint, to make a series of original and technically accomplished prints. Conceived in the great tradition of Chinese painting, they have, nevertheless, the vitality and freshness of a personal approach (illustration 487). Is it possible that out of the ferment and chaos of China a new popular print art may ensue, and that Japan when it recovers from the poison of imperialist militarism may again have the opportunity to cultivate a peaceful art worthy of its old tradition?

PLATES

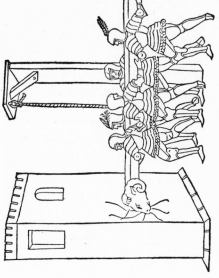

2. From Valturius, *De Re Militari*, Verona, 1472

4. From *Hypnerotomachia Poliphili*, Venice, 1499

1. From Turrecremata, *Meditations*, Rome, 1467

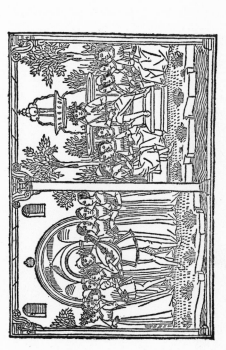

3. From Boccaccio, *Decameron*, Venice, 1491

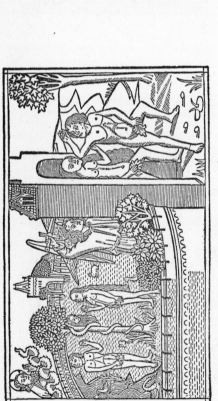

5. From Bible, Cologne, 1479

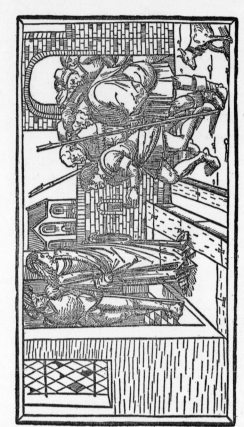

6. From Ingold, *Guldin Spil*, Augsburg, 1472

SAPHOS

7. From Boccaccio, *De Claris Mulieribus*, Ulm, 1473

8. From Bible, Lübeck, 1474

10. From Savonarola, *Compendio di Revelazione,* Florence, 1495

12. From Boccaccio, *Ninfale Fiesolano,* Florence

9. From Forestis, *De Claris Mulieribus,* Ferrara, 1497

11. From *Contrasto di Carnevale,* Florence

14. From Ketham, *Fasciculus Medicinae*, Venice,
1493

13. From Gafurius, *De Re Musica*, Milan,
1492

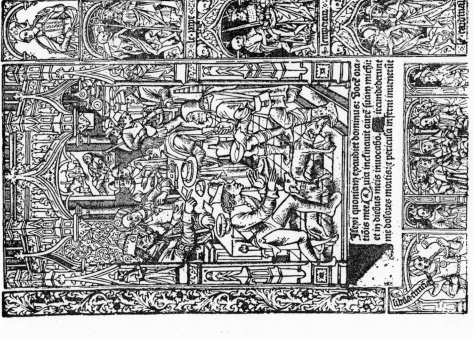

16. From *Horae*, Paris, 1498

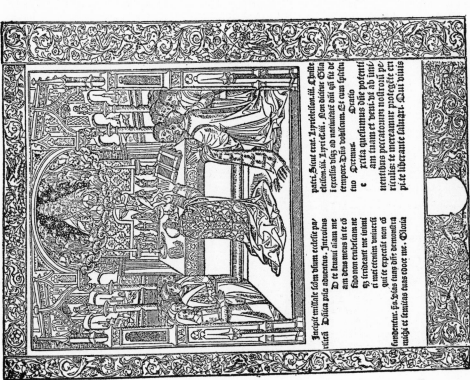

15. From *Missale Parisiense*, Paris, 1481

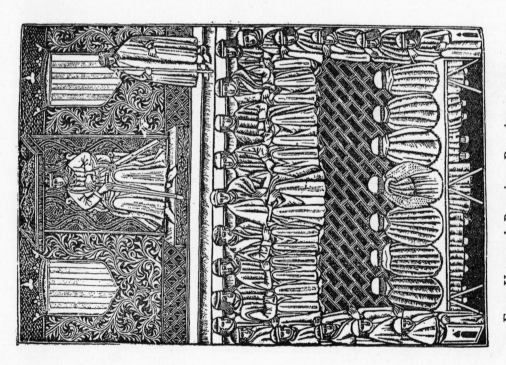

18. German School. Gossip during Mass, 15th Century (manière criblée)

17. From *Ustages de Barcelona*, Barcelona, 1495

19. German school. St. Christopher,
1423 (woodcut)

20. From *Buch der Weisheit*, Ulm, 1483

21. From Terence, Lyon, 1495

22. From Terence, Ulm, 1486

23. From *Le Chevalier Delibéré*,
Gouda, 1488

24. Dürer. From Brant, *Narrenschiff*,
Basel, 1494

25. Dürer. Four Riders of the
Apocalypse, 1498 (woodcut)

26. Dürer. Christ Appearing to Magdalen,
1511 (woodcut)

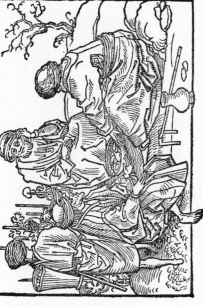

28. From Breydenbach, *Peregrinationes*, Mainz, 1486

30. From *Historie van Trojen*, Haarlem, 1485

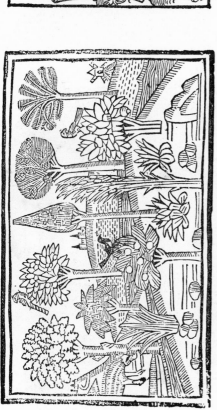

27. From *De Proprietatibus Rerum*, Toulouse, 1494

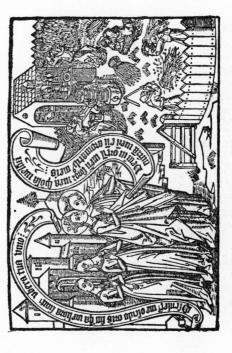

29. Dutch School. Canticum Canticorum, 15th Century (woodcut)

33. Altdorfer. Death of the Virgin (woodcut)

35. Baldung Grien. The Fifth Commandment (woodcut)

32. Holbein. Ruth and Boaz, Lyon, 1538 (woodcut)

31. Holbein. Dance of Death, Lyon, 1538 (woodcut)

34. From Marchant, *Danse Macabre*, Paris, 1485

36. Graf. Soldiers and Death   37. Cranach. Soldier and Woman (woodcut)
    (woodcut)

38. Burgkmair. Triumphal Procession (woodcut)

39. Boldrini, after Titian. Landscape (woodcut)

40. Baldung Grien. Horses, 1534 (woodcut)

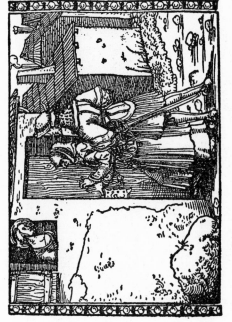

42. Weiditz. From *Calixtus und Melibea*, Augsburg, 1520

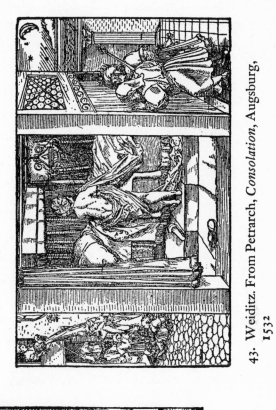

43. Weiditz. From Petrarch, *Consolation*, Augsburg, 1532

41. Altdorfer. Fountain (woodcut)

45. Boldrini, after Titian. Venus and Amor (woodcut)

44. Cranach. Venus (woodcut)

47. De Nanto, after Titian. Portrait of Ariosto, 1532 (woodcut)

46. Baldung Grien. Portrait of Brunfels (woodcut)

48. From de' Medici, *Nencia de Barberino*, Florence

49. From Dante, *Divina Commedia*, Florence, 1506

50. From *Bible en Françoys*, Paris

51. Graf. Arms of Unterwalden (wood engraving)

52. Baldung Grien. Nativity
(woodcut)

53. Baldung Grien. Ascension of
Christ (woodcut)

54. Baldung Grien. Adam and Eve
(woodcut)

55. Baldung Grien. The
Bewitched Groom
(woodcut)

56. Dale. Playing Card,
15th Century

57. Weiditz. From Brunfels,
Herbal, Strassburg, 1530

58. Flötner. Playing
Card (woodcut)

59. Viator. Interior, Toul 1505 (woodcut)

60. Tory. From *Horae*, Paris, 1525

61. Vicentino. From *Modo de Scrivere*, Rome, 1522

62. Flötner. Bed (woodcut)

63. From Vecellio, *Corona delle Nobili Donne*, Venice, 1591

64. Jegher, after Rubens. Temptation of Christ (woodcut)

65. Goltzius. Landscape (woodcut)

66. Deny, after Pillemont. Ornament (engraving)

67. Foin, after Lalonde. Barometer (engraving)

68. From Chapbook, *Robinson Crusoe*, 18th century

69. Papillon. Notre Dame de Bonne Déliverance (woodcut)

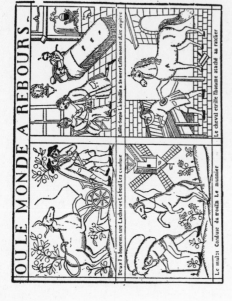

71. Image Populaire. World Upside Down, 18th century

72. Image Populaire. The Day of the Fall of Bastille, 18th century

70. Menzel. Voltaire and Frederick the Great (wood engraving)

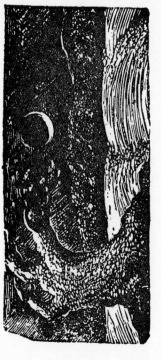

74. Blake. From Thornton's Virgil, 1821 (wood engraving, enlarged)

76. Calvert. Chamber Idyll (wood engraving, enlarged)

73. Blake. From Thornton's Virgil, 1821 (wood engraving, enlarged)

75. Calvert. The Return Home (wood engraving, enlarged)

80. Busch. From *Pater Filucius*, 1872 (wood engraving)

77. Bewick. From *British Birds*, 1826

78. Bewick. From *British Birds*, 1826

79. Daumier. Le Bourgeois Campagnard, 1840 (wood engraving)

81. From *Paul and Virginia*, Paris, 1838

82. Richter. Harvest Dance (wood engraving)

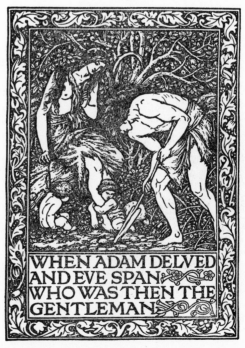

83. Doré. From *London, a Pilgrimage*, 1873

84. Burne-Jones. From *A Dream of John Ball*, London, 1892.

87. Maillol. From Virgil's *Eclogues* (woodcut)

89. Kent. Twilight of Man (wood engraving)

86. Weber. Mother and Child (woodcut)

85. Gill. Nowell (wood engraving)

88. Marc. Annunciation (woodcut)

90. Galanis. Still Life (wood engraving)

91. Gág. Cats at Window (wood engraving)

92. Skoczylas. Village Square (woodcut)

93. Nason. Ipswich Barns (wood engraving)

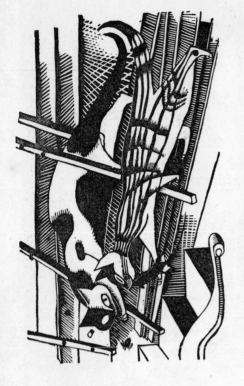

94. Feininger. Landscape (woodcut)

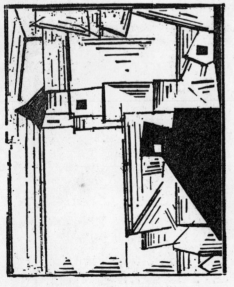

96. Murphy. Morning Gossip (wood engraving)

95. Marcks. Cats (woodcut)

97. Munch. Death Bed (woodcut)

98. Sakhnorskaya. Women in the 1905 Revolution (woodcut)

99. Masereel. The Strike (wood engraving)

100. Kravchenko. Dnieprostroi (wood engraving)

101. Lynd Ward. Spring
Idyll (wood
engraving)

102. Rethel. Death the Victor (woodcut)

103. Posada. Calavera (woodcut)

A VINGT ANS...

104. Vallotton. At Twenty Years (woodcut)

105. Chinese School. Procession, Wei Dynasty (stone rubbing)

106. Chinese School. Buddhist Image, 10th century (woodcut)

107. Coptic School. Textile Design, 6th century (woodcut)

108. Chinese School. Manjusri (woodcut)

109. Chinese School. Playing Card (woodcut)

110. Japanese School, Ise
Monogatari, about 1575
(woodcut)

111. Kano Tanyu. Chinese Sage,
1740 (woodcut)

112. Wu Tao Tzû. Confucius (stone rubbing)

113. Su Tung P'o. God of
Fortune (stone rubbing)

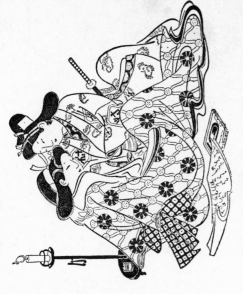

115. Moronobu. Lovers (woodcut)

117. Korin. Crows in Moonlight, 1707 (woodcut)

114. Sukenobu. Women Sketching (woodcut)

116. Mi Fei. Landscape, 1679 (woodcut)

118. Mantegna. Bacchanal (engraving)

119. Pollaiuolo. Battle of the Naked Men (engraving)

121. North Italian School. Primum Mobile
(engraving)

SIBYLLA LIBICA

ECCE VENIENTEM DIEM
ET LATENTIA APERIEN
TEM TENEBIT GREMIO
GENTIVM REGINA

120. Florentine School. Libyan Sibyl (engraving)

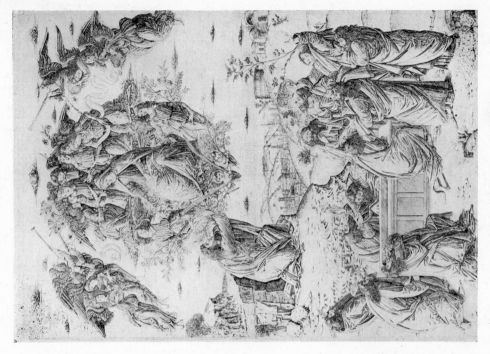

123. Botticelli School. Assumption of the Virgin (engraving)

122. Florentine School. The Planet Mercury (engraving)

125. Veit Stoss. Madonna and Child (engraving)

124. Master of the Playing Cards. Cyclamen Queen
(engraving)

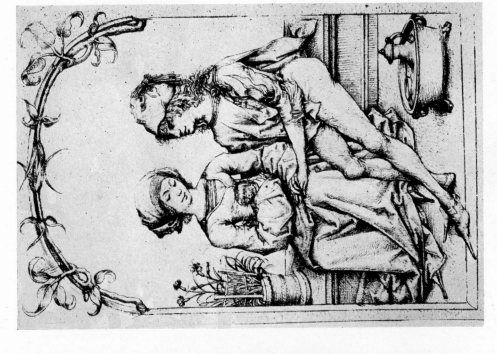

127. Master of the Amsterdam Cabinet. The Lovers (engraving)

126. Mantegna School. Entombment with Four Birds (engraving)

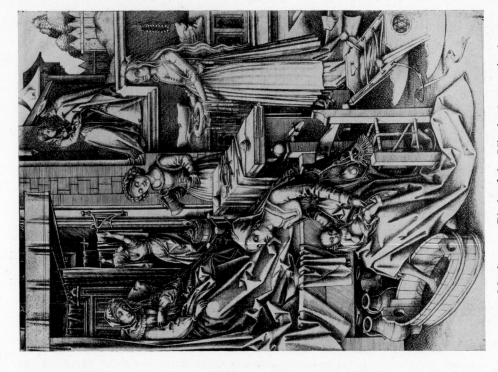

129. van Meckenem. Birth of the Virgin (engraving)

128. Schongauer. Nativity (engraving)

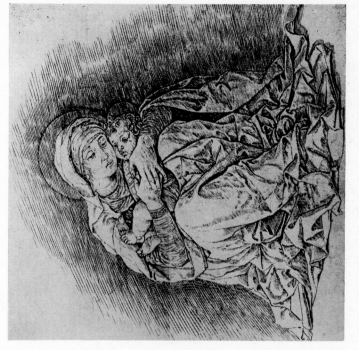

131. Mantegna. Virgin and Child (engraving)

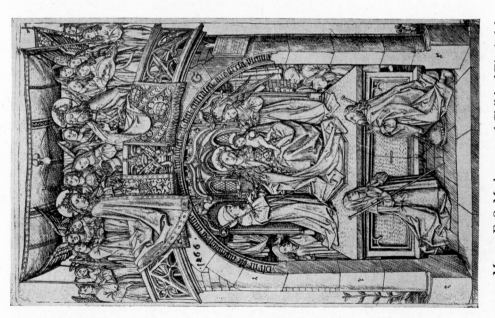

130. Master E. S. Madonna and Child of Einsiedeln
(engraving)

132. German School. St. Onuphrius (woodcut)

133. French School. Nativity (woodcut)

134. van Meckenem. Double Portrait (engraving)

135. Pollaiuolo School. Profile of
a Lady (engraving)

136. Da Vinci School. Profile of
a Lady (engraving)

137. Meister der Weibermacht. Satire on the Power of Women (engraving)

140. Master I. M. Architectural Ornament (engraving)

138. Peregrino. Ornament
(niello engraving)

139. Peregrino. Orpheus
(niello engraving)

141. Master E. S. Ornament (engraving)

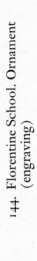

144. Florentine School. Ornament (engraving)

146. Raimondi. Two Fauns (engraving)

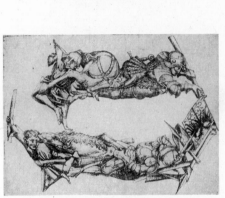

143. Master E. S. Grotesque Letter (engraving)

142. Romanesque School. Nativity (engraving)

145. Schongauer. Griffin (engraving)

148. Dürer. Virgin and Child with Monkey (engraving)

147. Dürer. Adam and Eve (engraving)

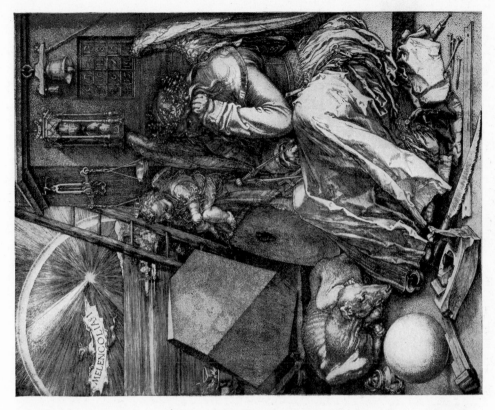

150. Dürer. Melancholia (engraving)

149. Dürer. Christ on Mount of Olives (etching)

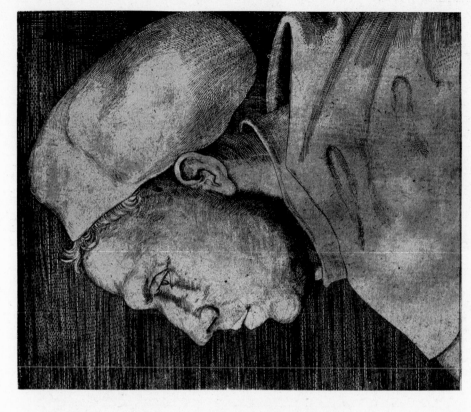

152. Cranach. Portrait of Luther (engraving)

BİLİBALDİ·PİRKEYMHERİ·EFFIGIES
·AETATIS·SVAE·ANNO·L·İİİ·
VIVITVR·INGENIO·CAETERA·MORTIS·
·ERVNT·
M·D·XX·IV

151. Dürer. Portrait of Pirkheimer (engraving)

154. van Leyden. Portrait of Maximilian (etching and engraving)

153. Agostino Caracci. Portrait of Titian (engraving)

155. Hirschvogel. Landscape (etching)

156. Dürer. The Cannon (etching)

DH.

DIE SPRICH SALOMO DAS XI CAPITEL
WER KORN INHELT DEM FLVCHEN DIE LEIT
ABER SEGEN KOMPT VBER DEN SO ES VERKAFFT
M DLX XIIII

157. D. Hopfer. Parable (etching)

158. van Leyden. Milkmaid (engraving)

159. Cousin. Entombment (engraving)

160. G. Campagnola. Christ and the Woman of Samaria (engraving)

161. Raimondi, after Raphael. Judgment of Paris (engraving)

162. Raimondi, after Raphael. Massacre of the Innocents (engraving)

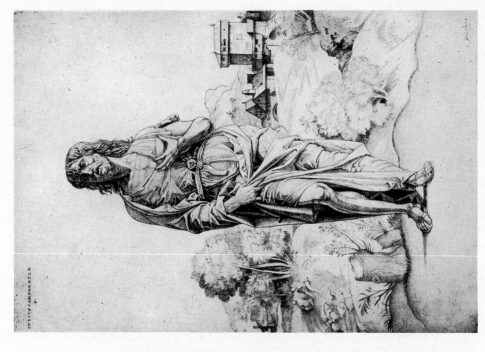

164. G. Campagnola. St. John the Baptist (engraving)

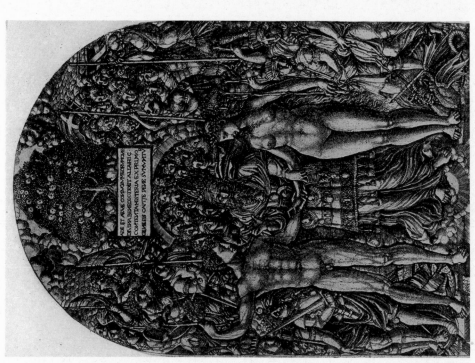

163. Duvet. Marriage of Adam and Eve (engraving)

166. Parmigiano. St. Thais (etching)

165. Baroccio. Annunciation (etching)

167. Da Carpi, after Parmigiano. Saturn (chiaroscuro woodcut)

168. Da Carpi, after Raphael. Draught of Fishes (chiaroscuro woodcut)

170. Cranach. St. Christopher (chiaroscuro woodcut)

169. Baldung Grien. The Witches (chiaroscuro woodcut)

171. Altdorfer. Virgin and Child
with St. Anne (engraving)

172. Vellert. Faun upon Wine
Barrel (engraving)

173. H. S. Beham. Drummer and
Standard Bearer (engraving)
(enlarged)

174. Master I. B. Luna
(engraving)

175. B. Beham. Bookplate
(engraving)

176. Delaune. Ornament
(engraving)

177. Aldegrever. Ornament with Lettering (engraving)

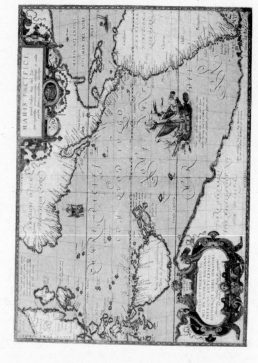

179. From *Nuremberg Chronicle*, 1493

180. Ortelius. Map of America, 1589 (engraving)

178. Fontana. Obelisk (engraving)

182. Balducci. Marriage of the Duke of Tuscany (etching)

181. Robetta. Allegory of Abundance (engraving)

Iulus, Augustus, nec non et Iunius Aestas .   *AESTAS* *Adolet* *Tenth imago*   Frugiferas aruis fert Aestas torrida meßeis .

183. Bruegel. Summer (engraving)

184. Bruegel. Justice (engraving)

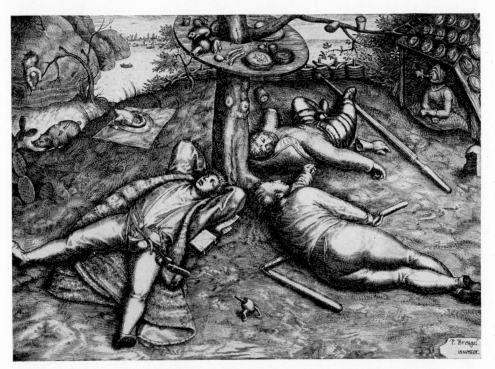

185. Bruegel. Luilekkerland (engraving)

186. Bruegel. Kermesse (engraving)

188. Rembrandt. Portrait of His Mother (etching)

187. Rembrandt. Self-Portrait Leaning on Stone Sill (etching)

190. Rembrandt. Woman with Arrow (etching)

189. Rembrandt. Dr. Faustus (etching)

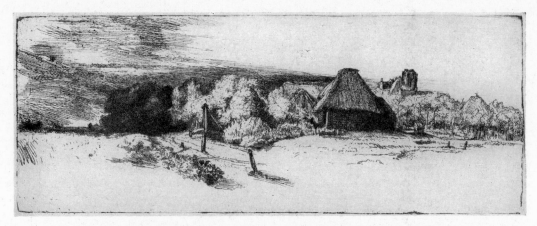

191. Rembrandt. Landscape with Trees, Farm Buildings, and Tower (etching)

192. Rembrandt. Three Trees (etching)

193. Rembrandt. Christ and Woman of Samaria (etching)

194. Rembrandt. Christ Preaching (etching)

195. Seghers. Rocky River Landscape with Road (etching)

196. Seghers. The Three Books (etching)

197. Ribera. Drunken Silenus (etching)

198. Goudt, after Elsheimer. Philemon and Baucis (engraving)

199. van Ostade. The Family (etching)

200. Buttewych. The Lovers (etching)

NICOLAVS CLAVDIVS FABRICIVS
DE PEIRESC SENATOR AQVENSIS

Cl. Mellan G. del. et fecit

202. Mellan. Portrait of Peiresc (engraving)

201. van Dyck. Portrait of de Momper (etching)

203. Claude. Rape of Europa (etching)

204. Bolswert, after Rubens. Village Dance (engraving)

205. Claude. Dance by the Waterside (etching)

206. Potter. Cowherd (etching)

207. Rembrandt. Beggar Warming
His Hands (etching)

208. Callot. Beggar with Head and
Feet Bare (etching)

209. Callot. Parterre at Nancy (etching)

210. Callot. Disasters of War (etching)

211. Callot. Disasters of War (etching)

212. de Bry. Spanish Exploitation in America (engraving)

213. Callot. Gypsies (etching)

214. Teniers. Kermesse (etching)

215. Bosse. Hearing (etching)

216. Bosse. Visite à l'Accouchée (etching)

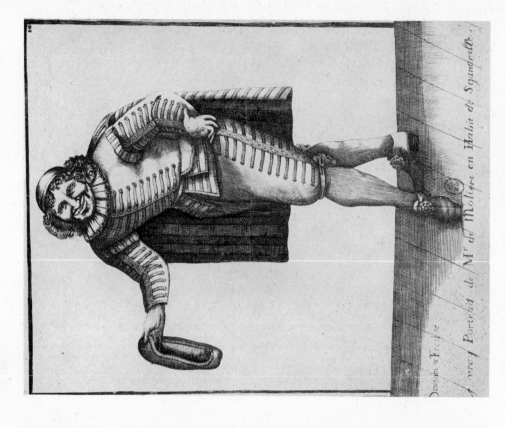

218. Simonin. Moliére as Sganarelle (engraving)

217. Callot. Pantaloon (etching)

220. Hollar. Winter (etching)

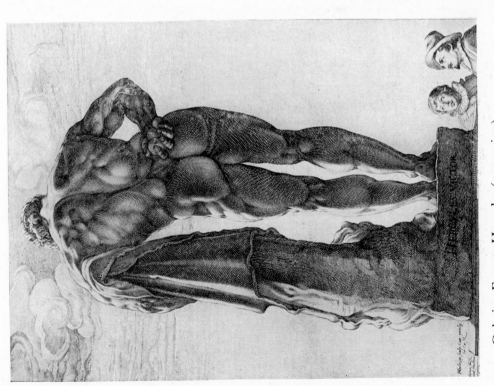

219. Goltzius. Farnese Hercules (engraving)

222. Rubens. St. Catherine (etching)

221. Guercino. St. Anthony (etching)

224. Salvator Rosa. St. William the Hermit (etching)

223. Cantarini. Flight into Egypt (etching)

225. Waterloo. The Linden Tree (etching)

226. Ruysdael. The Wheat Field (etching)

227. Backhuysen. Sea Piece (etching)

228. van Ostade. The Fisherman (etching)

230. Woeiriot. Design for Ring (engraving)

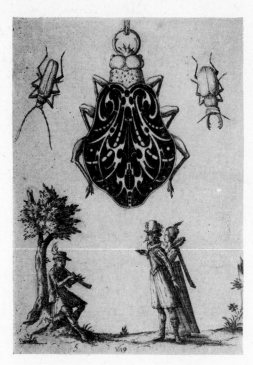

229. Tutin. Ornament (engraving)

231. Della Bella. Cartouche (etching)

232. Jacquard. Gunsmith's Shop (engraving)

233. Le Pautre. Ornament (engraving)

234. Le Clerc. Galerie des Gobelins (engraving)

235. Le Pautre. Grottoes and Fountains (engraving)

237. Leoni. Portrait of Galileo (engraving)

236. Goltzius. Portrait of Henri IV (engraving)

239. Drevet, after Rigaud. Portrait of de Cotte (engraving)

238. Nanteuil. Portrait of Louis XIV (engraving)

240. Fragonard. Bacchanal (etching)

241. Demarteau, after Boucher. Venus Desarmée par les Amours (engraving)

242. Le Prince. O Fortunatos Nimium (aquatint)

243. Tardieu, after Watteau. Embarquement pour Cythère (engraving)

245. Cars, after Lemoyne. Rape of Europa (engraving)

244. Cars, after Watteau. Fêtes Vénitiennes (engraving)

247. Simonet, after Baudouin. Soirée des Tuileries (engraving)

246. De Launay, after Fragonard. Les Hazards Heureux
d'Escarpolette (engraving)

249. De Launay, after Lavreince. Le Billet Doux (engraving)

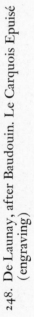

248. De Launay, after Baudouin. Le Carquois Epuisé (engraving)

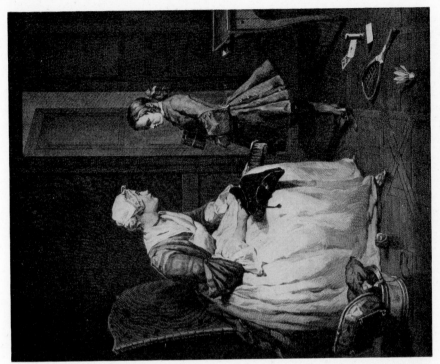

251. Lepicié, after Chardin. La Gouvernante (engraving)

250. Le Bas, after Chardin. Le Negligé (engraving)

253. Malbeste, after Moreau. Sortie de l'Opera (engraving)

252. Helman, after Moreau. Les Délices de la Maternité (engraving)

255. De Launay, after Moreau. Les Adieux (engraving)

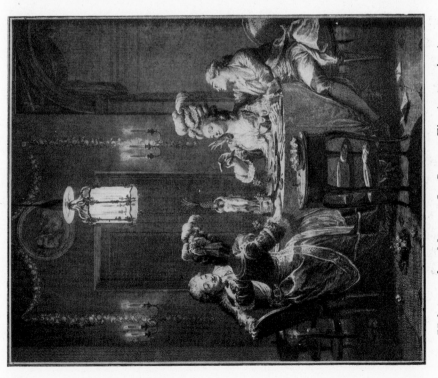

254. Helman, after Moreau. Le Souper Fin (engraving)

256. G. St. Aubin. Spectacle de Tuileries (etching)

257. G. St. Aubin. Les Nouvellistes (etching)

258. Hogarth. Marriage à la Mode (engraving)

259. Hogarth. The Enraged Musician (engraving)

261. G. St. Aubin. Théâtre Italien (etching)

260. Delafosse, after Carmontelle. The Mozart Family (engraving)

263. Cars, after Boucher. Tartuffe (engraving)

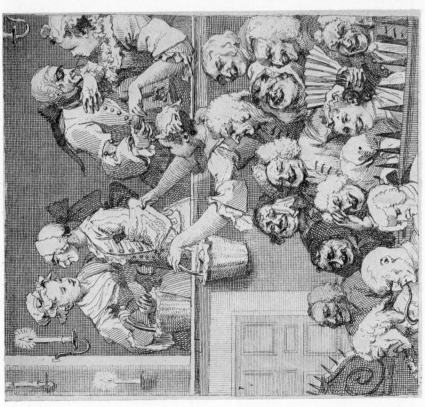

262. Hogarth. Laughing Audience (engraving)

265. Bonnet, after Boucher. Femme à la Rose (aquatint)

264. Pitteri. Portrait of Pompadour (engraving)

267. A. St. Aubin, after Cochin. Portrait of Franklin
(engraving)

266. Hogarth. Portrait of Lord Lovat (etching)

268. G. St. Aubin. Académie Particulier (etching)

269. Chodowiecki. Cabinet d'un Peintre (engraving)

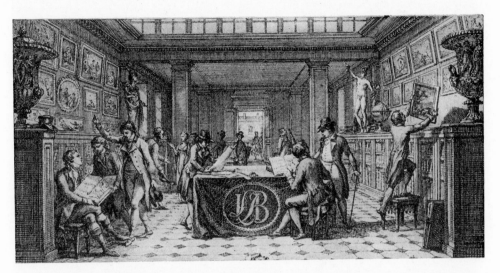

270. Choffard. The Shop of Basan (engraving)

271. Aveline, after Watteau. The Shop of Gersaint (engraving)

272. Gaucher, after Moreau. The Crowning of the Bust of Voltaire (engraving)

273. Berthault, after Fragonard *fils*. Revolutionary Committee under the Terror (engraving)

274. Lammerk. Vue d'Optique (engraving)

275. Revere. Boston Massacre (engraving)

276. Gainsborough. Landscape (soft ground etching)

277. Piranesi. The Baths of Titus (etching)

278. Piranesi. Via del Corso (etching)

279. Piranesi. Carcere (etching)

280. Canaletto. The Prison (etching)

281. Canaletto. The Terrace (etching)

282. G. B. Tiepolo. Caprice (etching)

283. D. Tiepolo. Flight into Egypt (etching)

287. Monnoyer. Flowers (engraving)

285. Chrétien. Portrait (engraving)

286. St. Menin. Portrait of Jefferson (engraving)

284. Chippendale. Furniture Design (engraving)

289. Wille, after Schalken. Family Concert (engraving)

288. Moreau-le-Jeune. Chanson de la Borde (engraving)

290. Jukes, after Rowlandson. Vauxhall (aquatint)

291. Debucourt. Promenade Publique (aquatint in color)

LA LIBERTÉ

293. Copia, after Prud'hon. La Liberté (engraving)

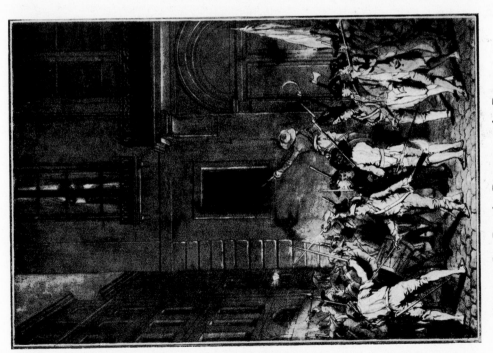

292. Sergent. Les Peuples Parcourant les Rues
(aquatint in color)

295. Smith, after Reynolds. Mrs. Carnac (mezzotint)

294. Turner, after Hoppner. Viscount Nelson (mezzotint)

297. Doughty, after Reynolds. Dr. Johnson (mezzotint)

296. Meyer, after Romney. Lady Hamilton (mezzotint)

299. Bartolozzi, after Cosway. Mrs. Abington (stipple engraving)

298. Earlom, after Huysum. Fruit and Flower Piece (mezzotint)

300. Turner. Liber Studiorum (etching and mezzotint)

301. Lucas, after Constable. Summer Evening (mezzotint)

302. Pugin, after Rowlandson. Microcosm of London (aquatint)

303. Rowlandson. Sign of the Four Alls (etching)

304. Rowlandson. Ballad Singers (etching)

305. Rowlandson. More Miseries (etching)

306. Reeve, after Newhouse. False Alarm on the Road to Gretna Green (aquatint)

307. Reeve, after Hodges. Hare Hunting (aquatint)

308. Langlois, after Redouté. Rose
(aquatint)

309. Havell, after Audubon. Trail's
Flycatcher (aquatint)

310. Currier and Ives. Clipper Ship "Contest" (lithograph)

311. Goya. Porque Fue Sensible
(aquatint)

312. Goya. Subir y Balar (aquatint)

313. Goya. Flying Men (aquatint)

314. Goya. Bravo Torro (lithograph)

315. Goya. Disparate de Bestia (aquatint)

316. Goya. Gracias à La Almorta (aquatint)

317. Goya. Y no hay Remedio (aquatint)

318. Raffet. Revue Nocturne (lithograph)

319. Goya. Estragos de la Guerra (aquatint)

321. Boilly. Portrait of Susemihl (lithograph)

320. Quaglio. Portrait of Senefelder (lithograph)

323. Delacroix. La Soeur de Dugesclin (lithograph)

322. Delacroix. Faust (lithograph)

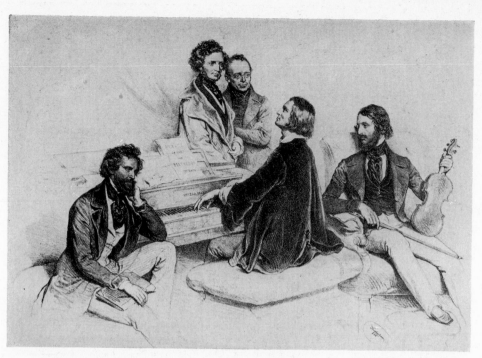

324. Kriehuber. Une Matinée chez Liszt (lithograph)

325. Géricault. Boxers (lithograph)

326. Denon. Denon Drawing a Portrait (lithograph)

327. C. Vernet. Delpech's Printing Shop (lithograph)

329. Eugène Isabey. Eglise de St. Nectaire (lithograph)

328. Bonington. Tour du Gros Horloge (lithograph)

330. Boys. Hôtel de Cluny (lithograph in color)

331. Bonnard. Paris Night (lithograph in color)

332. Daumier. Ventre Législatif (lithograph)

333. Daumier. Rue Transnonain (lithograph)

334. Daumier. Croquis d'Eté (lithograph)

335. Daumier. Exposition Universelle (wood engraving)

337. Daumier. Les Témoins (lithograph)

336. Daumier. European Equilibrium (lithograph)

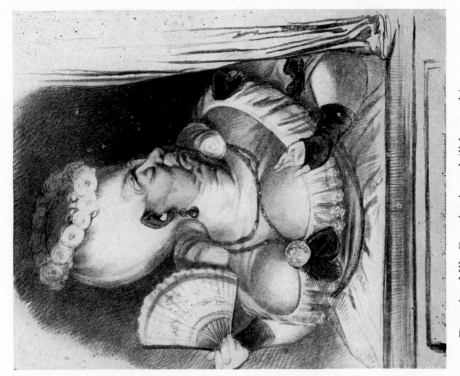

339. Daumier. Mlle Constitutionnel (lithograph)

338. Daumier. Steps of the Palace of Justice (lithograph)

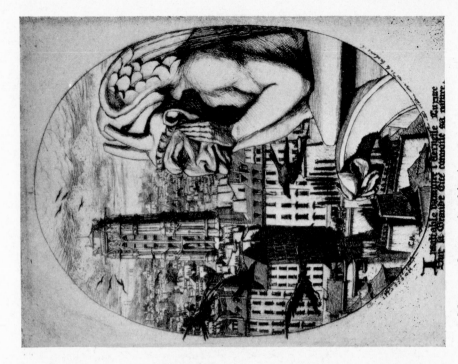

341. Meryon. Stryge (etching)

340. Meryon. The Morgue (etching)

343. Ensor. Cathedral (etching)

342. Legros. Mort de Vagabond (etching)

345. Blake. Tyger, Tyger (relief etching)

344. Blake. The Morning Stars (engraving)

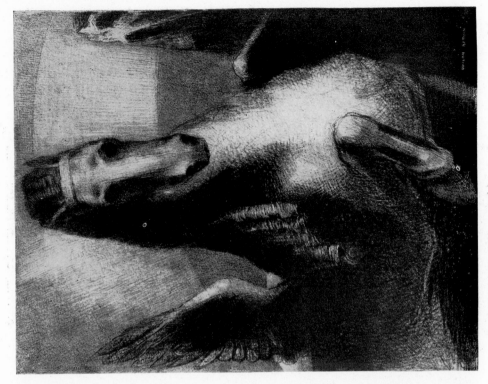

347. Redon. L'Aile (lithograph)

346. Bresdin. Comédie de la Mort (lithograph)

349. Whistler. Limeburner (etching)

348. Delacroix. The Blacksmith (aquatint)

351. Palmer. The Sleeping Shepherd (etching)

350. Buhot. Débarquement en Angleterre
(etching)

352. Whistler. Nocturne (lithograph)

353. Whistler. Nocturne (etching)

354. Haden. Egham Lock (etching)

355. Jongkind. Porte d'Honfleur (etching)

357. Manet. Le Printemps (etching)

356. Cassatt. Femme se Coiffant (aquatint in color)

359. Whistler. Annie Haden (drypoint)

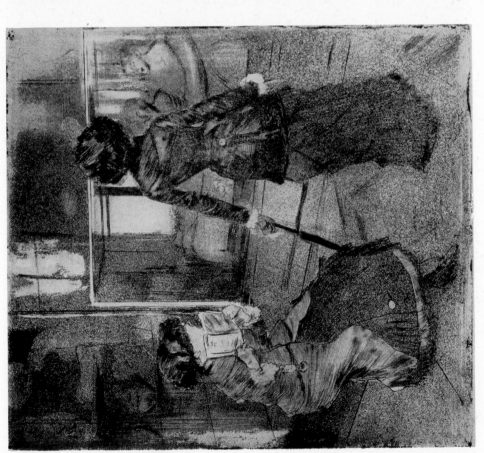

358. Degas. Au Louvre (aquatint)

360. Millet. The Diggers (etching)

361. Corot. Paysage Normande (etching)

362. Jacque. Pastoral (etching)

363. Pissarro. The Goose Girl (etching)

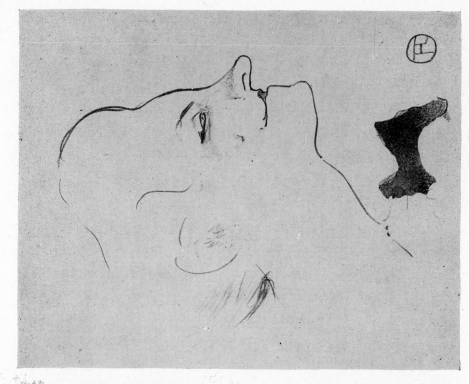

365. Lautrec. Portrait of Yvette Guilbert (lithograph)

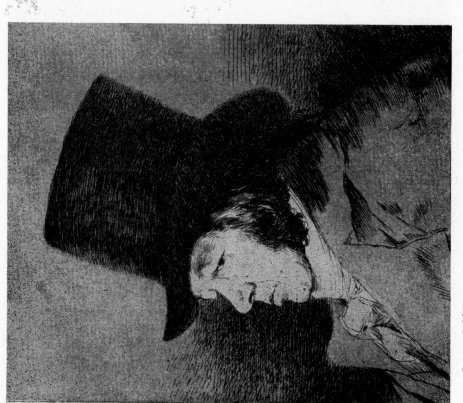

364. Goya. Self-Portrait (etching and aquatint)

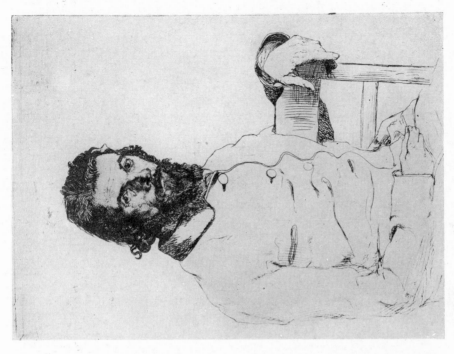

367. Bracquemond. Portrait of Meryon (etching)

366. Van Gogh. Portrait of Dr. Gachet (etching)

369. Lautrec. Etude de Femme (lithograph)

368. Degas. Sortie de Bain (etching)

371. Chassériau. Venus Anadyomène (lithograph)

370. Renoir. Bather (lithograph in color)

372. Cézanne. Bathers (lithograph in color)

373. Gauguin. Mahna No Varua Ino (wood engraving)

374. Ingres. Odalisque (lithograph)

375. Manet. Olympia (etching)

377. Courbet. Portrait of Journet (lithograph)

376. Gavarni. Portrait of the De Goncourts (lithograph)

379. Lautrec. Jane Avril (lithograph)

378. Degas. Mlle Bécat aux Ambassadeurs (lithograph)

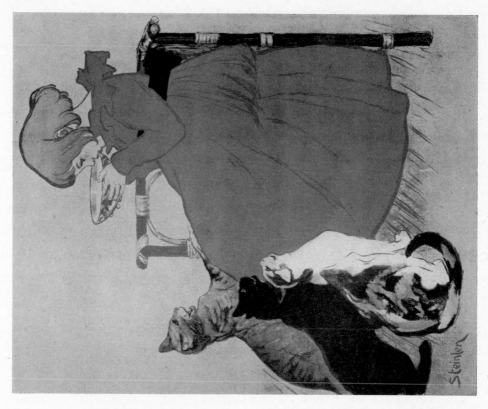

381. Steinlen. Lait Stérilisé (lithograph poster)

380. Lautrec. Jockey (lithograph)

383. Fantin. Siegfried and the Rhine Maidens (lithograph)

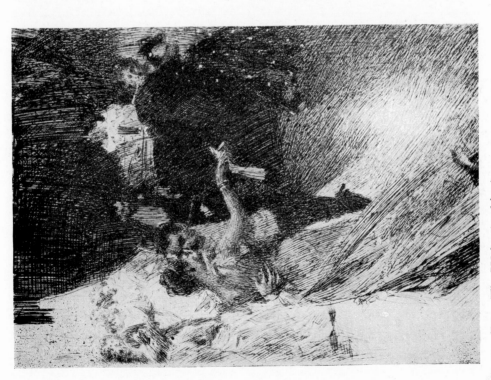

382. Zorn. The Waltz (etching)

384. Hill. Mrs. Jameson (photograph)

385. Atjet. Avenue des Gobelins (photograph)

386. Stieglitz. The Hand of Man (photograph)

387. Sickert. Gaité Montparnasse
     (etching)

388. Benson. Mallards at Evening
     (drypoint)

389. Davies. Nocturne
     (soft ground etching)

390. Griggs. The Almonry (etching)

392. Bone. Ship Building (lithograph)

391. Pennell. Piedro Miguel Lock, Panama (lithograph)

393. Hermes. Through the Windscreen
(wood engraving)

394. Marin. Downtown, New York (etching)

396. Marin. Sail Boat (etching)

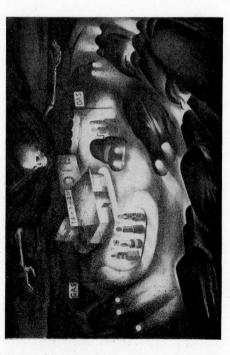

395. Spruance. Road to the Shore (lithograph)

397. Cook. Bridge (lithograph) 398. Lozowick. Tanks (lithograph)

399. Huntley. Coke (lithograph)

400. Sternberg. Construction (aquatint)

401. Benton. Locomotive (lithograph)

402. Kent. Pinnacle (lithograph)

403. Shannon. Swimmers (lithograph)

404. Bellows. A Stag at Sharkey's (lithograph)

405. Pascin. Cabaret (lithograph)

406. Forain. Témoins à l'Audience (etching)

408. Lepère. July in Picardy (etching)

407. Hopper. American Landscape (etching)

410. Bone. Ballantrae Road (drypoint)

409. Mahonri Young. Tewa (drypoint)

412. Segonzac. Curé de Soleil (etching)

414. Bauer. The Visit (etching)

411. Cameron. Doge's Palace (etching)

413. Arms. La Colegiata, Toro (etching)

416. Cook. Mexican Interior (etching)

415. Gág. Lamplight (lithograph)

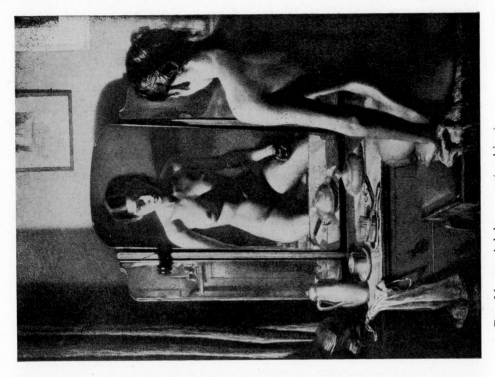

418. Brockhurst. Adolescence (etching)

417. Ganso. Nude at Mirror (aquatint)

419. Soyer. Mission (lithograph)

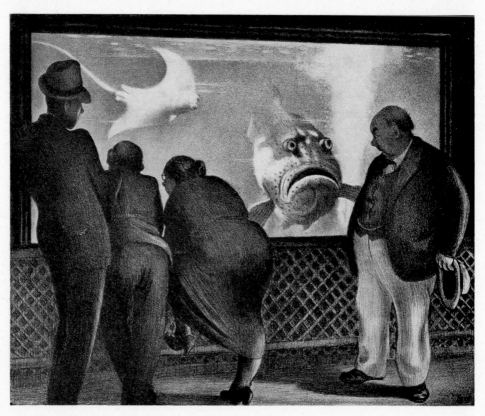

420. Dwight. Queer Fish (lithograph)

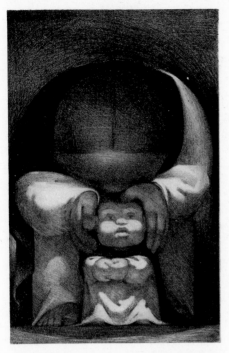

421. Charlot. First Steps (lithograph)

422. Covarrubias. Lindy Hop (lithograph)

423. Handforth. Lili (etching)

424. Bacon. The Patroness (drypoint)

426. Kollwitz. Death and the Mother (aquatint)

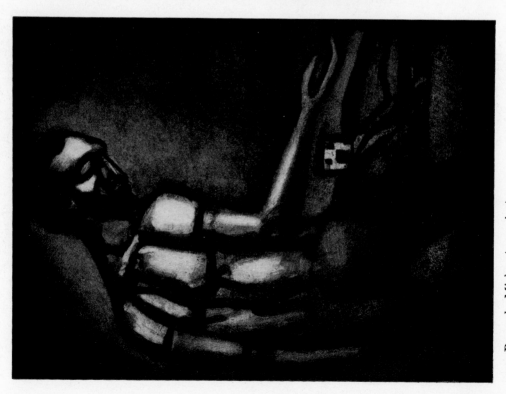

425. Rouault. Misère (aquatint)

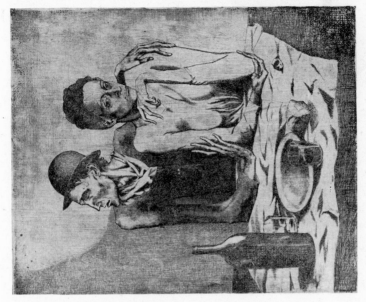

428. Picasso. Le Repas Frugal (etching)

427. Beckmann. The Curtain Falls (etching)

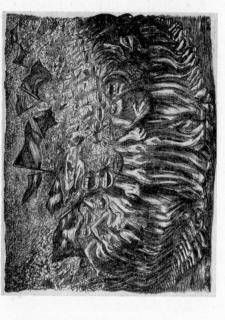

430. Orozco. Mouths (lithograph)

432. Kollwitz. The Strike (etching)

429. Dehn. All for a Piece of Meat (lithograph)

431. Gropper. The Judge (lithograph)

433. Baker. Religion (lithograph)

434. Grosz. The Robbers (lithograph)

435. Rivera. Fruits of Labor (lithograph)

436. Sternberg. Dance of the Machines (lithograph)

438. Kollwitz. News from the Front (lithograph)

437. Grosz. The Pimps of Death (lithograph)

439. Orozco. Requiem (lithograph)

440. Dix. Airplane Raid (etching)   441. Nevinson. Airplane (lithograph)

442. Dix. Dance of Death (aquatint)

443. Derain. Head (lithograph)

444. Kuniyoshi. Café (lithograph)

445. Matisse. Liseuse (lithograph)

447. Braque. Abstraction (etching)

449. Castellon. The Gordian Knot (lithograph)

446. Niles Spencer. Roof Tops (lithograph)

448. Kokoschka. The Resurrection (lithograph)

450. Picasso. Abstraction (color stencil)

451. Miro. Singers (color stencil)

452. Chagall. Grandfather's House (etching)

453. Chirico. Figure (lithograph)

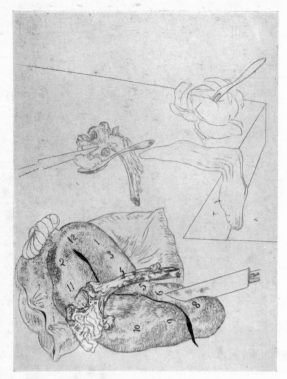

454. Dali. Chant de Maldoror (etching)

455. Klee. L'Homme Approximatif (etching)

456. Picasso. Minotauromachia (etching)

457. Kiyomasu. Samurai and
Attendant (woodcut)

458. Kiyonobu. Kamimura
Kichisaburo (woodcut)

459. Shigenaga. Girl with
Cherry Blossoms
(woodcut)

460. Shunsho. The Second
Ichikawa Monnosuke
(woodcut)

463. Buncho. Fox Dance (woodcut)

462. Masanobu. Self-Portrait (woodcut)

461. Toyonobu. Oiran in Night Attire (woodcut)

465. Harunobu. Girl with Lantern (woodcut)

464. Harunobu. Two Girls Playing Cat's Cradle (woodcut)

467. Kiyonaga. Iris Garden (woodcut)

466. Yeishi. Two Ladies and Child at Seashore
(woodcut)

468. Kiyonaga. Terrace by the Sea (woodcut)

469. Yeishi. Fête in Nobleman's Palace (woodcut)

470. Utamaro. Awabi Fishers (woodcut)

471. Kiyomitsu. Daimyo Procession Game (woodcut)

472. Kiyonaga.
Woman
Painting
Eyebrows
(woodcut)

473. Shunsho. Woman in
Red (woodcut)

474. Koriusai. Bather
(woodcut)

476. Utamaro. Yamauba and Kintoki (woodcut)

475. Sharaku. Actor in Role of Moronao (woodcut)

478. Hokusai. Iris (woodcut)

479. Hiroshige. Rain Storm at Shono (woodcut)

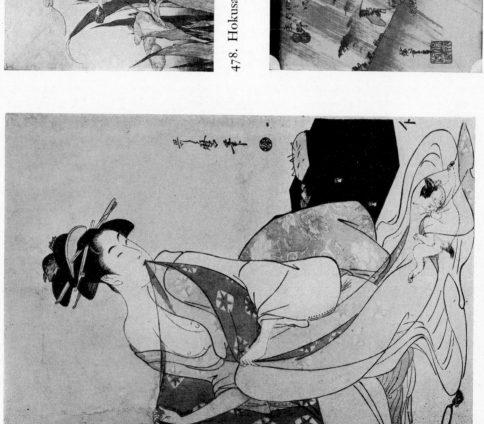

477. Utamaro. Young Woman Dressmaking (woodcut)

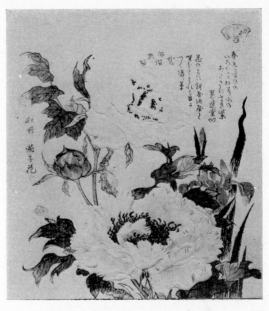

481. Shunman. Surimono (woodcut)

480. Shunyei. Wrestler (woodcut)

482. Choki. Lady and Child
Catching Fireflies
(woodcut)

483. Toyokuni. Woman Bathing
(woodcut)

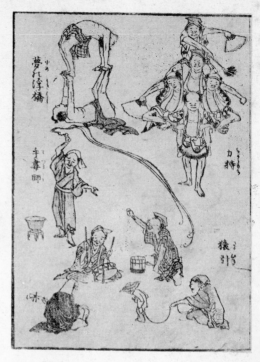

484. Hiroshige. Mt. Fuji from Willows
(woodcut)

485. Hokusai. Mangwa (woodcut)

486. Hokusai. The Wave (woodcut)

487. Teng-Kwei. Birds in Rain (lithograph)

488. Chinese School. From *Mustard Seed Garden* (woodcut)

INDEX OF PLATES

INDEX OF PLATES

400

404

405